# FEDERAL JURISDICTION IN AUSTRALIA

# Federal Jurisdiction in Australia

ZELMAN COWEN

*and*

LESLIE ZINES

*Second Edition*

1978

MELBOURNE
OXFORD UNIVERSITY PRESS
OXFORD WELLINGTON NEW YORK

*Oxford University Press*

OXFORD  LONDON  GLASGOW  NEW YORK
TORONTO  MELBOURNE  WELLINGTON  CAPE TOWN
DELHI  BOMBAY  CALCUTTA  MADRAS  KARACHI  LAHORE  DACCA
KUALA LUMPUR  SINGAPORE  JAKARTA  HONG KONG  TOKYO
NAIROBI  DAR ES SALAAM  LUSAKA  ADDIS ABABA
IBADAN  ZARIA  ACCRA  BEIRUT

*Oxford University Press, 7 Bowen Crescent, Melbourne*

ⓒ   Zelman Cowen and Leslie Zines

*First published 1959*
*Second edition 1978*


Cowen, Sir Zelman, 1919:—
  Federal Jurisdiction in Australia.

  2nd ed.
  Bibliography
  ISBN 0 19 550054 7

  1. Courts—Australia. 2. Jurisdiction—
  Australia. I. Zines, Leslie Ronald, 1930-,
  joint author. II. Title.

  347'.94'02'2


PRINTED IN AUSTRALIA BY BROWN PRIOR ANDERSON PTY LTD
MELBOURNE

THE framers of our own Federal Commonwealth Constitution (who were for the most part lawyers), found the American instrument of government an incomparable model. They could not escape from its fascination. Its contemplation damped the smouldering fires of their originality.

SIR OWEN DIXON

# FOREWORD TO THE SECOND EDITION

The first edition of this book was a work of single authorship. Over the period of almost twenty years which have elapsed since then, my activities and occupations have changed, and in the preparation of a second edition I sought the co-operation of a distinguished scholar in the complex field of federal jurisdiction. Professor Leslie Zines of the Australian National University is an acknowledged authority and he has agreed to join me as co-author of the second edition. The new writing is very much his work.

It is a great pleasure to record that Mr Frank Eyre, who was publisher to the Oxford University Press in Australia when the first edition was published but who has now retired from that office, has been retained to see this edition through the Press. It is a happy circumstance that it is so.

It is also a very happy circumstance that the publication of this book coincides in time with the five hundredth anniversary of the Oxford University Press with which I have had a long and cordial association.

*Zelman Cowen*


I am extremely grateful to my secretary Ms Rita Harding for her ability, care and unremitting labour in helping me with the manuscript of this book. Thanks are also due to Mr Mark Richardson, Miss Jane Connors, Mr Eric Lucas and Miss Rebecca Davies (who were all research assistants in the Law School of the Australian National University) for their assistance in lightening my burdens.

*Leslie Zines*

# CONTENTS

# INTRODUCTION TO THE SECOND EDITION

The introduction to the first edition of this book ended with the words that 'its most satisfying achievement would be its own relegation to the shelves of legal history'. The hope remains unfulfilled and the major problems of federal jurisdiction remain and are likely to remain with us for many years to come. Over the period of almost two decades since the book first appeared there have, however, been many developments in this area in consequence of judicial interpretation and legislative enactment. There has also been renewed interest on the part of governments and the legal profession in the structure and better ordering of the Australian judicial system. These developments in our view make it appropriate to bring the book up to date.

There has been an active debate on the propriety of maintaining notions of State and federal jurisdiction and it is argued that there is much to be said for a national judiciary whose role it would be to apply and administer the law from whatever source it may emanate. The former Attorney-General, Mr Ellicott, has reiterated the view once expressed by Sir Owen Dixon, that in Australian circumstances, at any rate, the concept of federalism has no legitimate place so far as the judiciary is concerned, and that what is needed is a national system of courts. A committee of the Australian Constitutional Convention was charged with examining this proposal and has recommended that further consideration be given to it.* It is clear that there are formidable political and emotional obstacles to be overcome before that object can be achieved. Apart from issues of States' rights, there is the justified pride of many members of the legal profession in the Supreme Courts of their States, well articulated by many during the celebration in 1974 of the 150th anniversary of the establishment of the Supreme Court of New South Wales.

Short of a change in the Constitution the various arguments and proposals made in this area lead to opposite goals. Over the past decade or so, members of the Commonwealth Parliament on both sides have put forward proposals for a federal court with authority over virtually the whole range of federal jurisdiction. The alternative proposal is to use existing State courts, subject to some exceptions, in all matters of federal and State jurisdiction, with the High Court as the final court of appeal in all

* 1977 Judicature Committee Report to Standing Committee D of the Australian Constitutional Convention, p. 34.

matters. This latter proposal comes closest to the notion of a national system within the present framework of the Constitution.

Under legislation introduced in 1976, the present system provides something of a compromise, but one which strengthens State courts. A recurring theme in the first edition was the point that there had been 'a remarkable willingness to confer original jurisdiction on the High Court under section 76 (ii)—matters arising under laws made by the Parliament' and it was argued that a rational ordering of jurisdiction required the original jurisdiction of the High Court to be confined to a small number of matters. This view has gained support and much of the jurisdiction that had previously been conferred on the High Court by particular Acts of Parliament has been transferred to the State Supreme Courts. In addition, the State Supreme Courts have been given back jurisdiction in *inter se* questions which had been denied to them for nearly sixty years.

The notion of a federal court of *general* jurisdiction has not, so far, been accepted. The two federal courts—the Federal Court of Australia and the Family Court of Australia—are courts of limited and specialized jurisdiction. In certain areas, such as industrial property and taxation, a new approach has been adopted conferring jurisdiction on the State Supreme Courts, from whose orders there is an appeal to the Federal Court of Australia.*

The Australian Founding Fathers departed from the United States model in a major respect by empowering the Commonwealth Parliament to confer federal jurisdiction on State courts. This was the 'autochthonous expedient' and legislation implementing it has produced the strange situation in which a State court is said to have both State *and* federal jurisdiction to deal with the same matter. In *Lorenzo v. Carey* (1921) 29 C.L.R. 243 the High Court declared that a State court could in these circumstances exercise State or federal jurisdiction at the suit of a party. It was not made clear which party had the choice and what the situation was if neither the court nor a party adverted to the question. In *Felton v. Mulligan* (1971) 124 C.L.R. 367 the High Court appears to have determined that where federal jurisdiction is conferred in respect of a matter, the State jurisdiction becomes inoperative by virtue of the operation of section 109 of the Constitution. In this, as in the earlier edition of the book, we examine the formidable difficulties of reasoning involved

---

* See generally Ellicott: The Exercise of Federal Jurisdiction—A Revision of the Federal Judicial Structure [1977] 1 Crim. L.J. 2.

in reaching such a conclusion. At least it can be said that that decision has avoided a situation which was patently absurd.

The use of State courts in matters involving federal jurisdiction has been made rather more difficult by such decisions as *Kotsis v. Kotsis* (1970) 122 C.L.R. 69 and *Knight v. Knight* (1971) 122 C.L.R. 114 which, to a large extent, prevent State courts from making the same use of registrars, masters and prothonotaries in federal jurisdiction, as they do in the exercise of State jurisdiction. The divisions in the High Court in *Russell v. Russell* (1976) 9 A.L.R. 103 have shown how difficult and elusive is the dividing line between altering the organization of a State court, which the Commonwealth may not do, and regulating its procedure, which is within Commonwealth power. To some extent, these decisions have impeded the policy of using State courts for purposes of federal jurisdiction.

Since 1959, the Commonwealth Parliament has dealt with and resolved some of the problems and questions raised in the first edition. For example: the enactment of section 39A of the Judiciary Act has made clear Parliament's intention that specific grants of federal jurisdiction, subsequent to the enactment of section 39 of the Judiciary Act, are subject to the conditions imposed by that section on the exercise of federal jurisdiction by State courts. As that section also applies those conditions to jurisdiction granted by the Judiciary Act, it would seem that they apply to section 68 of the Judiciary Act which deals with federal criminal jurisdiction. The amendment of section 39 (2) (a) in 1968 ensured that there could be no appeal in matters of federal jurisdiction to the Privy Council by special leave from State courts and sections 38A and 40A of the Judiciary Act were repealed in consequence.

The problems associated with the exercise of jurisdiction in the Territories have become even more complex than in 1959. In a series of cases, most of the Justices of the High Court have expressed their disagreement with the basic principle of *R. v. Bernasconi* (1915) 19 C.L.R. 629 which treats the Territories' power as a disparate and non-federal matter: see the *Boilermakers' Case* (1957) 95 C.L.R. 529, 545. At the same time they have upheld the actual decision and the view that territorial courts are not federal courts and do not exercise federal jurisdiction. The cases leave unanswered a number of questions and they appear to create substantial problems of jurisdiction in this case of a general Commonwealth law operating throughout Australia and beyond.

# INTRODUCTION TO THE FIRST EDITION

A RECENT American writer has remarked that 'questions of federal jurisdiction for many people involve no more than the application of technical formulae created only to confuse the uninitiated. More sophisticated students of government understand that these problems involve fundamental questions of power, and that the existence of democracy depends in no small part upon the proper allocation of such authority'.[1] Other American writers[2] echo this sentiment, though perhaps they may wish to substitute for the word democracy some such phrase as the proper balance of federalism. Australian lawyers—and few have much acquaintance with the law of federal jurisdiction, which has been described on the highest Australian authority as a peculiarly arid study[3]—will certainly agree with the first sentence of the American commentator's statement. There is no doubt that the Australian law of federal jurisdiction is technical, complicated, difficult and not infrequently absurd. It is doubtful whether any Australian lawyer will be found who will support the view that the study of the law of federal jurisdiction offers any insight into more fundamental aspects of the Australian federal system of government. The present writer would certainly not argue that case.

This does not mean that the study of federal jurisdiction in Australia is merely a dull catalogue of difficult and complex rules of law. There is a much deeper interest in the study. Much of our present discontent in this area arises from unintelligent and uncritical copying of the provisions of the United States Constitution. It is from that Constitution that we gleaned the notion of federal jurisdiction. From that source we also copied many of the subject-matters of federal jurisdiction and then, on a frolic of our own, assigned a formidable burden of original jurisdiction with respect to such matters to the High Court. The matters in secs 75 and 76 are a curious *mélange*; some, though not many, may be appropriate for the exercise of original jurisdiction by the

1 Kurland: Mr Justice Frankfurter, The Supreme Court and the Erie Doctrine in Diversity Cases (1957) 67 Yale L.J. 187.

2 See e.g. Hart and Wechsler: The Federal Courts and the Federal System (1953); Hart: The Relations Between State and Federal Law (1954) 54 Columbia L.R. 489.

3 Dixon: The Law and the Constitution (1935) 51 L.Q.R. 590, 608.

High Court, but others, when exposed to critical scrutiny, ought not to be there at all and their presence can only be explained in terms of a hypnotic fascination with the American Judicature Article. It is easy to be wise after the event and to charge the Founding Fathers with a stronger disposition to copy than to think, but there can be little doubt that much of the wider interest in the study of federal jurisdiction in Australia lies in an examination of what results from inapposite transcription of another federal model.

In this area of the law, the model was inappropriate. The tensions between State and federal governments in the United States, the desire for uniform interpretation of federal law, the problems thrown up by the need for judicial policing of a bill of rights, may well have called for the creation of two sets of courts, State and national. To have left the protection of the national interests in the hands of State courts, subject only to the ultimate appellate control of the Supreme Court of the United States, would have been risky. Chief Justice Marshall spoke in *Osborn v. Bank of the United States*[4] of 'the insecure remedy of an appeal upon a point after it has received that shape which may be given to it by another tribunal'. Contemporary writers have endorsed Marshall's view.[5]

The Australian situation is different. It is not that Australian federalism does not produce inter-governmental tensions and conflicts; it is that they do not significantly touch the court structures. In their great commentary on the Australian Constitution written in 1900, before the Constitution had begun to operate, Quick and Garran, discussing sec. 77 (iii) which authorizes the making of laws by the Parliament investing State courts with federal jurisdiction, observed that the judicial department of the Commonwealth was more national and less distinctively federal than either the legislative or the executive department. They drew attention to the fact that the High Court was not only a *federal* but also a *national* court of appeal; that it entertained appeals from State courts on matters of State law as well as federal matters. 'Confidence in the integrity and impartiality of the Bench prevents any jealousy or distrust of this wide federal juris-

---

4 (1824) 9 Wheat. 738, 822-3.
5 'The Supreme Court is the ultimate judicial exponent of federal rights, the lower federal courts are their vindicators. . . . It hardly seems open to doubt that a full system of independent federal courts plays a valuable part in furthering the rapid, widespread, yet uniform and accurate interpretation of federal law.' Mishkin: The Federal 'Question' in the District Courts (1953) 53 Columbia L.R. 157, 170-1.

diction; and the same confidence makes it possible to contemplate without misgiving the exercise of federal jurisdiction by State courts—subject, of course, to the controlling power of the Federal Parliament.'[6]

The Founding Fathers departed from American precedent by conferring general appellate jurisdiction on the High Court and by devising the 'autochthonous expedient',[7] as the High Court has described it, of authorizing the investment of State courts with federal jurisdiction. As in the United States, the Constitution made provision for the legislative creation of federal courts, but this power has been little used, except for the establishment of a very few courts of specialized jurisdiction. The pity is that, having accepted the State courts as a *general* base for the Australian legal system, and having established the High Court as a *general* court of appeal, the makers of the Constitution were led along false American trails to federal jurisdiction. It seems clear that with the establishment of the Commonwealth it was necessary to confer additional jurisdiction on the State courts to try matters in which the Commonwealth was a party defendant—to take an example—but why it was necessary to funnel jurisdiction into two separate channels, State and federal, is not clear. The High Court in *Lorenzo v. Carey*[8] said that it saw no difficulty in a court exercising either State or federal jurisdiction at the instance of a party, but as a practical matter State courts can run into difficulties, as was demonstrated by the case of *Booth v. Shelmerdine Bros Pty Ltd.*[9] But whether or not there are difficulties in the two-channel concept, is there any good sense in it? It may be that in a particular federal system there is a good practical case for the creation of two separate channels of jurisdiction in two separate sets of courts, but the establishment of separate channels within the same set of courts is irrational. The additional jurisdiction which had to be vested in State courts as a result of the establishment of the Commonwealth could have been conferred without bifurcation of channels. More recent federal constitutions have demonstrated how it may be done.[10]

The Commonwealth Parliament has added to the intricacies and the difficulties. A desire to shut out the appellate jurisdiction of the Privy Council at one end of the scale, a low opinion of the

---

6 The Annotated Constitution of the Australian Commonwealth at p. 804.

7 The *Boilermakers' Case* (1956) 94 C.L.R. 254, 268.

8 (1921) 29 C.L.R. 243, 252.

9 [1924] V.L.R. 276.

10 See Cowen: The Emergence of a New Federation in Malaya (1958) Tasmania U.L.R. at pp. 61-2.

capacities of honorary justices of the peace at the other end, and some views about the general organization of appeals, led to the enactment of sec. 39 of the Judiciary Act. The validity of that section as a whole is now apparently established, after an attack spread over many years, with many differences of judicial opinion and some lingering doubt. Sec. 39 was in large part political action designed to shut out as far as possible the appeal to the Privy Council. This is not the appropriate place to canvass the merits of the Privy Council appeal; but the pity is that this issue had to complicate the administration of justice within the *Australian* court system. Sir Owen Dixon, in an analysis of the organization of federal jurisdiction in Australia, described the confusion and difficulties to the Royal Commission on the Constitution in 1927:

> It is by no means easy to arrive at a clear understanding of the operation of these provisions from a mere consideration of the authorities but this merely serves to support the conclusion which we are desirous of suggesting to the Commission that as a result of the provisions of the Constitution and those of the Judiciary Act 'Federal jurisdiction' forms a grave impediment to the practical administration of justice. We think this confusion and all the difficulties which attend it ought to receive the serious attention of those interested in maintaining a Federal system of justice which is speedy, efficient and practical.[11]

Sec. 39 of the Judiciary Act is the Commonwealth Parliament's most handsome contribution to the complications which surround the law of federal jurisdiction, but there are other difficulties. There are problems affecting federal criminal jurisdiction; the relationship of secs. 39 and 68 of the Judiciary Act is not altogether clear, and there are questions whether specific grants of federal jurisdiction *subsequent* to the enactment of sec. 39 of the Judiciary Act are subject to the conditions imposed by that section on the exercise of federal jurisdiction by State courts.

In other areas of federal jurisdiction, the record of the Parliament has not been very notable. The Founding Fathers, in an excess of copying zeal, authorized the Parliament to confer Admiralty and maritime jurisdiction on the High Court. In 1914, the Parliament exercised this power conferred by sec. 76 (iii) of the Constitution. Between 1914 and 1939 the High Court grappled with the problems of this grant of jurisdiction in a series of difficult cases. One of the unresolved problems was the

[11] Royal Commission on the Constitution, Minutes of Evidence (1927) at p. 787.

B

connection between this grant of jurisdiction and the grant of
Admiralty jurisdiction to the High Court under the Imperial
Colonial Courts of Admiralty Act 1890. In 1939 the Parliament
revoked the grant of jurisdiction under sec. 76 (iii), though the
debates suggest some uncertainty of purpose. These difficulties,
it seems, live on elsewhere, as State courts are invested with
Admiralty and maritime jurisdiction by the vesting provisions of
sec. 39 of the Judiciary Act, and are also repositories of jurisdiction under the Colonial Courts of Admiralty Act. No one has
thus far essayed an explanation of the relationship of the two
grants of jurisdiction.

The Parliament has also shown a remarkable willingness to
confer original jurisdiction on the High Court under sec. 76 (ii)
—matters arising under laws made by the Parliament. The office
of the High Court must, on any rational principle, be almost
exclusively that of an appellate court; and it is given the broadest
appellate office by sec. 73 of the Constitution. The court already
has at least a potentially burdensome original jurisdiction under
secs 75 and 76 of the Constitution. Some of the heads of that jurisdiction are the result of unintelligent copying from the United
States Constitution by the Founding Fathers. The case for the
grant of original jurisdiction to the High Court can only be made
out, on a rational ordering of jurisdiction, in comparatively rare
cases. It may well be that the dignity of the parties to an action
demands a trial in the highest court, so that matters between
governments, State and State, and Commonwealth and State are
properly triable at first instance in the High Court. A power
such as that granted by sec. 40 of the Judiciary Act to remove into
the High Court a matter arising under the Constitution or involving its interpretation is also justified, so far as it permits of the
speedy resolution of issues with which the High Court is distinctively equipped to deal. But to load the High Court with
original jurisdiction in tax, patent, trade mark and like matters
is a maldistribution of functions. Why such matters should not be
tried by State courts is not clear; if the answer is that State courts
are overburdened or inexpert, the appropriate solution is the
creation of specialized courts. There is ample precedent for this,
in Australia as in the United States. It is altogether irrational
to load the ultimate court of appeal with a ragbag collection of
matters of originial jurisdiction.

In this book an attempt is made to examine a number of these
problems and questions. Much of the discussion is necessarily very
technical, because this is a complex and difficult area of the law,

with many unanswered questions. The book does not purport to exhaust all the topics and problems of federal jurisdiction. There is no detailed discussion of the definition of 'judicial power' which has been exhaustively discussed by many writers, including the present writer[12] and, except for incidental reference, the reader is referred to those writings. Choice of law problems in federal courts are also omitted. Here there are some very difficult questions, many of which are unanswered, and this question may await a later investigation.[13] The present study covers five topics: the original jurisdiction of the High Court; an extended discussion of diversity jurisdiction—jurisdiction in matters between residents of different States; the federal courts; the territorial courts and jurisdiction in the Territories; and the investment of State courts with federal jurisdiction. The inclusion of territorial jurisdictional problems calls for some explanation, for it would seem on the authorities that the territorial courts, or most of them, are not federal courts and do not exercise federal jurisdiction. But this topic is included because it is believed that there is a sufficiently close relationship between the problems discussed and those of federal jurisdiction.

The apology for the book is, firstly, the need for detailed exposition of a difficult body of law which is with us. In the second place, it is an argument against the present ordering of jurisdiction—an argument which was brilliantly and tersely stated before the Royal Commission on the Constitution by Sir Owen Dixon in 1927.[14] In this respect it puts a case for constitutional and legislative reform of matters which for the most part arouse no political passions and are distinctively matters of lawyers' law. If Sir Owen Dixon could not persuade, it is not likely that this book will succeed in the task, but its most satisfying achievement would be its own relegation to the shelves of legal history.

---

[12] See Wynes: Legislative, Executive and Judicial Powers in Australia (2nd ed., 1956) pp. 556-72; Sawer (1948) 1 Annual L.R. (Univ. of W.A.) 29; Cowen (1948) 26 Can.B.R. 829; Beasley (1949) 27 Can.B.R. 686.

[13] See Moore: Suits Between States within the British Empire (1925) 7 J.C.L. (3rd ser.) 155; Moore: The Federations and Suits Between Governments (1935) 17 J.C.L. (3rd ser.) 163; Cowen: Bilateral Studies: American-Australian Private International Law (1957) pp. 45-8.

[14] ante note 11 at p. 782 et seq.

= I =

# The Original Jurisdiction of the High Court

'If it be suggested that the volume of business that will flow
from the new head of jurisdiction established by this decision
is in itself not likely to be very heavy, it is pertinent to say
that it is true of the Court's business also that many a mickle
makes a muckle.'[1]

I

THE influence of American precedents on Australian constitution
making was considerable.[2] In no area, probably, was that influence stronger than on the judicature chapter of the Constitution.
At the preliminary Federal Conference, at Melbourne in 1890,
Alfred Deakin expressed the opinion that the American distribu-
tion of federal jurisdiction fitted Australian needs.[3] At the Sydney
Convention in 1891, the task of drafting the judicature provisions
of the federal bill was assigned to a committee under the chairmanship of Inglis Clark, who was an ardent admirer of the United
States Constitution. Although there were some important departures from the American model in this committee's proposals,
they largely consisted of quotations from the American Constitution.[4] Further changes were made in the course of the meetings
of the Convention of 1897-8, but it remained true that in the
Constitution as finally enacted 'the organization of the federal
courts, and, for the most part, their jurisdiction followed American precedent'.[5]

The copying of the American judicature provisions was not
slavish, and for present purposes it suffices to draw attention to
two major departures from the American model. In the first place,
the High Court of Australia was designed as a *general* court of
appeal, from State courts exercising *State* as well as *federal* juris-

---

[1] *per* Frankfurter J. in *Williams v. Austrian* (1947) 331 U.S. 642, 681.
[2] For a general study see Hunt: American Precedents in Australian Federation (1930).
[3] Debs. Melb. (1890), p. 89.
[4] Hunt, *op. cit.*, p. 188.
[5] Hunt, *op. cit.*, p. 199.

diction, and from inferior federal courts.[6] In this respect, its functions were very different from those of the Supreme Court of the United States whose appellate functions were much more narrowly confined.[7] This points to a very marked difference of attitude on the part of the Founding Fathers in the two federations. In the United States, there was a strong suspicion of the new central authority and it was not seriously argued that general appellate functions should be vested in the Supreme Court of the United States. In Australia, a desire for the establishment of a general court of appeal from State courts had been expressed as early as 1849. In 1870, the Victorian Government appointed a Royal Commission to consider and report on the expediency of establishing a general court of appeal for the Australian colonies, and this commission reported in favour of the project.[8] Even the most ardent admirers of the American judicial structure, Inglis Clark included, supported the establishment of a general court of appeal for the new Commonwealth of Australia. This difference of attitude was very clearly stated in the first great commentary on the Commonwealth Constitution in 1900:

> In Australia, as in Canada, the appellate jurisdiction is not one of those jealously guarded State rights which make anything more intimate than a federal union impossible. We are accustomed to a common court of appeal in the shape of the Privy Council: we are so assured of the independence and integrity of the Bench that the advantages of having one uniform Australian tribunal of final resort outweigh all feelings of localism, and the federal tribunal has been entrusted (subject to the rights reserved with respect to the Privy Council) with the final decision of all cases, whether federal or purely local in their nature.[9]

This trust in the new High Court was matched by a willingness to accept State courts as repositories of federal jurisdiction. In the United States Constitution, no provision was made for conferring federal jurisdiction on State courts, and the judicial power of the United States was vested in the Supreme Court of the United States and in such inferior *federal* courts as the Congress might from time to time create.[10] The Australian Constitution inferen-

---

[6] Commonwealth of Australia Constitution, sec. 73.

[7] United States Constitution Art. III, sec. 2.

[8] 'The decisions of the various Supreme Courts of the colonies upon purely colonial affairs would thereby be brought into harmony and uniformity of law be thus encouraged, to the great advantage of commerce.' Parliamentary Papers (Victoria) 1870, vol. 2, p. 711.

[9] Quick and Garran: The Annotated Constitution of the Australian Commonwealth, p. 725.

[10] Art. III, sec. 1.

tially authorized the establishment of inferior federal courts *and* also the investment of State courts with federal jurisdiction.[11]

Having regard to these differences in the two constitutional schemes, it might have been thought that there was little need for an extensive *original* jurisdiction for the High Court. But the Commonwealth Constitution both grants and authorizes the grant of an extensive original jurisdiction to the High Court.[12] It is much broader than the original jurisdiction conferred on the Supreme Court of the United States[13] which is 'narrowly confined and strictly construed'.[14] Several matters which in the United States Constitution are assigned to federal jurisdiction, but lie within the original jurisdiction of *inferior* federal courts, are by the Australian Constitution assigned to the original jurisdiction of the High Court.

This matter does not appear to have been elaborately discussed in the Australian Constitutional Conventions. No doubt the difference may be explained in this way. The theory which underlay the assignment of particular matters to federal jurisdiction was that for varying reasons it was thought desirable to have such matters decided by *national* rather than *State* courts. In the American system, a hierarchy of distinctively national or federal courts was envisaged, and this object could be achieved by assigning original jurisdiction for the most part to inferior federal courts, leaving only very special cases to the original jurisdiction of the Supreme Court of the United States. The Australian constitutional system provided for the establishment of inferior federal courts and for the investment of State courts with federal jurisdiction, but the intendment was that the State courts should be used, and this was what was done. This meant that, apart from particular federal courts with specialized functions, the only established national court was the High Court. If subject-matters of federal jurisdiction were to be assigned as a matter of original jurisdiction to a *national* court, the High Court was therefore the inevitable repository.

This reasoning is intelligible, but it is doubtful whether it carries much conviction. It assumes the desirability or the necessity of referring the various matters of federal jurisdiction to a national court. In view of the differences in the two Constitutions,

---

11 Sec. 71.

12 Secs. 75, 76.

13 Art. III, sec. 2.

14 Freund: The Supreme Court of the United States (1950) 29 Canadian B.R. 1080, 1083.

and particularly in view of the general appellate jurisdiction conferred on the High Court and of the grant of federal jurisdiction to State courts—both of which were very significant departures from the American model—it might have been thought that there was very much less call for the allocation of original jurisdiction to a national court in Australia. Moreover, the Australian Federal Conventions do not appear to have subjected the particular subject-matters of original jurisdiction assigned to the American federal courts to very close scrutiny in considering their suitability for allocation to the original jurisdiction of the High Court. It will be argued that many of these do not warrant assignment to original federal jurisdiction in Australia.

The result is that the Commonwealth Constitution places a considerable burden on the High Court. Not only is it invested with important constitutional functions and with a general appellate jurisdiction, but it has been loaded with an original jurisdiction, which, if it were invoked to the full, would impose an intolerable burden on the court. This, Sir Owen Dixon said, stands in the way of 'the efficient, speedy and orderly administration of the law'.[15] As the population of Australia grows, and as its activities diversify, the burden imposed upon the High Court both in respect of its appellate and original jurisdiction will become very great. It is submitted that the original jurisdiction of the Court ought to be severely curtailed, and that there is a good case for amendment of Chapter III of the Constitution in this respect.

In 1974 a standing committee of the Australian Constitutional Convention recommended amendments of the Constitution to considerably reduce the High Court's original jurisdiction at present conferred under sec. 75 of the Constitution.[16]

## II

The original jurisdiction of the High Court is conferred by secs. 75 and 76 of the Constitution which provide:

75. In all matters—
    (i) Arising under any treaty:
    (ii) Affecting consuls or other representatives of other countries:
    (iii) In which the Commonwealth, or a person suing or being sued on behalf of the Commonwealth, is a party:

---

[15] Then Mr Dixon, K.C., in Royal Commission on the Constitution, Minutes of Evidence (1927), p. 785.

[16] Australian Constitutional Convention 1974 Standing Committee D Report to Executive Committee.

    (iv) Between States, or between residents of different States, or between a State and a resident of another State:

    (v) In which a writ of Mandamus or prohibition or an injunction is sought against an officer of the Commonwealth:

the High Court shall have original jurisdiction.

76. The Parliament may make laws conferring original jurisdiction on the High Court in any matter—

    (i) Arising under this Constitution, or involving its interpretation:

    (ii) Arising under any laws made by the Parliament:

    (iii) Of Admiralty and maritime jurisdiction:

    (iv) Relating to the same subject-matter claimed under the laws of different States.

It will be seen that sec. 75 conferred original jurisdiction on the High Court by direct operation of the Constitution, while sec. 76 authorized the Commonwealth Parliament to confer additional original jurisdiction on the Court. These sections have to be read together with sec. 77 which authorizes the Parliament, with respect to any of the matters mentioned in secs. 75 and 76, to make laws (i) defining the jurisdiction of any federal court other than the High Court; (ii) defining the extent to which the jurisdiction of any federal court shall be exclusive of that which belongs to or is invested in the courts of the States; and (iii) investing any court of a State with federal jurisdiction. Under this section, jurisdiction in matters which constitute the actual or potential original jurisdiction of the High Court may be vested in State courts exercising federal jurisdiction or in inferior federal courts. Sec. 77 (i) and (iii) contemplate the possibility of *concurrent* original jurisdiction in State and federal courts *and* in the High Court. Under sec. 77 (ii), reading the words 'any federal court' as including the High Court,[17] there is power to make the jurisdiction of the High Court *exclusive* of that of State courts in respect of any matter in which it either has or is invested under sec. 76 with original jurisdiction. It is interesting to note that the matters in respect of which jurisdiction may be conferred on State courts or inferior federal courts are all matters within the description of the actual or potential *original* jurisdiction of the High Court. This raises the interesting question whether it is possible under sec. 77 (i) and (iii) to vest inferior federal courts and State courts with *appellate* jurisdiction in respect of these matters.[18]

17 *Pirrie v. McFarlane* (1925) 36 C.L.R. 170, 176.
18 See *Ah Yick v. Lehmert* (1905) 2 C.L.R. 593, 604; see also *Collins v. Charles Marshall Pty Ltd* (1955) 92 C.L.R. 529. See pp. 130 ff.

The Commonwealth Parliament has never fully exercised its power under sec. 76 to invest the High Court with original jurisdiction. By the Judiciary Act, sec. 30, the High Court was invested with original jurisdiction in all matters arising under the Constitution or involving its interpretation, and in trials of indictable offences against the laws of the Commonwealth. The Judiciary Act 1914 invested the Court with jurisdiction in all matters of Admiralty *or* maritime jurisdiction, but this was repealed by the Judiciary Act 1939. There has never been any *general* investment of original jurisdiction in any matter arising under any laws made by the Parliament[19] for the obvious reason that this would impose an intolerable burden on the Court. Specific statutes have from time to time conferred original jurisdiction on the Court in respect of matters arising under particular laws made by Parliament such as those relating to patents, trade marks and income tax. A great deal of this jurisdiction has been transferred to State courts.[20] The Attorney-General has stated the intention of the Government to divest, with some possible exceptions, the remaining original jurisdiction of the High Court conferred under separate legislation.[21]

There is some doubt as to whether the Parliament may delegate its powers under secs. 76 and 77 of the Constitution. This matter will be dealt with in relation to the investing of State courts with federal jurisdiction.[22] Assuming, however, that an Act can validly authorize the making of legislation conferring jurisdiction on courts, the High Court will require the clearest possible language before holding that that was the intention of Parliament.

In *Willocks v. Anderson*[23] the High Court held invalid, as not being authorized by the Act under which they were made, regulations purporting to confer jurisdiction on the High Court to determine disputes relating to the election of members of a statutory board. The judgement of six members of the Court expressed their concern that the Court's ability to carry out its chief functions as constitutional interpreter and final court of appeal should not be impaired by the grant of additional original jurisdiction. They said:

---

[19] *R. v. Bevan, ex parte Elias* (1942) 66 C.L.R. 452, *per* Starke J.

[20] Income Tax Assessment Act (No. 3) 1973, Patents Amendment Act 1976 and Trade Marks Amendment Act 1976.

[21] Ellicott: The Exercise of Federal Jurisdiction—A Revision of The Federal Judicial Structure [1977] 1 Crim. L.J. 2, 15.

[22] Chapter 5 *post*.

[23] (1971) 124 C.L.R. 293.

Under the Constitution this Court is entrusted with the most important of judicial functions. To confer additional original jurisdiction upon it may well impair its ability to discharge its major functions with despatch. The question whether in any particular circumstances, original jurisdiction should be conferred on this Court is of such great significance as to warrant the careful attention of the Parliament. Even if the power to do so may be validly delegated to the Governor-General it is not a matter to be left to the initiative of the Executive except after that attention has been given to the question by the Parliament. If after such consideration the Parliament for reasons sufficiently compelling in a particular case should decide to delegate the power, its intention to do so should be expressly and clearly stated. It cannot be held that the Parliament intended that the time of this Court should be taken up in hearing in its original jurisdiction appeals against elections to commodity boards, such as the Australian Apple and Pear Board, without a clear and unmistakable expression of such an intention. General words should not readily be construed as expressing the necessary intention.[24]

The jurisdiction conferred by the Judiciary Act, sec. 30 (c), in trials of indictable offences against the laws of the Commonwealth raises some interesting points which were discussed in *R. v. Kidman*.[25] That was an indictment for conspiracy to defraud the Commonwealth. Both Griffith C.J. and Isaacs J. indicated that the jurisdiction of the High Court in respect of indictable offences against the laws of the Commonwealth might derive from sec. 75 (iii) of the Constitution—matters in which the Commonwealth is a party. Isaacs J. was of opinion that sec. 75 (iii) covered all justiciable issues both in civil and criminal actions and that it therefore included matters in which the King in right of the Commonwealth complained of some breach of public law to which a penal consequence was attached. In his view this was not confined to such breaches of public law as were created by statute but applied also to offences at common law.[26] To the extent that sec. 75 (iii) covers jurisdiction in trials of indictable offences against the laws of the Commonwealth, sec. 30 (c) of the Judiciary Act is unnecessary, since under sec. 75 the High Court possesses original jurisdiction without need for further parliamentary action. In *R. v. Kidman*, Griffith C.J. also drew attention to the difficulties involved in basing sec. 30 (c) of the Judiciary Act upon the power conferred by sec. 76 (ii) of the Constitution—matters arising under any laws made by the Parliament. He observed that the Judiciary Act provision was concerned with offences against the laws of the Commonwealth, and that there

[24] at pp. 299, 300.          [25] (1915) 20 C.L.R. 425.          [26] at p. 444.

was no warrant for treating laws of the *Commonwealth* (Judiciary Act, sec. 30) and laws made by the *Parliament* (Constitution, sec. 76 (ii)) as necessarily synonymous.[27] This view assumes that there is a common law of the Commonwealth in the sense that there are offences against Commonwealth law that do not derive from statutes of the Commonwealth Parliament. A majority of the High Court, however, has never pronounced on the question and it remains doubtful.[28]

It has already been said that the Constitution contemplates the vesting of *exclusive* and *concurrent* original jurisdiction in the High Court. Under sec. 77 (ii) Parliament may make laws defining the extent to which the jurisdiction of a federal court shall be exclusive of that of a State court. Parliament may make the jurisdiction of the High Court exclusive of that of inferior federal courts by appropriate exercise of its powers under sec. 77 (i) in defining the jurisdiction of inferior federal courts. By sec. 38 of the Judiciary Act, Parliament exercised its powers under sec. 77 (ii) to prescribe five matters in which the jurisdiction of the High Court should be exclusive of the jurisdiction of the several courts of the States. They were (*a*) matters arising directly under any treaty; (*b*) suits between States, or between persons suing or being sued on behalf of different States, or between a State and a person suing or being sued on behalf of a State; (*c*) suits by the Commonwealth, or any person suing on behalf of the Commonwealth, against a State or any person being sued on behalf of a State; (*d*) suits by a State or any person suing on behalf of a State, against the Commonwealth, or any person being sued on behalf of the Commonwealth; (*e*) matters in which a writ of *mandamus* or prohibition is sought against an officer of the Commonwealth or a federal court.

In respect of the matters with which it dealt, sec. 38 of the Judiciary Act made the jurisdiction of the High Court exclusive of that of *all* State courts.[29]

----

27 'Having regard to the sense in which the term "the laws of the Commonwealth" is used in the Constitution e.g. in secs 61 and 120, and the terms "any law of the Commonwealth" in sec. 80, I think it is impossible to contend successfully that they can be treated as synonymous. The only result would be that the enactment (i.e. in the Judiciary Act, sec. 30) was unnecessary' (p. 439).

28 Wynes: Legislative, Executive and Judicial Powers in Australia (5th ed., 1976) pp. 58-60.

29 It should be noted also that the Judiciary Act, sec. 57, specifically provides that claims by a State against the Commonwealth in contract or in tort may be brought in the High Court and sec. 59 makes similar provision in the case of suits between States.

Between 1907 and 1976 sec. 38A of the Judiciary Act provided that in matters (other than trials of indictable offences) involving any question however arising as to the limits *inter se* of the constitutional powers of the Commonwealth and those of any State or States, or as to the limits *inter se* of the constitutional powers of any two or more States, the jurisdiction of the High Court shall be exclusive of the jurisdiction of the Supreme Courts; so that the Supreme Court of a State shall not have jurisdiction to entertain or determine any such matter, either as a court of first instance or as a court of appeal from an inferior court. Sec. 40A provided machinery for the removal of such *inter se* questions when they arose in the Supreme Court of a State. It was declared that it was the duty of the court to proceed no further in the cause which was automatically removed to the High Court. Sec. 41 provided that when a cause was removed into the High Court, the Court should proceed as if the cause had been originally commenced there.

Secs. 38A and 40A were originally enacted in 1907. They were designed to give effect to a legislative policy that *inter se* questions should be finally determined in Australia by the High Court and that no appeal should lie to the Privy Council except on the certificate of the High Court. This policy had been expressed in sec. 74 of the Constitution which provides that on an *inter se* question no appeal shall be permitted from the High Court to the Privy Council unless the High Court grants a certificate authorizing such an appeal. This embodied the compromise on appeals to the Privy Council which was reached between the Australian delegation and the United Kingdom Government in 1900.[30] An attempt was made to circumvent sec. 74 by taking an appeal from the Supreme Court of a State *direct* to the Privy Council without going to the High Court at all.[31] To cover this gap in the scheme, it was thought necessary to prevent *inter se* questions from being decided by State Supreme Courts and this was done by enacting secs. 38A and 40A of the Judiciary Act.

Secs. 38A, 40A and 41 were held valid in *Pirrie v. McFarlane*[32] to the extent that they related to *inter se* questions as between the

---

30 For an account of the negotiations and matters in dispute, see Garran: Cambridge History of the British Empire, vol. vii at pp. 451-2 (1933) and La Nauze: The Making of the Australian Constitution (1972) pp. 248-69.

31 See *Webb v. Outrim* [1907] A.C. 81; *Baxter v. Commissioner of Taxation (N.S.W.)* (1907) 4 C.L.R. 1087; *Pirrie v. McFarlane* (1925) 36 C.L.R. 170, 177, 195-6.

32 (1925) 36 C.L.R. 170.

Commonwealth and the States. The Parliament had, under sec. 76 (i) of the Constitution, vested the High Court with jurisdiction in any matter arising under the Constitution or involving its interpretation (sec. 30 (c) of the Judiciary Act) and under sec. 77 (ii) it had power to define the extent to which the jurisdiction of any federal court should be exclusive of State courts.

Secs. 38A and 40A were repealed by the Judiciary Amendment Act 1976. It was clear by then that the condition in sec. 39 (2) (a) of the Judiciary Act, prohibiting appeals to the Privy Council from any State court exercising federal jurisdiction, was valid. It was considered therefore that secs. 38A and 40A were no longer necessary for achieving the object of preventing appeals to the Privy Council in relation to *inter se* questions. The validity of sec. 39 (2) (a) will be discussed later.[33] It follows that the jurisdiction of the High Court to deal with these matters is now concurrent with State Supreme Courts as well as with other courts.

Sec. 40 of the Judiciary Act provides for the removal of a cause or a part of a cause from a federal, Territory or State court into the High Court. Where the cause is one arising under the Constitution or involving its interpretation, the High Court may order its removal into the High Court on the application of a party on such terms as the Court thinks fit. It is further provided that an order of removal shall be made as of course on the application by the Attorney-General of the Commonwealth or of a State (sec. 40 (1)).

In the case of other causes pending in a federal or Territory court or in a State court exercising federal jurisdiction the cause may be removed into the High Court by order of that Court upon application of a party or of the Commonwealth Attorney-General (sec. 40 (2)). As the causes that may be so removed include those with respect to which the High Court has not otherwise been invested with jurisdiction (for example, a matter arising under a law made by Parliament), sec. 40 (3) confers jurisdiction to hear and determine the cause that is removed 'to the extent that jurisdiction is not otherwise conferred on the High Court'. In the case of an order for removal under sec. 40 (2)—i.e. non-constitutional matters—the High Court is prohibited from making an order unless all parties consent to it or the Court is satisfied that it is appropriate to make the order having regard to all the cir-

---

[33] See pp. 206 ff *post.*

cumstances, including the interests of the parties and the public interest (sec. 40 (4)).

Before 1976, power to remove causes into the High Court under sec. 40 of the Judiciary Act was confined to the removal from State courts of matters arising under the Constitution or involving its interpretation. There was no power to order removal from federal or Territory courts. As is the case at present in relation to constitutional questions, it was provided that the order should be made as of course on the application of the Attorney-General of the Commonwealth or of a State.

The special standing of a Commonwealth or State Attorney-General was referred to by Isaacs J. in *Ex parte Walsh and Johnson; In re Yates*.[34] 'If a party applies, he must show sufficient cause, and must submit to terms if the Court thinks fit. But an Attorney-General—of the Commonwealth, if he things Commonwealth interests involved, or of a State, if he thinks State interests involved—may obtain the order as of course. Parliament recognizing that, if the Commonwealth or a State desires the removal, that is in itself sufficient guarantee of materiality in the first instance.'

The validity of sec. 40, in the form in which it was then, was upheld by the High Court in that case. To understand the argument, it is necessary to refer to sec. 39 of the Judiciary Act. Sec. 39 (1), which is an exercise of Commonwealth legislative power under sec. 77 (ii) of the Constitution, declared that the jurisdiction of the High Court, so far as it was not already exclusive of the jurisdiction of any State court under secs. 38 and 38A of the Judiciary Act, should be exclusive of the jurisdiction of the several courts of the States except as provided in this section. Sec. 39 (2), which is an exercise of power under sec. 77 (iii), then invested State courts with federal jurisdiction in all matters in which the High Court has original jurisdiction or may have original jurisdiction conferred upon it, except as provided in secs. 38 and 38A, and subject to conditions which are set out in paras. (a) to (d) of the sub-section. Under paras. (a) to (c) appeals from State courts exercising federal jurisdiction were specially regulated, and sec. 39 (2) (d) prescribed the constitution of State courts of summary jurisdiction when exercising federal jurisdiction. (Sec. 39 is in similar form today except that sec. 38A has been repealed as well as the condition in paragraph (b) of sec. 39 (2)

---

[34] (1925) 37 C.L.R. 36, 73.

which provided for an appeal to the High Court from a State court where an appeal lay to the State Supreme Court.)[35]

The nub of the section is sec. 39 (2) (a) which was designed to ensure that appeals from State courts exercising federal jurisdiction should not by-pass the High Court. This section, like sec. 38A, was part of a legislative scheme designed to shut out appeals to the Privy Council. The validity of this elaborate legislative scheme, so far as it purported to regulate these appeals, was considered and upheld in decisions of the High Court.[36] The enactment of sec. 39 meant that State courts were deprived of *State* jurisdiction in respect of certain matters and invested with *federal* jurisdiction in respect of those very matters. It also meant that in certain matters the High Court and the courts of the States exercised concurrent original federal jurisdiction. For example: the section deprived State courts of their pre-existing *State* jurisdiction in matters between residents of different States and then invested them with federal jurisdiction in these matters. The High Court and the State courts have concurrent original federal jurisdiction in these matters.[37]

In *Ex parte Walsh and Johnson*,[38] the High Court pointed out that jurisdiction in matters arising under the Constitution or involving its interpretation had been taken away from State courts as a matter of State jurisdiction by sec. 39 (1) and invested in State courts as a matter of federal jurisdiction by sec. 39 (2). The power to invest State courts with federal jurisdiction under sec. 77 (iii) authorized the imposition of conditions on the exercise of such jurisdiction. Starke J. said:

> The Judiciary Act, sec. 40, simply provides for the removal from the State Courts in certain cases of any cause or part of a cause arising under the Constitution or involving its interpretation. But as the jurisdiction exercised by the State Courts is, as we have seen, Federal jurisdiction, the provisions of secs 76 and 77 of the Constitution contain ample authority, in my opinion, for the Parliament to withdraw any matter from that jurisdiction, and remove it into the High Court or any other Federal Court, and to provide for its remission again, as in sec. 42 to the State Courts. I entertain no doubt of the validity of the provisions of sec. 40 of the Judiciary Act.[39]

As has been mentioned, sec. 40 now goes beyond constitutional matters and permits removal from a State court of any cause in-

---

[35] Judiciary Amendment Act 1976.
[36] See pp. 199 ff.
[37] See pp. 87-8 *post*.
[38] (1925) 37 C.L.R. 36.
[39] at p. 129.

volving the exercise of federal jurisdiction by that court or of any cause pending in a federal or Territory court.

So far as removal from State courts is concerned the reasoning in *Ex parte Walsh and Johnson* regarding the validity of sec. 40 in its old form may not be fully applicable to the present section. When sec. 40 was confined to matters arising under the Constitution or involving its interpretation, it was clear that the State court could be exercising only federal jurisdiction because any State jurisdiction had been excluded by sec. 39 (1) and federal jurisdiction conferred by sec. 39 (2). However, in respect of matters within sec. 76 of the Constitution, where original jurisdiction has not been conferred on the High Court by the Parliament, sec. 39 (1) could not, of course, operate. But under sec. 39 (2) federal jurisdiction was conferred on State courts in *all* matters enumerated in secs. 75 and 76 and is authorized by sec. 77 (iii) of the Constitution. It was suggested in a number of cases that in certain matters State courts could exercise both federal and State jurisdiction with different requirements as to the composition of courts of summary jurisdiction and with different rights of appeal depending on whether the case was tried in *State* or *federal* jurisdiction.[40]

If this were the case the operation of sec. 40 (2) in respect of, for example, a matter arising under a Commonwealth law would depend on whether the State court was in respect of the particular matter exercising federal jurisdiction or State jurisdiction. If it were State jurisdiction sec. 40 (2) would not operate, nor could it constitutionally do so. It seems probable, however, that the High Court will hold that where a State court can possibly exercise State or federal jurisdiction in respect of the same matter, sec. 109 of the Constitution operates to deprive the State court of its State jurisdiction.[41] This raises problems that will be discussed later.[42] When the cause is removed into the High Court, sec. 40 (3) confers on the High Court jurisdiction to hear and determine the matter if the High Court does not otherwise have jurisdiction, i.e. when it is not a matter coming within sec. 75 of the Constitution, sec. 30 of the Judiciary Act or within any other law conferring jurisdiction on the High Court.

There would seem no doubt as to the constitutional validity of sec. 40 in so far as it deals with the removal of causes from federal or Territory courts. Clearly, if the cause is pending in a federal

---

[40] See, for example, *Booth v. Shelmerdine* [1924] V.L.R. 276; pp. 224-5 *post.*
[41] *Felton v. Mulligan* (1971) 124 C.L.R. 367.
[42] See pp. 224 ff. *post.*

C

court, it must be a matter within federal jurisdiction. So far as Territory courts are concerned, this will be dealt with later.[43]

It will be seen from the foregoing account that the High Court possesses a substantial original jurisdiction, part of which is exclusive and part concurrent. The constitutional power to make jurisdiction exclusive under sec. 77 (ii) is a power to make it exclusive of State courts, and sec. 77 (i), which confers power to define the jurisdiction of federal courts other than the High Court, would, if the power to create an American type hierarchy of federal courts were exercised, authorize Parliament to define the extent to which the original jurisdiction of the High Court should be exclusive of that of other federal courts. But since the power to create federal courts under sec. 71 has been very sparingly exercised, sec. 77 (ii) has been the vehicle by which the exclusive original jurisdiction of the High Court has been defined under Chapter III of the Constitution.

The original jurisdiction of the Supreme Court of the United States is much more narrowly confined. Art. III, sec. 2 provides:

> The judicial power shall extend to all Cases, in Law and Equity, arising under this Constitution, the Laws of the United States, and Treaties made, or which shall be made, under their Authority;—to all Cases affecting Ambassadors, other public Ministers and Consuls;—to all Cases of admiralty and maritime Jurisdiction;—to controversies to which the United States shall be a Party; to Controversies between two or more States;—between a State and Citizens of another State;—between Citizens of different States;—between Citizens of the same State claiming lands under Grants of different States, and between a State, or the Citizens thereof, and foreign States, Citizens or Subjects.
>
> In all Cases affecting Ambassadors, other public Ministers and Consuls, and those in which a State shall be a Party, the Supreme Court shall have original jurisdiction. In all the other Cases before mentioned, the Supreme Court shall have appellate jurisdiction both as to Law and Fact, with such Exceptions, and under such Regulations as the Congress shall make.

Art. III, sec. 2 has to be read subject to the Eleventh Amendment, ratified in 1795, which provides that 'the Judicial power of the United States shall not be construed to extend to any suit in law or equity, commenced or prosecuted against one of the United States by Citizens of another State, or by Citizens or Subjects of any Foreign State'. This amendment was adopted following the decision in *Chisholm v. Georgia*[44] where it was held that there was jurisdiction to try a case which a citizen of one State might bring

---

43 See Chapter 4 *post*.
44 (1793) 2 Dall. 419.

against another State notwithstanding the refusal of consent by the defendant State to the assumption of jurisdiction. It is now the law that in these circumstances a State may only be sued with its consent, although it may freely bring an action as plaintiff. A proposal to include a provision comparable to the Eleventh Amendment in the Judicature Chapter of the Commonwealth Constitution was made at the Constitutional Convention of 1897.[45] The clause provided that 'nothing in this Constitution shall be construed to authorize any suit in law or equity against the Commonwealth or any person sued on behalf of the Commonwealth, or against a State or any person sued on behalf of a State by any individual person or corporation, except by the consent of the Commonwealth, or of the State, as the case might be', but it was unceremoniously struck out.[46]

The original jurisdiction of the Supreme Court of the United States is specifically conferred by the Constitution, so that there is no power in Congress to restrict it. The same is true of the original jurisdiction conferred by sec. 75 of the Commonwealth Constitution. On the other hand, there is no American counterpart to sec. 76 of the Australian Constitution authorizing parliamentary extension of the original jurisdiction of the High Court, and the Supreme Court ruled early in *Marbury v. Madison*[47] that Congress has no such power. Art. III, sec. 2, in prescribing the original jurisdiction of the Supreme Court, has not been read as conferring a necessarily exclusive original jurisdiction, and it is now well settled that Congress may provide that matters within the original jurisdiction may be concurrently vested in inferior federal courts, and may reach the Supreme Court on appeal.[48] The Judiciary Act 1789 first delimited the exclusive and concurrent original jurisdiction of the Supreme Court. The present situation is that the Supreme Court possesses *exclusive original* jurisdiction in all controversies between two or more States and in all actions or proceedings *against* ambassadors or other public ministers of foreign states or their domestic servants, which are not inconsistent with the law of nations.[49] The Court has *concur-*

---

45 Debs. (1897), pp. 989-90.
46 Hunt, *op. cit.*, p. 196.
47 (1801) 1 Cranch 137.
48 See Wagner: The Original and Exclusive Jurisdiction of the United States Supreme Court (1952) 2 St Louis University L.J. 111; Surridge: Jurisdiction over Suits against Foreign Consuls in the United States (1932) 80 U. of Pennsylvania L.R. 972; note (1926) 39 Harvard L.R. 1084; Hart and Wechsler: The Federal Courts and the Federal System (1953) pp. 218-87.
49 28 U.S.C. s. 1251.

*rent* original jurisdiction in all actions or proceedings brought by ambassadors or other public ministers of foreign states or to which consuls or vice-consuls of foreign states are parties, in all controversies between the United States and a State, and in all actions or proceedings by a State against the citizens of another State or against aliens. In general, it will be seen that the existing and potential original jurisdiction of the High Court of Australia is considerably larger than that of the Supreme Court of the United States. Only in respect of the jurisdiction against aliens is the American jurisdiction wider, for the Commonwealth Constitution does not in terms confer original jurisdiction on the High Court in suits between States and non-resident aliens. Under sec. 75 (iii) in a case in which the Commonwealth is a party, the High Court has original jurisdiction, and it is possible that the other party may be an alien. Likewise, under one or other of the heads of jurisdiction in sec. 76, a case may arise in which a State and a non-resident alien will be parties.

It is to be noted that the original jurisdiction of the High Court under secs. 75 and 76 arises only in respect of *matters*. In *In re Judiciary and Navigation Acts*,[50] it was held that sec. 88 of the Judiciary Act 1903-20 was invalid. This purported to give the High Court jurisdiction to 'hear and determine' any question referred to it by the Governor-General as to the validity of any enactment of the Parliament of the Commonwealth. The Court construed the section as a grant of judicial power invalidly conferred because secs. 75 and 76 of the Constitution defined the jurisdiction of the High Court by reference to 'matters' which postulated the existence of a *lis inter partes*. 'We do not think that the word "matter" in sec. 76 means a legal proceeding, but rather the subject-matter for determination in a legal proceeding. In our opinion there can be no matter within the meaning of the section unless there is some immediate right, duty or liability to be established by the determination of the Court.'[51] The terms of the Constitution, on this reading, precluded the giving of advisory opinions. Art. III, sec. 2 of the United States Constitution, which adopts the language of cases and controversies rather than of matters, has likewise been construed as forbidding the giving of advisory opinions by the Supreme Court of the United States.[52]

It has been questioned whether the power to give an advisory

---

[50] (1921) 29 C.L.R. 257.

[51] *In re Judiciary and Navigation Acts* (1921) 29 C.L.R. 257, 265.

[52] See The Constitution of the United States of America: Analysis and Interpretation (Ed. Small & Jayson, 1964) at pp. 616-617.

opinion might be more appropriately described as non-judicial and therefore the purported grant of such power would be invalid as a result of the doctrine in the *Boilermakers' Case*.[53] In the *Boilermakers' Case* itself it was not necessary for either the Privy Council or the High Court to determine that question. The doctrine of the *Boilermakers' Case* has itself been questioned by two judges of the High Court[54] and it has been argued that the Court should refuse to follow that case. If it is held that a federal court can be given non-judicial functions but that its judicial functions are restricted to the matters specified in Chapter III of the Constitution, the correctness of the classification of advisory opinions in *In re Judiciary and Navigation Acts* could become important. It has been reaffirmed by Jacobs J. [55]

The rigour of this rule preventing the conferring on federal courts of power to give advisory opinions has been mitigated by the broad scope which the High Court has given to the declaratory judgement remedy in public law litigation. The Court has infrequently directed its attention to the justiciability of the particular issue—certainly less frequently than does the Supreme Court of the United States—and there are cases in which the High Court has entertained suits for declarations in circumstances where, as has been aptly said, 'the prematurity and breadth of the challenge, and the abstract manner in which the legal issues were presented, make the suit resemble a proceeding for an advisory opinion'.[56] It seems probable that the High Court has been influenced in these cases, which are exceptional, by the importance of the legislation challenged, the desirability of a speedy determination of its validity, and in some cases by the inconvenience attendant on delaying a decision until after the enactment had come into full operation.[57] Such a case was *Attorney-General for Victoria v. Commonwealth*[58] where an application was made in the original jurisdiction of the High Court for a declaration that the Pharmaceutical Benefits Act 1944 was unconstitutional and void, on the ground that it was *ultra vires* the Commonwealth Parliament. The Act had not been proclaimed and it was unsuccess-

---

[53] *Attorney-General for the Commonwealth v. The Queen; ex parte The Boilermakers' Society of Australia* (1957) 95 C.L.R. 529, 541 (P.C.). See also (1956) 94 C.L.R. 254, 272-4 (H.C.).

[54] *R. v. Joske* (1974) 130 C.L.R. 87, 90, 102.

[55] *Commonwealth v. Queensland* (1975) 7 A.L.R. 351, 372-3.

[56] Foster: The Declaratory Judgment in Australia and the United States (1958) 1 Melbourne U.L.R. 347, 391.

[57] ibid.

[58] (1945) 71 C.L.R. 237, esp. at 277-9.

fully argued on the authority of *In re Judiciary and Navigation Acts* that there was no 'matter' before the Court but merely an abstract question of law. It was pointed out that the Act would shortly be proclaimed, and that the necessary preliminary steps were being taken so that it could be brought into effective operation. It followed that the question would shortly arise whether the public in the various States was entitled to the benefits and subject to the obligations imposed by the Act. The cause of action was founded on the right of an individual in some instances, and in others of the public, or a section of the public, to restrain a public body clothed with statutory powers from exceeding those powers. On this view there was a 'matter' for decision, and the Attorney-General had standing to sue on behalf of the public of the State of Victoria. There are other cases of this type.[59] Some judges have gone further and stated that a State may challenge the constitutional validity of Commonwealth Acts, even where no injury to the public is shown, on the ground that the nature of the Constitution is such that the Commonwealth and each State has a right to the observance of constitutional limits by the other.[60]

In *Attorney-General for Australia ex rel. McKinlay v. Commonwealth*[61] the Commonwealth Attorney-General granted a fiat to permit a challenge to Commonwealth legislation. No question of standing was raised. Jacobs J. in *Commonwealth v. Queensland*[62] stated that the Commonwealth Attorney-General could seek a declaration as to the validity of a Commonwealth Act. If this is so, there is, as His Honour pointed out, scarcely any difference in substance between that procedure and the provisions of sec. 88 of the Judiciary Act that were invalidated. The difficulty with that view is that the other party to the suit would be the Commonwealth and there would be little guarantee that the suit would be an adversary one. Under the invalidated provisions, notice of the hearing was required to be given to the Attorney-General of each State, who was given a right to appear and to be repre-

---

59 See e.g. *Union Label Case* (1908) 6 C.L.R. 469; *Commonwealth v. Queensland* (1920) 29 C.L.R. 1; *South Australia v. Commonwealth* (1942) 65 C.L.R. 373; *Australian National Airways Ltd v. Commonwealth* (1945) 71 C.L.R. 29; *Bank of New South Wales v. Commonwealth* (1948) 76 C.L.R. 1; *Australian Communist Party v. Commonwealth* (1951) 83 C.L.R. 1; see Foster, *ante* note 56 at 373 *et seq.*; *Attorney-General (Vict.) v. Commonwealth* (1962) 107 C.L.R. 529.

60 *Victoria v. Commonwealth* (1975) 7 A.L.R. 277, 314-6, *per* Gibbs J.; 330-1 *per* Mason J.

61 (1975) 7 A.L.R. 593.

62 (1975) 7 A.L.R. 351, 373.

sented at the hearing. Sec. 78A of the Judiciary Act, as amended in 1976, gives a right to the Attorneys-General of the Commonwealth and the States to intervene in proceedings relating to the Constitution and sec. 78B requires a court, other than the High Court, in such matters not to proceed until the court is satisfied that notice has been given to the Attorneys-General. In the circumstances, therefore, if the Attorney-General of the Commonwealth may seek a declaration as to the validity of Commonwealth legislation, it may be, as Jacobs J. suggested in *Attorney-General for New South Wales ex rel. McKellar v. Commonwealth*[63] that *In re Judiciary and Navigation Acts* does no more than affect the manner of bringing constitutional questions before the court. The practice of the High Court in such cases is more liberal than that of the Supreme Court of the United States.

### III

The High Court of Australia, unlike the Supreme Court of the United States, is peripatetic, and it is therefore necessary to prescribe rules of venue. The principal registry of the Court is at present in Sydney[64] and there are district registries in Canberra and in the capital cities of the various States.[65] The general rule is that an action in the original jurisdiction of the High Court may be brought in any registry of the Court,[66] but a defendant who neither resides nor carries on business in the State of the registry may elect to appear at the principal registry rather than the registry in which the writ is issued.[67] If he elects to appear at the principal registry, the trial of the action shall take place there.[68] It is further provided that a party may make an application to the High Court for an order that the cause be transferred to another registry, and the Court, in its discretion, may make or refuse the order.[69] The High Court of its own motion may direct a transfer at any stage of the suit.[70] In *Queen v. Langdon*,[71] which was a custody application brought in the original diversity jurisdiction of the High Court under sec. 75 (iv) of the Constitution, the original application was made to a justice in the New South Wales registry.

[63] (1977) 12 A.L.R. 129.
[64] Judiciary Act, sec. 10. Commonwealth Gazette No. 80, 2 July 1973.
[65] ibid., sec. 11.
[66] High Court Procedure Act, sec. 6 (1).
[67] ibid., sec. 6 (2).
[68] ibid., sec. 6 (3).
[69] ibid., sec. 7.
[70] ibid., sec. 25.
[71] (1953) 88 C.L.R. 158.

The judge adjourned the hearing, which was transferred to the Victorian registry, and the case was tried there.[72]

The trial of indictable offences against laws of the Commonwealth in the High Court is by a justice with a jury,[73] but in other cases, unless the Court or justice otherwise directs, the trial of an action in the High Court is by a justice without a jury.[74]

In general, the original jurisdiction of the High Court may be exercised by a single justice,[75] who may state a case or reserve any question for the consideration of a Full Court, which shall thereupon have power to hear and determine the case or question.[76] This procedure is frequently adopted in constitutional cases. In general, a Full Court may be constituted by two or more justices,[77] but a Full Court consisting of less than all the justices may not give a decision on a question affecting the constitutional powers of the Commonwealth, unless at least three justices concur in the decision.[78]

The authority of decisions of single justices of the High Court, exercising original jurisdiction, in State Supreme Courts, was briefly considered by Macfarlan J. of the Supreme Court of Victoria in *R. v. Sodeman*.[79] That was a murder case, involving a defence of insanity. Macfarlan J. referred to Dixon J.'s charge to the jury in *R. v. Porter*,[80] a murder trial in the original jurisdiction of the High Court at Canberra, and said that he did not think that Dixon J. intended to lay down any new rule on the burden of proof in insanity. If, however, Dixon J. intended to state a rule which departed from English authority, Macfarlan J. said that he 'should decline to follow him'.[81] In cases of concurrent original jurisdiction in the High Court and State courts, the theory of federal jurisdiction supports the view that they are for

72 See also *Gleeson v. Williamson* (1972) 46 A.L.J.R. 677.

73 High Court Procedure Act, sec. 15A; Constitution, sec. 80.

74 High Court Procedure Act, sec. 12. See *Huntley v. Alexander* (1922) 30 C.L.R. 566; *Henry v. Commonwealth* (1937) 43 A.L.R. 409; *McDermott v. Collien* (1953) 87 C.L.R. 154; *Inglis v. Commonwealth Trading Bank of Australia* (1969) 119 C.L.R. 334.

75 Judiciary Act, sec. 15.

76 ibid., sec. 18.

77 ibid., sec. 19.

78 ibid., sec. 23. It is also provided in sec. 22 of the Judiciary Act that application for a certificate authorizing an appeal to the Privy Council in a case involving an *inter se* question shall be heard and determined by a Full Court consisting of not less than three judges.

79 [1936] V.L.R. 99.

80 (1933) 6 A.L.J. 394-5.

81 [1936] V.L.R. at p. 103.

this purpose co-ordinate, and that the litigant may choose between a State and a federal court. Practically speaking, the only
federal tribunal exercising substantial original jurisdiction is
the High Court, and for the rest, federal jurisdiction—apart from
the specialized jurisdiction of the Federal Court of Australia and
the Family Court of Australia—is conferred on State courts. There
may be occasions where a litigant's choice is between the High
Court and a State court exercising non-federal jurisdiction,[82] but
most often it is between the High Court and a State court exercising federal jurisdiction. But whether the State court is exercising non-federal or federal jurisdiction, in those cases in which the
High Court has concurrent original jurisdiction, the litigant
chooses as between a State court and the High Court. It does not
appear unreasonable that a State Supreme Court should in a
proper case decline to follow the decision of a single justice of the
High Court exercising its original jurisdiction. That original
jurisdiction may also be exercised by a Full High Court on a
reference by a single justice stating a case under sec. 18 of the
Judiciary Act. Such a reference, say, in a diversity case, would still
involve the exercise of concurrent original jurisdiction, but having regard to the position of the High Court as a general court
of appeal under sec. 73 of the Constitution—where it must be a
Full Court[83]—it could not be sensibly argued that a State Supreme

---

82 This may possibly arise in Admiralty where the High Court exercises
jurisdiction conferred by the Colonial Courts of Admiralty Act. State Supreme
Courts also have conferred on them Admiralty jurisdiction derived from the
same Imperial source, which is non-federal. By operation of sec. 39 (2) of
the Judiciary Act, it would seem that they may exercise federal jurisdiction in
Admiralty and maritime matters within the meaning of sec. 76 (iii) of the
Constitution. It has been assumed in many cases that the civil jurisdiction
exercised by State courts in Admiralty matters is that derived from the
Colonial Courts of Admiralty Act. The issue of criminal jurisdiction in Admiralty of State Supreme Courts was the subject of disagreement among the
judges of the High Court in *R. v. Bull* (1974) 131 C.L.R. 203. In *Oteri v. R.*
(1976) 11 A.L.R. 142, the Privy Council considered that the exercise of
criminal jurisdiction of Admiralty was regulated in Australian State Courts
by the Admiralty Offences (Colonial) Act 1849 and the Courts (Colonial)
Jurisdiction Act 1874. They granted special leave to appeal from the Supreme Court of Western Australia. This they would have been unable to
do if it was considered that the Western Australian Court was exercising
jurisdiction under sec. 39 of the Judiciary Act, because of the limitation in
sec. 39 (2)(a). In the light of *Felton v. Mulligan* (1971) 124 C.L.R. 367 (discussed
pp. 225-8 *post*.) , it is arguable that a State court cannot exercise non-federal
jurisdiction if it is invested with federal jurisdiction to deal with the matter
(see pp. 224 ff. *post*.) .

83 Judiciary Act, secs. 20, 21.

Court could decline to follow a decision of a Full High Court, whatever the jurisdiction in which the High Court was sitting.

## IV

In a discussion of the various heads of federal jurisdiction under Art. III, sec. 2 of the United States Constitution, the Supreme Court of the United States observed that 'it is apparent upon the face of these clauses that in one class of cases the jurisdiction of the courts of the Union depends on the character of the cause, whatever may be the parties, and in the other on the character of the parties, whatever may be the subject of controversy'.[84] The subject-matters of original jurisdiction of the High Court of Australia under secs. 75 and 76 of the Constitution are similarly classified. Sec. 75 (i) matters arising under any treaty, sec. 76 (i) matters arising under this Constitution or involving its interpretation, sec. 76 (ii) matters arising under any laws made by the Parliament, 76 (iii) matters of Admiralty and maritime jurisdiction and 76 (iv) matters relating to the same subject-matter claimed under the laws of different States are all concerned with 'the character of the cause, whatever may be the parties'. Sec. 75 (ii) matters affecting consuls or other representatives of other countries; sec. 75 (iii) matters in which the Commonwealth or a person suing or being sued on behalf of the Commonwealth is a party; sec. 75 (iv) matters between States or between a State and a resident of another State are matters depending 'on the character of the parties whatever may be the controversy'. Sec. 75 (v) matters in which a writ of *mandamus* or prohibition or an injunction is sought against an officer of the Commonwealth, which as a matter of original jurisdiction has no counterpart in the United States Constitution, has traces of both elements, since it depends partly upon the character of the remedy sought and partly upon the character of the parties.[85]

It is clear that in selecting the subject-matter of federal jurisdiction, the framers of the Commonwealth Constitution relied heavily on American precedent. The main departure was sec. 75 (v) which forms 'no part of Article III but (was) inspired by the provisions of the American Judiciary Act held invalid in *Marbury v. Madison*'.[86] This was more fully explained by Barton J. in

---

[84] *United States v. Texas* (1892) 143 U.S. 621, *per* Harlan J.

[85] See *Carter v. Egg and Egg Pulp Marketing Board* (Vic.) (1942) 66 C.L.R. 557, 579, *per* Latham C. J.

[86] *Collins v. Charles Marshall Pty. Ltd.* (1955) 92 C.L.R. 529, 544.

*Ah Yick v. Lehmert.*[87] In *Marbury v. Madison*,[88] the Judiciary Act provision which was held invalid authorized the Supreme Court in its original jurisdiction to issue a *mandamus* against a non-judicial officer of the United States. Since the Constitution did not specifically confer *original* jurisdiction on the Supreme Court to issue a *mandamus* in such a case, it was held that the purported congressional grant of power was *ultra vires*.[89] But even here the American influence was so strong that two leading lawyer members of the 1897-8 Convention, who subsequently became justices of the High Court, were led into error. For reasons which will appear later, this clause was under heavy attack by Mr Isaacs. In the course of the debate, Mr Higgins said: 'The provision was in the Bill of 1891 and I thought it was taken from the American Constitution.'[90] Mr Barton was equally ill informed: 'I fancy it is in some part of the American Constitution.'[91] In this situation, when leading lawyer members of the Convention were so obviously vague and ill-informed about the purpose and origins of the clause, Mr Isaacs carried the day and the clause was struck out. Mr Barton, better briefed, came back a little later to explain the point of the clause by reference to *Marbury v. Madison*. Mr Isaacs pressed his objections, but the clause was restored in its present form.[92]

Another clause—sec. 76 (iv): matters relating to the same subject-matter claimed under the laws of different States—does not appear to have an obvious counterpart in the United States Constitution. When Mr Barton was questioned about this clause at Melbourne in 1898 he offered the answer: 'It is in the American Constitution,'[93] and went on to say 'This is similar to the power in the American Constitution, which is described as controversies between two or more States. It was thought that the words "two

87 (1905) 2 C.L.R. 593, 609.

88 (1801) 1 Cranch 137.

89 'It is well known that there is a difference between our Constitution and that of the United States, because in the former, original jurisdiction is by sec. 75 (v) given to the High Court in matters in which mandamus is sought against a non-judicial *(quaere)* officer of the Commonwealth. That case was not provided for in the United States Constitution, and hence the decision in *Marbury v. Madison* that mandamus to a non-judicial officer was outside the powers of the Constitution and that therefore the Act of Congress purporting to authorize the grant of such a mandamus was not valid.' *Ah Yick v. Lehmert* (1905) 2 C.L.R. 593, 609, *per* Barton J.

90 Debs. Melb. (1898), vol. 1, p. 321.

91 ibid., p. 321.

92 ibid., vol. 2, p. 1875; La Nauze, *op. cit.*, pp. 233-4.

93 Debs. Melb. (1898), vol. 1, p. 321.

or more" were unnecessary.'[94] There was a little more discussion, but this apparently satisfied the Convention and the clause was agreed to. It has not given equal satisfaction to later commentators on the Constitution. In his evidence before the Royal Commission on the Constitution in 1927, Mr Owen Dixon, K.C., said of sec. 76 (iv) that: 'so far, the meaning of this and the application of it has been elucidated by no one.'[95] Another writer, confessing perplexity, has suggested that under sec. 76 (iv) the High Court might be invested with original jurisdiction in all matters of interstate private international law.[96] On Mr Barton's explanation that the clause was intended to provide jurisdiction in controversies between States, it is obviously redundant for that matter is fully covered by sec. 75 (iv). The Commonwealth Parliament has never attempted an interpretation of sec. 76 (iv), for no action has been taken to confer original jurisdiction on the High Court under it. It is to be noted that under sec. 39 (2) of the Judiciary Act, the State courts are invested with federal jurisdiction in matters falling within sec. 76 (iv).

Sec. 75 (i) and (ii) very clearly reflect the influence of the American model. Art. III, sec. 2 conferred federal jurisdiction in all cases arising under treaties made under the Constitution and laws of the United States and in all cases affecting ambassadors, other public ministers and consuls. The Supreme Court was given original jurisdiction in cases involving ambassadors, other public ministers and consuls. In the Commonwealth Constitution, the High Court was given original jurisdiction in all matters arising under any treaty and in matters affecting consuls or other representatives of other countries. Sec. 38 of the Judiciary Act added a complication by providing that in matters arising *directly* under any treaty, the jurisdiction of the High Court should be exclusive of that of the State courts. This means, in the absence of competent federal courts, that it is the exclusive forum for such cases in Australia. In matters arising, otherwise than *directly*, under a treaty, and in matters affecting consuls or other representatives of other countries, the Judiciary Act sec. 39 (1) and (2) operates to confer concurrent original jurisdiction on the High Court and State courts, which can exercise only federal jurisdiction in respect of such matters. In cases in which ambassadors and public ministers are *defendants*, the Supreme Court of the United States has exclusive original jurisdiction. When ambassadors and public

---

94 ibid., p. 322.
95 Royal Commission, Minutes of Evidence, p. 786.
96 Wynes: The Judicial Power of the Commonwealth (1938) 12 A.L.J. 8, 9.

ministers are *plaintiffs* and when consuls are *parties*, there is con-current original jurisdiction in the Supreme Court and inferior federal courts.

In The Federalist Papers, Hamilton expounded the case for conferring original jurisdiction on the Supreme Court in respect of ambassadors, public ministers and consuls as follows:

> Public Ministers of every class are the immediate representatives of their sovereigns. All questions in which they are concerned are so directly connected with the public peace, that as well for the preserva-tion of this, as out of respect to the sovereignties they represent, it is both expedient and proper that such questions should be submitted in the first instance to the highest judiciary of the nation. Though con-suls have not in strictness a diplomatic character, yet as they are the public agents of the nations to which they belong, the same observa-tions are in a great measure applicable to them.[97]

This touches the question of the proper forum in actions affecting ambassadors and public ministers. It does not touch the question of diplomatic immunity, that is, whether such persons may *claim* immunity from judicial process in any court. As the law stands, diplomatic immunity may be invoked to exclude the jurisdiction of the courts altogether where actions are brought against diplomatic representatives and their diplomatic families, and the decision on waiver of privilege rests with the sovereign, and not with the diplomatic representative.[98] Moreover, consuls appear to bob along in the rear, drawn in by the magnetic influ-ence of superior foreign representatives. It has been suggested that the rationale of the rule which attracts the original jurisdiction of the Supreme Court to cases affecting consuls is that they are appointed to and received by the Union and not by the States, which abandoned all their international law personality to the United States.[99] Here also, there are problems of consular immunities.[100]

Alexander Hamilton, of course, argued his case in the light of the conditions and circumstances which attended the making of the United States Constitution. It has already been pointed out that federal and State elements distrusted each other; that it was not considered possible or desirable to create an integrated judicial system in which the Supreme Court of the United States

[97] Federalist Papers, No. 81.

[98] See Wagner: The Original and Exclusive Jurisdiction of the United States Supreme Court (1952) 2 St Louis L.J. 111; Hart and Wechsler, *op. cit.* at pp. 264-7.

[99] Wagner, *op. cit.*, p. 132.

[100] See Beckett: Consular Immunities (1944) 21 British Y.B.I.L. 34.

would exercise *general* appellate jurisdiction, or in which the State courts would discharge national (i.e. federal) judicial functions. Since the foreign relations of the United States were the preserve of the national government, it followed that State courts had to be prevented from tampering with national foreign policies. So far as foreign diplomatic representatives were concerned this object was achieved by excluding the jurisdiction of the State courts.[101] It is a little surprising that the American Founding Fathers thought it necessary that certain cases affecting ambassadors and public ministers should be tried in the original jurisdiction of the Supreme Court, but were quite prepared to relegate cases arising under treaties to the original jurisdiction of inferior federal courts. It might have been thought, having regard to the importance of foreign relations, that it was at least as important to direct justiciable issues arising out of treaties into the original jurisdiction of the supreme federal court. In the Australian scheme, matters arising directly under treaties were assigned to the exclusive original jurisdiction of the High Court, but there was no provision for exclusive jurisdiction in the case of matters affecting consuls and other representatives of other States.

Having regard to the very different circumstances which attended the making of the Australian Constitution—specifically the difference in attitude to the jurisdiction of the High Court as a general court of appeal and to the investment of State courts with federal jurisdiction—it has to be asked whether the reasoning which led to the assignment of these matters to federal jurisdiction in the United States has any application to Australian circumstances. An explanation of the treaty jurisdiction was offered by Latham C.J. in *R. v. Burgess*.[102] After considering the plan of the Constitution which, as interpreted, conferred power on the Executive to make treaties (sec. 61) and on the Legislature to implement them (sec. 51 (xxix)), he said:

> Questions may arise under treaties with other countries, and accordingly the plan is completed by a provision in sec. 75 of the Constitution that the High Court shall have original jurisdiction in all matters arising under a treaty. Thus in the provisions of the Constitution dealing with the three functions of government, executive, legislative and judicial, the same principle is found. O'Connor J. said

[101] For a time from 1875 to 1911 the State courts were given concurrent jurisdiction in cases involving consuls. See Surridge: Jurisdiction over Suits against Foreign Consuls in the United States (1932) 80 U. of Pa L.R. 972; Hart and Wechsler, *op. cit.* at p. 269.

[102] (1936) 55 C.L.R. 608, 643-4.

in 1908 that the powers of the Constitution 'vest in the Common-wealth the power of controlling in every respect Australia's relations with the outside world'.

This, with respect, is hindsight. The Australian Founding Fathers at no stage envisaged that sec. 61 of the Constitution would be the source of executive power to conclude treaties, for the very simple reason that they did not contemplate that the treaty-making function would pass out of Imperial into Colonial hands. The original form of the legislative power was 'external affairs and treaties', and the words 'and treaties' were struck out, since treaties were not a matter for colonial action.[103] When sec. 75 (i)—matters arising under any treaty—was under discussion at the Melbourne meeting of the Convention in 1898, one member moved to have the clause struck out on the ground that 'the court cannot decide upon a treaty, otherwise it might abrogate the Im-perial law or polity upon the question at issue'.[104] To this, an apparently satisfactory answer was given by Mr Symon of South Australia: 'Some day hereafter it may be within the scope of the Commonwealth to deal with matters of this kind. . . . It cannot do any harm to leave this provision in the clause.'[105]

It is fairly clear that the Founding Fathers were not very sure of what they were doing here. Moreover they overlooked one very important point which was made by Mr Dixon in his evidence before the Royal Commission on the Constitution:

> No one yet knows what is meant by the expression 'matter arising under a treaty'. The word 'matter' refers to some claim the subject of litigation. It must, therefore, be a claim of legal right, privilege or immunity. Under a British system, the executive cannot, by making a treaty, regulate the rights of its subjects. A state of war may be ended or commenced, and the rights and duties of persons may be affected by the change from one State to another, but this results from the general law relating to peace and war, and not from the terms of the treaty. If a treaty is adopted by the legislature and its terms are converted into a statute, it is the statute and not the treaty which affects the rights and duties of the persons.[106]

The judicial power with respect to treaties has a more obvious meaning in the United States where a treaty may be self-executing under the terms of Art. VI, sec. 2, so that on being made in proper form under Art. II, sec. 2 it may become the law of the land without any necessity for congressional implementation.

103 Debs. Melb. (1898), vol. 1, p. 30.
104 ibid., p. 320.
105 ibid., p. 320.
106 Royal Commission, Minutes of Evidence, p. 785.

This situation was quite clearly envisaged by the American Founding Fathers.[107] Australia, on the other hand, adopted the British distinction between treaty *making* and treaty *implementation*. This distinction was stated in the Privy Council by Lord Atkin:

> Within the British Empire there is a well established rule that the making of a treaty is an executive act, while the performance of its obligations, if they entail alteration of the existing domestic law, requires legislative action. Unlike some other countries, the stipulations of a treaty duly ratified do not within the Empire, by virtue of the treaty alone, have the force of law.[108]

This being the case, it is not easy to see when a matter will arise under a treaty within the terms of sec. 75 (i). A problem may arise whether legislation in purported implementation of a treaty is validly enacted under sec. 51 (xxix), but that would appear to be a matter in which the High Court would have original jurisdiction under sec. 76 (i) of the Constitution (Judiciary Act, sec. 30 (a)) as a matter arising under the Constitution or involving its interpretation. If there is a question arising out of the legislative implementation of a treaty, which does not involve constitutional interpretation, the appropriate head of jurisdiction might be sec. 76 (ii): matters arising under any laws made by the Parliament, but in this case there has been no general grant of original jurisdiction to the High Court. It is difficult to formulate a justiciable issue which would arise squarely under the terms of sec. 75 (i), and it is more difficult still to give a meaning to the word 'directly' in the case of matters arising directly under any treaty, which are assigned to the exclusive original jurisdiction of the High Court by the Judiciary Act, sec. 38.

An attempt was made in *Bluett v. Fadden*[109] to interpret sec. 75 (i) and the corresponding clause in sec. 38 of the Judiciary Act. In proceedings in the Supreme Court of New South Wales, the plaintiffs challenged an order made by the Commonwealth Treasurer vesting certain shares in the Controller of Enemy

---

107 See Sutherland: Restricting the Treaty Power (1952) 65 H.L.R. 1305, 1315. One of the first great cases involving the self-executing operation of the U.S. treaty power was *Ware v. Hylton* (1796) 3 Dall. 199.

108 *Attorney-General for Canada v. Attorney-General for Ontario* [1937] A.C. 326, 347; see also a statement of the same principle in *R. v. Burgess, ex parte Henry* (1936) 55 C.L.R. 608, 644, *per* Latham C.J.; *Bradley v. Commonwealth* (1973) 47 A.L.J.R. 504 at p. 514. See Chafee: Amending the Constitution to Cripple Treaties (1952) 12 Louisiana L.R. 345.

109 [1956] S.R. (N.S.W.) 254. See also Civil Aviation (Carriers' Liability) Act 1959, sec. 19.

Property under authority conferred by the Trading with the Enemy Act 1939-1952. The defendants argued that the shares were German enemy assets within the meaning of Art. 6 of the Agreement on Reparation from Germany on the Establishment of an Inter-Allied Reparation Agency and on the Restitution of Monetary Gold, to which the Commonwealth of Australia was a party, and that the order in question was made pursuant to a regulation authorized by the Act for the purpose of giving effect to Art. 6 of the Agreement. The defendants argued further that the suit involved a matter directly arising under a treaty, within sec. 38 of the Judiciary Act, with the consequence that it lay within the exclusive original jurisdiction of the High Court.

McLelland J. adverted to the matters already discussed, and to the different legal situation with respect to treaties in the United States and Australia. He concluded however that sec. 75 (i) covered the case where the decision involved the interpretation of a treaty.

> Section 75 must, I think, be taken to refer to cases where the decision of the case depends upon the interpretation of the treaty. In such cases, the matter in question arises under the treaty.
> It is, of course, primarily the legislation which has to be interpreted but, where the terms of the treaty have by legislation been made part of the law of the land, it is in a very real sense the treaty which is being interpreted. I may add that I find it difficult to ascertain any subject-matter falling within s. 75, if s. 75 does not refer to the type of case I have mentioned.[110]

The defendants were subsequently allowed to amend to plead that the dealings with the shares were for the fraudulent purpose of cloaking German enemy interests and thus saving them harmless from the effects of control measures regarding German enemy interests, and that they were German enemy assets within the meaning of Art. 6 of the Agreement. McLelland J. held that this raised a question of the interpretation of the treaty, and that the matter was one directly arising under a treaty, so that it fell within the *exclusive* original jurisdiction of the High Court.

There are difficulties in this reading of sec. 75 (i). The issue in this case, whether there was any legal authority for divesting the plaintiffs of title to their shares, depended upon Commonwealth legislation, and the reference in that legislation to Article 6 of the Agreement did not, it is submitted, affect the situation. If the draftsman had spelled out the provisions of the Article in the legislation, but without specific reference to the Agreement as

[110] at p. 261.

D

such, it would have been difficult to argue that any matter arose
under a treaty. The fact that the draftsman adopted a shorthand
technique of direct reference to the Article cannot, intelligibly,
affect the situation. In either case, any rights, claims, or obligations arose, and arose only under authority of the legislation. If
this is so, it follows that the issues in *Bluett v. Fadden* were
matters arising under a law made by the Parliament and not
under a treaty. This may well mean, as McLelland J. observed,
that it is difficult to give any meaning to sec. 75 (i) and the corresponding clause in sec. 38 of the Judiciary Act. But this is the
result of unintelligent copying of an inappropriate American
precedent.[111]

It is to be noted that McLelland J.'s decision in *Bluett v.
Fadden* denied jurisdiction to the Supreme Court of New South
Wales, and that he allowed the defendants (though penalized in
costs) to amend specifically to raise a jurisdictional plea. If the
High Court differed from McLelland J.'s interpretation of sec. 75
(i) and sec. 38 of the Judiciary Act, it would on the particular
facts of *Bluett v. Fadden* still retain jurisdiction under sec. 75
(iii), as the Commonwealth was a defendant. In these circumstances, it is to be noted, the State Supreme Court would have
concurrent jurisdiction. But if it had not been possible to discover
another head of original jurisdiction for the High Court, and if
that Court had dissented from McLelland J.'s reading of sec. 75
(i) and sec. 38 of the Judiciary Act, the High Court would have
been obliged to dismiss the suit for want of jurisdiction. The case
would then, perforce, have come up a *third* time, this time in a
State jurisdiction, for the *first* trial on the merits. This seems to
demonstrate pretty clearly the case for the most careful scrutiny
of the original and especially the exclusive original jurisdiction of
the High Court.

The Founding Fathers were aware of the differences in treaty-
making and treaty-implementation power in the American and
Australian schemes. These were mentioned in another context in
the Convention Debates.[112] But in the Judicature Chapter they
appear to have followed the American precedent without appre-
ciating these differences, and without any apparent awareness of
any specific purpose that this grant of original jurisdiction to the
High Court might serve.

Sec. 75 (ii) is not a perfect transcription from the American

111 Lumb and Ryan: The Constitution of the Commonwealth of Australia
(2nd ed., 1977) pp. 263-4.
112 Debs. Sydney (1891) at p. 240.

Constitution. Ambassadors and public ministers disappear in the Australian text, and consuls, who are at the bottom of the American hierarchy, are at the head in the Australian clause. As Quick and Garran pointed out in 1901, there was good reason for this variation, as the diplomatic relations of Australia were conducted by the United Kingdom Government. More than twenty years later, three justices of the High Court found it 'difficult to imagine an Ambassador to Australia'.[113] At the date of federation, Australia's independent external relations were conceived as primarily commercial in character. The difference in the form of the Australian clause raises a question of interpretation. If consuls were deliberately put at the head of the list, and ambassadors and public ministers deliberately omitted, is it proper, even in the changed circumstances of today, to read the words 'other representatives of other countries' as including ambassadors, ministers and other distinctively diplomatic representatives? It might fairly be argued that in these circumstances it would not be proper to read the words 'other representatives of other countries' as including superior diplomatic representatives. Should the problem arise, however, it is likely that the court would read those words as including 'all persons officially accredited to the Commonwealth by foreign governments'.[114] This was the meaning suggested by Quick and Garran, who never, of course, envisaged that such representatives would include ambassadors and ministers.

There are other problems of interpretation. The Australian clause followed American precedent in copying the word '*affecting*' consuls. When does a matter *affect* a consul? This has occasioned some difficulty in the United States.[115] Is the jurisdiction of the High Court attracted by a matter in which a consul is affected in his *private* capacity? Quick and Garran pointed to this uncertainty and expressed the opinion that the clause applied only to consuls and other representatives in their official capacities.[116] These difficulties and obscurities were mentioned by Mr Dixon in his evidence before the Royal Commission in 1927.

> When does a matter affect a consul? He may be prosecuted in the police court for failing to register his dog; he may be sued for money borrowed. He may, and often does, conduct an independent business as well as exercise the office of consul. Do all proceedings arising out

---

113 *Commonwealth v. New South Wales* (1923) 32 C.L.R. 200, 208, *per* Isaacs, Rich and Starke JJ.

114 Quick and Garran, *op. cit.* at p. 772.

115 The Constitution of the United States of America, *op. cit.* at p. 645.

116 *op. cit.*, p. 772. See also Lumb and Ryan, *op. cit.* at p. 264 *contra*; Lane: The Australian Federal System (1972) at p. 468.

of the business affect him so that in all his legal relations he is the subject of federal jurisdiction? If he is an employer, and the party to an industrial dispute, and is summoned to a compulsory conference in the Arbitration Court, does this raise a question under sec. 75 (ii)?[117]

Quick and Garran's view that a matter arises under sec. 75 (ii) only when a consul is acting in his official capacity has the clear merit of restricting the jurisdiction, but the matter is still unresolved. It is unfortunate that the Founding Fathers, who had sufficient perspicacity to see that the American model was in some respects inapplicable to Australian conditions in 1900, did not apparently see these other difficulties and obscurities in the clause. Once again they transcribed blindly. It does not appear to have occurred to them to ask Mr Dixon's question: 'Why should a State court be any the less fit to entertain litigation affecting . . . (a consul) . . . than it was when it was a court of a colony?'[118] Had they asked that question, it seems doubtful whether the clause would have been written into the Constitution.

Sec. 75 (iii) and (iv) deal with matters in which the Commonwealth or States are parties. Sec. 75 (iv) also provides for jurisdiction in matters between residents of different States. In this particular case, except for the substitution of the word 'residents' for 'citizens', and for the investment of original jurisdiction in the High Court instead of in an inferior federal court, the Australian Founding Fathers once again transcribed the American diversity jurisdiction provisions without any enquiry as to their applicability to Australian conditions or needs. The diversity clause will be considered in detail at a later stage.[119]

Sec. 75 (iii) confers original jurisdiction on the High Court in matters in which the Commonwealth, or a party suing or being sued on behalf of the Commonwealth, is a party. Sec. 75 (iv), excluding the diversity clause, confers jurisdiction in matters between States or between a State and a resident of another State. Secs. 38, 57 and 59 of the Judiciary Act make special provision with respect to State courts. Sec. 56 (1) of the Judiciary Act provides that a person making a claim against the Commonwealth, whether in contract or tort, may in respect of the claim bring a suit against the Commonwealth in the High Court, the Supreme Court of a State or Territory in which the claim arose or any court of competent jurisdiction of the State or Territory where the claim arose. 'Court of competent jurisdiction' includes

---

117 Minutes of Evidence at p. 785.
118 ibid.
119 See Chapter 2.

any court exercising jurisdiction in the capital city of a State or the principal or only city or town of a Territory which would be competent to hear the suit if the Commonwealth were and had at any time been a resident in that city or town.

Sec. 58 makes provision for suits against a State, whether in contract or tort, in matters within federal jurisdiction, but requires the claim to be brought in the High Court (if it has original jurisdiction) or in the Supreme Court of the State. Until 1960 a person suing the Commonwealth was also compelled to choose the Supreme Court of a State as an alternative to the High Court. While sec. 56 was amended to provide as a forum a wider range of State courts, no similar amendment has been made to sec. 58 where, for example, there is a suit between a State and a resident of another State. It is difficult to see why this distinction has been made.

Art. III, sec. 2 of the United States Constitution declared that controversies to which the United States was a party were matters of federal jurisdiction. It also included controversies between two or more States, and between a State and a citizen of another State, as matters of federal jurisdiction, and declared further that all cases of federal jurisdiction in which a State was a party should fall within the original jurisdiction of the Supreme Court of the United States. It is interesting to note that in this respect suits involving the *United States* and *States* as parties were differently treated. The principle on which controversies involving the United States as a party were assigned to federal jurisdiction was stated by Story in terms of the proposition that a sovereign must have the power to sue in his own courts, and that unless such a power were given, the enforcement of the rights of the national government would be at the mercy of the States. This 'would prostrate the Union at the feet of the States. It would compel the national government to become a supplicant for justice before the judicature of those who were by other parts of the Constitution placed in subordination to it.'[120] This has very little relevance to Australian conditions, as was shown by the willingness of the Commonwealth Parliament to submit most cases involving the Commonwealth as a party to the concurrent jurisdiction of State courts. No doubt, the explanation for its inclusion in the Australian Constitution was the disposition to copy the American heads of federal jurisdiction without overmuch thought. Perhaps here there was some general feeling that it was appropriate that cases involving the Commonwealth as a party should properly find

120 Commentaries, sec. 1674.

their way into the original jurisdiction of the one constitutionally entrenched national tribunal.

The assignment to the original jurisdiction of the Supreme Court of the United States of cases in which a State is a party was justified by Hamilton on the basis that 'in cases in which a State might happen to be a party, it would ill suit its dignity to be turned over to an inferior tribunal'.[121] The dignity of the United States was, apparently, less easily outraged. As the plan of original jurisdiction was elaborated, the Supreme Court was given *exclusive* original jurisdiction in suits between States, while this original jurisdiction was made *concurrent* in the case of suits between the United States and a State and in actions and proceedings by a State against the citizens of another State or against aliens. The Eleventh Amendment foreclosed a suit by a citizen of another State or an alien against a State.

In Australia, the case of suits between States appears to be one in which there is good sense in the grant of original jurisdiction to the High Court. The position of the States in the Australian constitutional framework is such that it seems most appropriate to have justiciable disputes between them tried in the High Court. Similar considerations apply to suits between the Commonwealth and a State. In all these cases, as we have seen, the jurisdiction of the High Court is effectively exclusive. On the other hand, it is doubtful whether in suits between a State and a resident of another State there was any particular justification for conferring original jurisdiction. Here the considerations of policy were substantially the same as those involved in the grant of diversity jurisdiction—the fear of partiality or bias on the part of a State court. The arguments against the grant of original jurisdiction in diversity matters in Australia[122] apply equally in this case.

The terms of sec. 75 (iii) were rather different from those of Art. III, sec. 2. In the first place, in the United States Constitution, federal jurisdiction was conferred in controversies 'to which the United States shall be a party'. In the Australian clause, the High Court's original jurisdiction extended to matters in which the Commonwealth *or a person suing or being sued on behalf of the Commonwealth* is a party. The italicized words indicate that it was part of the constitutional plan that the Commonwealth should be *liable* to suit, and sec. 78 of the Constitution specifically authorized the making of laws conferring rights to proceed

---

121 Federalist Papers, No. 81.
122 See pp. 83-6 *post.*

against the Commonwealth or a State in respect of matters within the limits of the judicial power. As Dixon J. said in *Bank of New South Wales v. Commonwealth* (the *Bank Nationalization Case*):[123] 'The purpose of s. 75 (iii) obviously was to ensure that the political organization called into existence under the name of the Commonwealth and armed with enumerated powers and authorities, limited by definition, fell in every way within a jurisdiction in which it could be impleaded and which it could invoke.' He went on to observe that this clause should be read together with sec. 75 (v), conferring jurisdiction in matters in which *mandamus* or prohibition or an injunction is sought against an officer of the Commonwealth, 'which, it is apparent, was written into the instrument to make it constitutionally certain that there would be a jurisdiction capable of restraining officers of the Commonwealth from exceeding Federal power'.[124]

This leads to a more precise examination of the scope of sec. 75 (iii). Quick and Garran, in their commentary on the clause, insisted that it was simply a grant of jurisdiction, and did not, in itself, confer any right of action against the Commonwealth. Any such right of action must arise *aliunde*, and when and if it arose the High Court was a competent original forum under sec. 75 (iii). In view of the case law, however, the position cannot be stated with any certainty. In *Commonwealth v. New South Wales*[125] there was a strong expression of opinion by the majority in the High Court that sec. 75 (iii) itself imposed a substantive liability in tort on the Commonwealth. In that case, the Commonwealth brought an action in the original jurisdiction of the High Court claiming damages in respect of a collision between ships belonging to the plaintiff Commonwealth and the defendant State. The majority in the High Court overruled the defendant State's objection to the jurisdiction, and expressed the opinion that sec. 75 (iii) enabled the Commonwealth to sue a State in tort without need for legislation under sec. 78, which, in their view, applied to sec. 76 but not to sec. 75 of the Constitution. It was said that sec. 75 of the Constitution, which bound Commonwealth and States alike, imposed tortious liability on the Crown in right of the Commonwealth or a State. The majority thought that the word 'matters' in sec. 75 included actions in tort, and on the reasoning of the Privy Council in *Farnell v. Bowman*[126] it was said

---

[123] (1948) 76 C.L.R. 1, 363.
[124] ibid. at p. 363. See also *per* Starke J. at p. 321.
[125] (1923) 32 C.L.R. 200.
[126] (1887) 12 A.C. 643.

that the provision of jurisdiction to entertain such actions also imposed substantive liability in tort on the Crown. Higgins J. dissented, arguing that sec. 75 (iii) conferred jurisdiction only, and that the source of substantive tortious liability must be found elsewhere. If the view of the majority is correct, it applies equally to cases arising under sec. 75 (iv), as was pointed out by Evatt J. in *New South Wales v. Bardolph*,[127] which was an action in the original jurisdiction of the High Court between a resident of South Australia and the State of New South Wales.

The reasoning of the majority in *Commonwealth v. New South Wales* was sharply criticized by Mr Dixon in his evidence before the Royal Commission[128] and this criticism was adopted in the Report of the Commission.[129] On the other hand, it was approved by Evatt J. on a number of occasions in the High Court.[130] There has, however, been considerable judicial criticism of the reasoning in the High Court, notably by Dixon J. He pointed to some of the difficulties in *Musgrave v. Commonwealth*,[131] and in *Werrin v. Commonwealth*[132] he elaborated this criticism:

> If it were not for the views expressed in the joint judgement (in *Commonwealth v. New South Wales*) I should have felt little or no hesitation in saying that the Federal Parliament had complete authority over all ordinary causes of action against the Commonwealth and over the remedies for enforcing them. I should have thought that the right of the subject to recover from the Crown in right of the Commonwealth, whether in contract or in tort, is the creation of the law which the Federal Parliament controls. No doubt when a jurisdiction is conferred like that given by sec. 75 (iii) and (iv) the source whence the substantive law is to be derived for determining the duties of the governments presents difficulties. But I should not have thought that sec. 75 itself could be the source of the substantive liability.

*Werrin v. Commonwealth* exposed a peculiar difficulty arising from the majority reasoning in *Commonwealth v. New South Wales*. *Werrin's Case* involved a money claim against the Commonwealth, and raised the question whether the Commonwealth

[127] (1934) 52 C.L.R. 455. See also *Daly v. State of Victoria* (1920) 28 C.L.R. 395, 400.

[128] at p. 785.

[129] at pp. 102-3. See however Moore: Suits Between States Within the British Empire (1925) 7 Journal C.L. 155, 161.

[130] *New South Wales v. Commonwealth* (No. 1) (1932) 46 C.L.R. 155, 210-1, 215; *New South Wales v. Bardolph* (1934) 52 C.L.R. 455, 458-9; *Heimann v. Commonwealth* (1935) 54 C.L.R. 126, 129; *Musgrave v. Commonwealth* (1937) 57 C.L.R. 514.

[131] (1937) 57 C.L.R. 514, 546.

[132] (1938) 59 C.L.R. 150, 167.

Parliament might legislatively extinguish a cause of action against the Commonwealth. In *Musgrave v. Commonwealth* Dixon J. had observed that if the reasoning in *Commonwealth v. New South Wales* were correct, so that tort liability was imposed on the Commonwealth by force of the Constitution itself, this liability could not, presumably, be impaired or controlled by legislation. In *Werrin's Case* he again adverted to this difficulty, but said that this consequence was probably not intended by the majority in *Commonwealth v. New South Wales*. In any event, Dixon J. said that he was 'not prepared to interpret the joint judgement as deciding that sec. 75 provides a source of substantive liability so that no Act of the Commonwealth Parliament can extinguish a cause of action which has accrued against the Commonwealth'.[133] Dixon J. and other judicial and non-judicial critics of *Commonwealth v. New South Wales* have preferred to base Commonwealth liability in contract and tort on sec. 56 of the Judiciary Act, which provides that any person making a claim in contract or tort against the Commonwealth may bring the action in the High Court or various other State and Territory courts specified in the section. This seems to be legislation under sec. 78 though it does not impose liability in express terms. In *Washington v. Commonwealth*[134] Jordan C.J., delivering the judgement of the Full Supreme Court of New South Wales in a case involving a claim in tort against the Commonwealth, referred to the authorities and said: 'I think that the better opinion is that the section (that is, Constitution, sec. 75 (iii)) is concerned with the jurisdiction of a Court and not with the rights or liabilities of persons who may be litigants in the Court. It says, in effect, that if any person desires to litigate a legal claim which he may conceive himself to have against the Commonwealth or the Commonwealth to litigate a legal claim which it may conceive itself to have against any person, he or it may do so by means of an original proceeding in the High Court; but it neither invests them with substantive rights nor subjects them to substantive liabilities. . . . I am of opinion that s. 56 (Judiciary Act) . . . is of itself sufficient to subject the Commonwealth to the law of torts.'[135] This approach was taken by Windeyer J. (sitting as a single judge in the original jurisdiction of the High Court) in *Suehle v. Commonwealth*.[136] Other judges have regarded Commonwealth lia-

---

[133] at p. 168.
[134] (1939) 39 S.R. (N.S.W.) 133, 140, 142.
[135] See also *James v. Commonwealth* (1939) 62 C.L.R. 339.
[136] (1967) 116 C.L.R. 353. See also *Asiatic Steam Navigation Co. Ltd. v. Commonwealth* (1956) 96 C.L.R. 397, 419-20.

bility as based on a combination of secs. 56 and 64 of the Judiciary Act or on section 64 alone.[136A] Section 64 provides that 'in any suit to which the Commonwealth or a State is a party, the rights of the parties shall be nearly as possible the same . . . as in a suit between subject and subject'.

It seems clear that the better view is that sec. 75 does no more than confer a jurisdiction on the High Court in matters in which the Commonwealth or a State is a party; that the jurisdiction is conferred by the Constitution and cannot be taken away by Commonwealth or State legislation but that the section does not, of itself, impose any substantive liability on the Commonwealth or a State.[137]

It is to be noted that sec. 75 (iii) confers jurisdiction in a matter in which a person suing or being sued on behalf of the Commonwealth is a party. These words do not appear in Art. III, sec. 2 of the United States Constitution which simply includes within the scope of federal jurisdiction cases to which the United States is a party. It was early settled that this head of federal jurisdiction did not, of itself, authorize suit against the United States without the consent of Congress expressed in a general or special enactment.[138] The harshness of this rule was mitigated by the rule that a servant or agent of the United States Government was personally liable and could not defend simply on a plea of authorization or direction by the executive government. As Dixon J. noted in the *Bank Nationalization Case*,[139] this gave rise to a readiness to admit proceedings against officers or agencies of the United States in respect of claims in which they had little or no personal interest, and in which the United States was the party really affected. There was a disposition in the cases to determine the question whether the United States was a party to a case by reference to the actual party on the record, even though it might be clear that the named party (e.g. the Postmaster-General) was not, and the United States was, the substantial party in interest

---

[136A] *Maguire v. Simpson* (1977) 18 A.L.R. 469.

[137] See Wynes: Legislative, Executive and Judicial Powers in Australia (5th ed., 1976) at p. 461; Paton: Liability of the Crown in Tort (Australia) (1944) 22 Canadian B.R. 729, 732; Renfree: A Brief Conspectus of Commonwealth Liability in Tort (1948) 22 A.L.J. 102, 103; Lane, *op. cit.* at pp. 397-8; Hogg: Suits Against the Commonwealth and the States in Federal Jurisdiction (1970) 44 A.L.J. 425.

[138] See Constitution of the United States of America, *op. cit.*, pp. 666-71. See also *Bank of N.S.W. v. Commonwealth* (1948) 76 C.L.R. 1, 364 *et seq.*, *per* Dixon J.

[139] (1948) 76 C.L.R. 1, 364.

to the actual controversy. As Higgins J. observed in *R. v. Murray and Cormie*,[140] 'it was no doubt because of these decisions that in sec. 75 (iii) of the Constitution the words were added "or a person suing or being sued on behalf of the Commonwealth" '. This ensured that the scope of the jurisdiction was wide enough to cover cases in which the Commonwealth was a named party and also those in which officers and agencies of the Government were suing or being sued in their official or governmental capacities.[141] As the course of American authority evolved, considerable difficulty was experienced, and it was not found possible to maintain the test based simply on the party disclosed on the face of the record. It was found necessary to draw a distinction between cases in which a suit was brought against officials in respect of acts for which they were personally responsible—where the action would lie against the official only—and cases in which suit was brought against an official 'in respect of acts . . . in which it is sought to affect the interests of the United States by suing him in his official capacity'.[142] In the latter situation it was held that the action was, in effect, against the United States and could not be brought without congressional consent.[143]

The meaning of the words 'person suing or being sued on behalf of the Commonwealth' fell to be considered by the High Court in the *Bank Nationalization Case*. The problem arose out of provisions which authorized the acquisition of the assets of private trading banks by the Treasurer of the Commonwealth. The assets so acquired were vested in the Commonwealth Bank which was an incorporated body. Liability to pay compensation for assets so acquired was imposed on the Commonwealth Bank. Failing agreement, the quantum of compensation was to be determined *exclusively* by a Court of Claims established under sec. 71 of the Constitution and invested with jurisdiction as a superior court of record under sec. 77. The object was to shut out the original jurisdiction of the High Court. It was clearly not possible to do this if the case fell within sec. 75 (iii), as the original jurisdiction of the High Court under sec. 75 was constitutionally

---

[140] (1916) 22 C.L.R. 437, 468.
[141] *Bank Nationalization Case* (1948) 76 C.L.R. 1, 367, *per* Dixon J.
[142] ibid. at p. 365.
[143] 'This extreme view (i.e. that the United States was only a party where it was named on the record) has been modified in more recent decisions; and it may be accepted that the same result has been achieved by judicial decisions as in sec. 75 (iii) of our Constitution by express words,' *per* Higgins J. in *R. v. Murray and Cormie* (1916) 22 C.L.R. 437, 468.

guaranteed. The question then was whether the Commonwealth Bank was a person being sued on behalf of the Commonwealth.

The problem was posed by Dixon J. in these terms:

> Does the third paragraph of s. 75 intend to give a jurisdiction confined to matters in which the Crown . . . is itself a party, whether suing or sued in the name of the King *or by the Attorney-General or some other officer or nominal party authorized for the purpose as a matter of procedure*[144] or, on the other hand, does the paragraph intend to place within the jurisdiction of the High Court all matters in which a claim of right is made by or against any part of the central government of the country in its executive department including the corporate and other agencies by which it is administered?[145]

Four members of the Court, Rich, Starke, Dixon and Williams JJ., had no doubt that the latter alternative was to be preferred. The question then arose whether the Commonwealth Bank was an agency or instrumentality of the Commonwealth so as to bring it within the definition of a person being sued on behalf of the Commonwealth and these four judges had little difficulty in holding, after examination of its structure and functions, that the Commonwealth Bank was such an agency or instrumentality. As Starke J. put it, this was 'manifest'[146] from a study of the provisions of the relevant Acts.[147] Latham C.J. and McTiernan J. dissented. The Chief Justice said that in order to determine whether a case fell within the terms of sec. 75 (iii) it was necessary to find out who was actually being sued and then to ask whether that person was being sued on behalf of the Commonwealth. If it were the Attorney-General or a minister or a nominal defendant, the answer would be easy. Here, however, the defendant was the Bank and any allegation with respect to any alleged liability of the Commonwealth was irrelevant. 'Accordingly, in my opinion, in such an action the corporation which was the defendant (the Commonwealth Bank) would be shown by the record not to be a person being sued on behalf of the Commonwealth, and the action would not come within the provisions of s. 75 (iii).'[148] Latham C.J. went on to examine the structure of the Bank to determine whether it might be properly described as a department of the Commonwealth Government.

The approach of the majority in the *Bank Nationalization Case*

---

144 Italics supplied.
145 *Bank Nationalization Case* (1948) 76 C.L.R. 1, 358.
146 at p. 322.
147 Commonwealth Bank Act 1945; Banking Act 1945; Banking Act 1947.
148 (1948) 76 C.L.R. 1, 226.

was followed in *Inglis v. Commonwealth Trading Bank of Australia*[149] where the Court held (Barwick C.J., Kitto and Windeyer JJ.; Owen J. dissenting) that a suit against the Commonwealth Trading Bank was a matter within sec. 75 (iii) of the Constitution. Kitto J. (with whom the other two majority judges agreed) regarded the conclusion of the majority in the *Bank Nationalization Case* as based on the following statement by Dixon J.—'the purpose of providing a jurisdiction which might be invoked by or against the Commonwealth could not, in modern times, be adequately attained and secured against colourable evasion, unless it was expressed so as to cover the enforcement of actionable rights and liabilities of officers and agencies in their official and governmental capacity, when in substance they formed part of or represented the Commonwealth'.[150] Dixon and Starke JJ., in arguing for a broad interpretation of the scope of the jurisdiction conferred by sec. 75 (iii), took the view that an authority did not have to be within the shield of the Crown in the strict sense to attract the jurisdiction. Rich and Williams JJ. were prepared to hold that in regard to the activities involved in that case the bank was an agent of the Crown in the strict sense. This aspect was not discussed in the *Inglis Case*. It is suggested, however, that if the purpose of the jurisdiction is taken to be that stated in the passage from Dixon J.'s judgement, set out above, the principles relating to whether a body is within the shield of the Crown cannot be conclusive. As His Honour pointed out, the question whether a statutory instrumentality should be given the privileges and immunities of the Crown is one for Parliament to determine.[151] But if one of the purposes of sec. 75 (iii) is to secure jurisdiction 'against colourable evasion' parliamentary intention cannot be the test.

The divisions of the Court in both the *Bank Nationalization Case* and *Inglis v. The Commonwealth Trading Bank of Australia* show that a party invoking the jurisdiction under sec. 75 (iii) must take the risk that the Court will not agree with his characterization of the party being sued. Assuming the general appellate jurisdiction of the High Court under sec. 73 it can be strongly argued that there is no need for the High Court to be invested with original jurisdiction in these matters. It would be more satisfactory to require a party to bring its action against the Commonwealth (or *vice versa*) in a State court.

149 (1969) 119 C.L.R. 334.
150 at p. 367.
151 at p. 359. See also *Maguire v. Simpson* (1977) 18 A.L.R. 469 *per* Jacobs J. at p. 502.

However, as mentioned below, the State courts probably do not have any State jurisdiction in matters where the Commonwealth is a defendant, even apart from the operation of sec. 39 of the Judiciary Act.[152] So, if matters in which the Commonwealth is a party was not a head of jurisdiction conferred on the High Court by virtue of the Constitution, it could be argued that the Commonwealth would not be amenable to suit. That would be so even if that particular head of jurisdiction was in sec. 76 rather than in sec. 75 and Parliament refrained from conferring the jurisdiction on the High Court or the State courts. Indeed, as the High Court's jurisdiction in respect of matters arising under the Constitution or involving its interpretation is not constitutionally guaranteed, but is based on legislation pursuant to sec. 76 (i), sec. 75 (iii) and (v) ensure that there is a jurisdiction to deal, among other things, with the constitutional validity of Commonwealth legislation and executive action.

If one is talking in terms of constitutional amendment, however, there is no need for the High Court to be given original jurisdiction in matters in which the Commonwealth or an agency of the Commonwealth is a party provided the State courts have such jurisdiction and the High Court can exercise its appellate jurisdiction should the case warrant such an appeal.

There can, however, be little doubt about the propriety of the grant of original jurisdiction to the High Court in suits between governments. It is appropriate that justiciable disputes between governments should be submitted in the first instance to the highest national tribunal and sec. 75 (iii) and (iv) provide for such cases.

Suits between governments have provided the great body of case law in the original jurisdiction of the Supreme Court of the United States. It was established in *United States v. Texas*[153] that the Supreme Court had original jurisdiction in suits between the United States and a State. The most spectacular modern instances of the jurisdiction authorized by *United States v. Texas* were the famous *Tidelands Oil* disputes.[154] There have been many important cases involving suits between States. Such cases, as we have seen, lie within the exclusive jurisdiction of the Supreme Court. Boundary disputes were the first cases between States in which the Supreme Court exercised this jurisdiction. Latterly, other

---

[152] See p. 177 *post*.

[153] (1892) 143 U.S. 621.

[154] *U.S. v. California* (1947) 332 U.S. 19; *U.S. v. Louisiana* (1950) 339 U.S. 699; *U.S. v. Texas* (1950) 339 U.S. 707. See Hart and Wechsler, *op. cit.* at pp. 228-9.

problems have loomed large, and the great development of irrigation, flood control and hydro-electric power has given rise to many disputes over water rights. Other cases have arisen out of disputes over sewage disposal, claims to natural gas, double taxation, etc. Up to 1919 there had been some seventy cases in the Supreme Court of the United States involving disputes between States, and between that date and 1954 there were more than fifty.[155] The first of the boundary cases was *Rhode Island v. Massachusetts*.[156] There the Court asserted its power to decide a boundary dispute despite the refusal of the respondent State to enter an appearance. A further challenge to the jurisdiction, on the ground that the questions involved in boundary disputes were political and not justiciable, was unsuccessfully raised in *Virginia v. West Virginia*.[157] Some doubts have been expressed, both judicially and extra-judicially, as to the effectiveness and utility of this jurisdiction. As Frankfurter J. observed in *Texas v. Florida*:[158]

> There are practical limits to the efficacy of the adjudicatory process in the adjustment of inter-state controversies. The limitations of litigation—its episodic character, its necessarily restricted scope of inquiry, its confined regard for considerations of policy, its dependence on the contingencies of a particular record, and other circumscribing factors—often denature and even mutilate the actualities of a problem and thereby render the litigious process unsuited for its solution.[159]

Nonetheless, Frankfurter J. and other judges have pointed out that this jurisdiction serves important ends in the working of American federalism.[160]

155 See Scott: Judicial Settlement of Controversies Between States of the American Union (1919); Barnes: Suits Between States in the Supreme Court (1954) 7 Vanderbilt L.R. 494; Hart and Wechsler, *op. cit.*, pp. 248-51; Heady: Suits by States Within the Original Jurisdiction of the Supreme Court (1940) 26 Washington U.L.Q. 61; Wagner: The Original and Exclusive Jurisdiction of the United States Supreme Court (1952) 2 St Louis U.L.J. 111.

156 (1838) 12 Pet. 657.

157 (1871) 11 Wall. 39.

158 (1939) 306 U.S. 398, 428.

159 See also *Pennsylvania v. West Virginia* (1923) 262 U.S. 553, *per* Brandeis J. See note in (1926) 39 Harvard L.R. 1084, 1087-8: 'The method of settling interstate disputes by original suit in the Supreme Court must be regarded as subordinate to the other method provided in the Constitution, that of compacts.' See also Heady: (1940) 26 Washington U.L.Q. 61.

160 *Texas v. Florida* (1939) 306 U.S. 398, 428. See also Scott: Judicial Settlement of Controversies Between States of the Union, *passim*; Caldwell: The Settlement of Interstate Disputes (1920) 14 A.J.I.L. 38, 68; Heady: Suits by States Within the Original Jurisdiction of the Supreme Court (1940) 26 Washington U.L.Q. 61; Barnes: Suits Between States in the Supreme Court (1954) 7 Vanderbilt L.R. 494.

In Australia there have been many actions between Commonwealth and States, and between States.[161] In many of these, substantive constitutional questions have been involved. Others, like *Commonwealth v. New South Wales*,[162] involved a simple tort claim as between the parties. The only Australian case raising a boundary dispute was *South Australia v. Victoria*.[163] The action was framed as a claim for possession of the land in dispute, for an injunction to restrain the defendants from further acts of trespass and other similar remedies. The defendants raised an objection to jurisdiction on the ground that the matter was not justiciable before federation, that it was 'undoubtedly political'[164] and that the proper authority to decide the dispute was the King-in-Council. It was argued further that the American authorities supporting the existence of original jurisdiction in boundary disputes were distinguishable.

The High Court stated that its jurisdiction was limited to the determination of *justiciable* disputes, and noted that the American and Australian situations, as at the date of federation, were not identical. At the date of federation in the United States there were existing boundary disputes between several States. Moreover the American federation was a union of sovereign States whose boundary disagreements were analogous to disputes between independent nations, and subject to no clearly established binding law. When the United States Constitution was enacted provision was made as a matter of necessity for the settlement of these disputes by conferring jurisdiction on the Supreme Court in controversies between States. In Australia the situation was different, because the States were subject to the authority of imperial law. It was suggested that this might make for a difference in the character of the boundary disputes which could be decided by the courts in the two federations.[165] Nonetheless the Commonwealth

---

161 See Moore: The Federation and Suits Between Governments (1935) 17 Journal C.L. (3rd series) 163; Campbell: Suits Between the Governments of a Federation (1971) 6 Syd. L. Rev. 309.

162 (1923) 32 C.L.R. 200.

163 (1911) 12 C.L.R. 667.

164 at p. 672.

165 'When, in the framing of the United States Constitution, the power to adjudicate in "controversies between the States" was conferred on the Supreme Court of the United States, it was clearly intended to vest in that tribunal all the power of settlement and adjudication which up to then had been exercised by the Confederation, that is to say, the power to determine matters not justiciable as well as matters justiciable. . . . The Australian Constitution, on the other hand, limits the power of settling disputes between States in boundary disputes, as in other cases, to those in which the matters in contro-

Constitution by sec. 75 (iv) conferred original jurisdiction in plain terms in matters between States. It followed that boundary disputes fell within the scope of the clause provided that they were, as here, capable of being determined on recognized legal principles. The test of justiciability in disputes between States was propounded by Griffith C.J.:

> In my opinion a matter between States, in order to be justiciable, must be such that a controversy of like nature could arise between individual persons, and must be such that it can be determined upon principles of law. This definition includes all controversies relating to the ownership of property or arising out of contracts.[166]

It was held that the claim in this case satisfied the test of justiciability.

Having regard to the point of distinction between the original jurisdiction of the Supreme Court of the United States and the High Court which was made in this case, it should be noted that the Supreme Court has, on a number of occasions, shown reluctance to assume jurisdiction in suits between States. It has refused leave to file an original complaint on the ground that the State has failed to allege sufficient injury, that the controversy is not justiciable, that it is premature, and so forth.[167] The Supreme Court has also been faced with the problem of deciding whether a State is a real party in interest in such an action. Jurisdiction has been denied in suits which, on their face, appear to be suits between States, but which are brought by a State on behalf of individual citizens.[168] The assumption of jurisdiction in such cases would defeat the object of the Eleventh Amendment which forbids suits by citizens of one State against another State. The principle upon which jurisdiction will be assumed or declined has been stated as being that the State has the right as *parens patriae* to protect its citizens in respect of its quasi-sovereign interests and to invoke the original jurisdiction of the Supreme Court for that purpose; but it does not have standing as *parens patriae* to represent a citizen for the purpose of enforcing his individual claims in contract, tort or under statute.[169] This problem is of no sig-

---

versy can be determined by the application of recognized legal principles,' *per* O'Connor J. at pp. 708-9.

[166] at p. 675.

[167] See Barnes (1954) 7 Vanderbilt L.R. at pp. 508 *et seq.*

[168] See *New Hampshire v. Louisiana* (1883) 108 U.S. 74. Compare *South Dakota v. North Carolina* (1904) 192 U.S. 286. See also *North Dakota v. Minnesota* (1923) 263 U.S. 365.

[169] See J. W. Moore: Commentary on the U.S. Judicial Code (1949) at pp. 624-5.

E

nificance in Australia, as an individual resident of a State may freely bring an action against another State in the original jurisdiction of the High Court under sec. 75 (iv). The Eleventh Amendment has no Australian counterpart.

Sec. 75 (v): matters in which a writ of *mandamus* or prohibition or an injunction is sought against an officer of the Commonwealth was, as we have seen, written into the Commonwealth Constitution because it was *not* in the United States Constitution; and the power of the Supreme Court of the United States to issue *mandamus* in its original jurisdiction against a non-judicial officer of the United States had been expressly denied in *Marbury v. Madison*.[170] It appears to have been accepted that a State court exercising State[171] jurisdiction could not issue a *mandamus* against an officer of the Commonwealth. In *Ex parte Goldring*[172] it was held by the Supreme Court of New South Wales that in the exercise of its State jurisdiction it had no power to grant an application to make absolute a rule nisi for *mandamus* against the Commonwealth Collector of Customs. The Court relied on American authority, and the principle was stated by Stephen A.C.J.: 'We cannot compel a federal officer to discharge a duty which he owes to the Federal Government. . . . He owes no duty to the State Government.'[173] The proposition goes beyond the single case of *mandamus*, and the accepted view is that in its State jurisdiction a State court could not entertain a suit against the Commonwealth, or grant prohibition against an officer of the Commonwealth.[174]

Some reference has already been made to the history of this clause in the Federal Conventions.[175] Its most redoubtable opponent was Mr Isaacs who argued[176] first that it was unnecessary because sec. 75 (iii) provided all necessary power, and second that the mention of the particular remedies named in sec. 75 (v) might raise the implication that the High Court had no jurisdiction with respect to other remedies not mentioned—such as *habeas*

---

170 See p. 15 *ante*.
171 Clearly if a State court were invested with *federal* jurisdiction under sec. 77 (iii) in respect of the matters covered by sec. 75 (v), the situation would be different.
172 (1903) 3 S.R. (N.S.W.) 260.
173 at p. 262. See also Harrison Moore: Commonwealth of Australia (2nd ed., 1910) at pp. 212-3; Bailey: The Federal Jurisdiction of State Courts (1940) 2 *Res Judicatae* at p. 111.
174 Bailey, *op. cit.* at p. 111.
175 See pp. 22-3 *ante*.
176 Convention Debates Melbourne at pp. 1879, 1882.

*corpus* and *certiorari*. At one stage, Mr Isaacs carried the day and the clause was deleted, but when his lawyer colleagues, particularly Mr Barton, had come back with some better understanding of the clause, it was reinstated.[177]

Mr Isaacs was primarily concerned to ensure that the jurisdiction of the High Court should not be *restricted* by the incorporation of this clause. But he was wrong on both his points. In the first place, sec. 75 (iii) does not cover the same ground. As Quick and Garran pointed out: 'it seems clear . . . that . . . [sec. 75 (iii)] . . . only applies where the Commonwealth is the real party, and some person sues or is sued as representing the Commonwealth. In applications for *mandamus*, that is never the case, because a *mandamus* cannot issue against the Crown, or against any person representing the Crown. A suit 'against an officer of the Commonwealth' is a very different thing to a suit against 'a person sued on behalf of the Commonwealth'.[178] Isaacs J. made the point himself in *R. v. Murray and Cormie, ex parte Commonwealth*[179] where he contrasted the duty of an officer under the law with his duty as representing the State, which is then supposed to be itself performing the duty by his agency.

Nevertheless it may be that the phrase 'person . . . being sued on behalf of the Commonwealth' in secs. 75 (iii) overlaps with 'officer of the Commonwealth' in sec. 75 (v). It is true that a prerogative writ cannot issue against a person who in relation to the particular matter is a strict agent of the Crown and whose duty is owed to the Crown and not to the public.[180] If, however, sec. 75 (iii) extends to officers and bodies that are not in the strict sense agents of the Crown so as to come within its shield, some of those officers and bodies may be sued under sec. 75 (iii) and yet may be subject to a suit for a prerogative writ under sec. 75 (v). As Dixon J. said in the *Bank Nationalization Case*,[181] the question whether the Commonwealth Bank came within the terms of sec. 75 (iii) must depend on the relation found to exist between it and the Executive Government, but 'that is not the same thing as inquiring whether the corporate entity is established for the use and service of the Crown' so that, for example,

---

[177] See p. 23 *ante*.

[178] *op. cit.*, p. 779. See *R. v. Governor of the State of South Australia* (1907) 4 C.L.R. 1497.

[179] (1916) 22 C.L.R. 437, 456.

[180] Benjafield and Whitmore: Principles of Australian Administrative Law (4th ed., 1970) p. 214.

[181] (1948) 76 C.L.R. 1, 358.

its occupation of property is for the behoof of the Crown and that its employees are servants of the Crown.[182]

The decisions of the High Court also make it clear that the fears of Mr Isaacs that the naming of certain remedies might by implication shut out the power of the High Court to grant others were groundless. On one occasion, the Court drew attention to the fact that sec. 75 (v) did not refer to *certiorari*.[183] But it is clear even with respect to the named remedies that the original jurisdiction of the High Court is not limited to the cases specified in sec. 75 (v).

In *R. v. Registrar of Titles for Victoria, ex parte Common-wealth*[184] Griffith C.J. and Isaacs J. held that the Court might in appropriate circumstances issue *mandamus* to the Registrar of Titles for Victoria to compel him to register a lease of land to the Commonwealth by a Victorian municipality. As the majority of the Court held in that case that there was no such duty on the Registrar, they did not deal with the jurisdictional question.

In *Collett v. Loane*[185] the Court ordered the issue of a *mandamus* to a State stipendiary magistrate in relation to an application for registration as a conscientious objector under the National Service Act. It would appear that the jurisdiction of the Court was based on sec. 75 (iii) as the Minister for Labour and National Service was made a respondent.

In *R. v. Murray and Cormie, ex parte Commonwealth* an application was made in the original jurisdiction of the High Court for prohibition directed to a judge of a State court. It was held by Isaacs, Higgins, Gavan Duffy and Rich JJ., with Griffith C.J. and Barton J. dissenting, that jurisdiction was not attracted under sec. 75 (v) because a State judge exercising federal jurisdiction was not an 'officer of the Commonwealth' for the purpose of that provision. It was then argued that the Court had jurisdiction under sec. 75 (iii). Although in the circumstances it was held that the Court did not have jurisdiction under that provision, a majority of the Court—Griffith C.J., Barton, Isaacs and Powers JJ. held that where the Commonwealth was a real party in interest, the Court had jurisdiction by virtue of sec. 75 (iii).

It was agreed that jurisdiction under sec. 75 (iii) was not attracted merely because the King was a party on the face of the

---

182 Cf. L. Katz, 3 Mon U.L.R. 89. See also *Maguire v. Simpson* (1977) 18 A.L.R. 469 *per* Jacobs J. at p. 502.

183 *Waterside Workers' Federation of Australia v. Gilchrist, Watt and Sanderson* (1924) 34 C.L.R. 482, 526, *per* Isaacs and Rich JJ.

184 (1915) 20 C.L.R. 379.

185 (1966) 117 C.L.R. 94.

record. The essential feature in the view of the majority was that the Commonwealth should be an applicant for the writ. The reason it was held that the Court had no jurisdiction in the circumstances to issue the writ was that Isaacs J. found that no 'matter' had arisen because the Commonwealth had on the facts no substantial interest in the subject matter relating to the excess of jurisdiction. It now seems clear that if the Commonwealth is a real party in interest, the Court has jurisdiction to issue prerogative writs on the Commonwealth's application under sec. 75 (iii).

It has been suggested that the Crown in seeking a prerogative writ of prohibition is not at common law required to show any personal interest at all in the proceedings impugned.[186] If that is so, Isaacs J. in *R. v. Murray and Cormie, ex parte Commonwealth* was incorrect in stating that, if the Crown was not a real party in interest, an application by the Commonwealth for the issue of a writ would not constitute a 'matter' within the terms of sec. 75. His Honour stated that 'The interest which every sovereign has in the lawful discharge of public duties by persons individually entrusted with them is not an interest which can be made the subject of litigation'.[187] If under common law rules and procedure the Crown has standing to apply for a writ of prohibition against a tribunal without having any property or other personal interest in the proceedings, then it is clear that it is the proper subject matter of a suit and therefore a 'matter' within the terms of sec. 75. Even then, of course, it will be necessary to have regard to the federal structure of the Constitution. Such a Crown right in relation to the Commonwealth could not extend to State courts or officers. But it is suggested that, although an absence of personal interest might not prevent the proceedings from being a 'matter', it would nevertheless not attract jurisdiction under sec. 75 (iii). For the purposes of that provision, it seems clear that a distinction has to be made between the King in right of the Commonwealth 'in his character of supreme guardian of the administration of royal justice' and the Commonwealth 'as a suitor interested in the subject matter'.[188] Sec. 75 (iii) applies only in the latter case. On the other hand, given the correctness

---

[186] de Smith: Judicial Review of Administrative Action (3rd ed., 1973) 368. This matter was brought to the authors' attention by Mr L. Katz, Senior Lecturer at Sydney Law School.

[187] (1916) 22 C.L.R. 437 at p. 454.

[188] ibid., at p. 456.

of the view expressed regarding the standing of the Commonwealth, there would seem no reason why the Court should not have jurisdiction under sec. 75 (v) if the Crown in the right of the Commonwealth applies for a writ referred to in that provision against a Commonwealth officer even though it lacks any interest other than as 'guardian of the administration of royal justice'.

It is clear that not only has the High Court jurisdiction to grant the named remedies in pursuance of jurisdiction granted outside the provisions of sec. 75 (v), it also has original jurisdiction to issue other writs in appropriate circumstances.[189] The Judiciary Act, sec. 33, confers specific power on the High Court to make orders or direct the issue of writs of *mandamus* and *habeas corpus*, (*inter alia*), and sec. 33 (2) declares that the section shall not be taken to limit by implication the power of the High Court to make any order or direct the issue of any writ. It is clear that the power to issue *mandamus* conferred by this section is not a general one, but is controlled by the Constitution.[190] The section also assumes that the High Court may grant writs of *habeas corpus*, and this has been affirmed by the Court.[191] As in the case of *mandamus*, sec. 33 cannot be read as conferring an unconfined and general power on the High Court to grant *habeas corpus*, but the power must be read as operating in aid of one or other of the heads of jurisdiction conferred on the High Court by the Constitution, or by Parliament pursuant to the authority of the Constitution. As Starke J. said in *Jerger v. Pearce*:[192] 'It must not be taken for granted that this Court has a general power to direct the issue of writs of *habeas corpus* under sec. 33 of the Judiciary Act, but I apprehend that the Court has jurisdiction to exercise this power in aid of its appellate or original jurisdiction.' There are cases of applications for *habeas corpus* in matters arising under the Constitution or involving its interpretation (Constitution, sec. 76 (i) and Judiciary Act, sec. 30 (a))[193] and in matters between residents of different States (Constitution, sec.

---

189 P.H.L.: High Court's Jurisdiction to Issue Writs (1967) 41 A.L.J. 130.

190 See *R. v. Governor of the State of South Australia* (1907) 4 C.L.R. 1497. See also *Ex parte Australian Timber Workers' Union; Veneer Co. Ltd and Another* (1937) 37 S.R. (N.S.W.) 52.

191 See *Jerger v. Pearce* (1920) 28 C.L.R. 588; *Ex parte Walsh and Johnson, in re Yates* (1925) 37 C.L.R. 36; *Ex parte Williams* (1934) 51 C.L.R. 545; *R. v. Carter, ex parte Kisch* (1934) 52 C.L.R. 221; *R. v. Bevan, ex parte Elias* (1942) 66 C.L.R. 452.

192 (1920) 28 C.L.R. 588, 590; see also *Ex parte Williams* (1934) 51 C.L.R. 545, 548, 551, 552; *R. v. Bevan, ex parte Elias* (1942) 66 C.L.R. 452.

193 See cases cited in note 191.

75 (iv)).[194] Similarly there is little doubt that the Court can issue a writ of *certiorari* where the case is otherwise within the jurisdiction of the Court. As Windeyer J. said in *R. v. District Court, ex parte White*,[195] 'It is at least questionable whether certiorari to quash proceedings of an inferior tribunal can issue from this Court as a substantive remedy *not ancillary to some proceeding otherwise within the original jurisdiction of the Court*'.[196]

It is rather surprising that injunctions are coupled with *mandamus* and prohibition in sec. 75 (v). As Quick and Garran observe: 'The necessity for the mention of injunctions here is not quite apparent. An injunction is on a different footing altogether from *mandamus* and prohibition: it is an ordinary remedy in private suits between party and party. It was probably added because of the analogy which exists, in effect, between a *mandamus* and an injunction.'[197]

The omission of *certiorari* from sec. 75 (v) has been of little practical importance in many cases because the High Court has liberally granted prohibition where *certiorari* would be an appropriate remedy and has thereby extended the scope of prohibition considerably beyond its generally accepted limits in England.[198] In respect of at least one ground for the issue of *certiorari*, however, namely error of law on the face of the record, prohibition is not available.

Apart from *certiorari*, the other glaring omission from sec. 75 (v) is the declaratory judgement or declaration, which has been

---

[194] *Queen v. Langdon* (1953) 88 C.L.R. 158; *Queen v. Macdonald* (1953) 88 C.L.R. 197. See Cowen: Diversity Jurisdiction: The Australian Experience (1955) 7 *Res Judicatae* at p. 5.

[195] (1966) 116 C.L.R. 644, 655.

[196] Italics supplied.

[197] *op. cit.*, p. 783.

[198] See Anderson: The Application of Privative Clauses to Proceedings of Commonwealth Tribunals (1956) 3 U. of Queensland L.J. 34 at pp. 34-5. 'So long as the decision of the tribunals the validity of which is questioned has a continuing effect on the rights and duties of the persons affected—as of course is usually the case—the High Court regards prohibition as an appropriate remedy for invalidity, even after the decision has been made, and even where enforcement of the rights and duties created by the decision lies with some other tribunal or court, so that the tribunal in question might well be regarded as *functus officio*. Prohibition lies not only to the tribunal which made the invalid decision but also to prohibit any party to the proceedings before it from taking steps to enforce the decision. As a result of this liberality with prohibition, *certiorari* is rarely applied for in the High Court. No doubt this development is at least in part due to the fact that s. 75 (v) gives a constitutional guarantee of prohibition—to what extent, I propose to consider—but not of *certiorari*.'

a popular remedy in recent times because it is free from many of the difficulties associated with the other remedies. In his evidence before the Royal Commission, Mr Dixon remarked that the specific reference to injunctions in sec. 75 (v) might prevent the High Court from doing under that section what a State court might well do—refuse the injunction but still make a declaration of right.[199]

The naming of the remedies of sec. 75 (v), however, raises another problem mentioned by Mr Dixon in his evidence before the Royal Commission. He said that it was by no means clear how much of the common law governing the character and nature of these remedies, the procedure by which they are administered, the occasions upon which they may be granted, is stereotyped and made immutable by this provision.[200]

The Commonwealth Administrative Review Committee, under the chairmanship of Mr Justice Kerr (as he then was), recommended in 1971 new statutory remedies to replace the existing common law and equitable remedies including those referred to in sec. 75 (v). The existing remedies were criticised as involving technicalities that were 'both unwieldy and unnecessary'.[201] It seems, as Mr Dixon pointed out, that as a result of sec. 75 (v) many of the common law rules and technicalities must remain as far as this head of jurisdiction is concerned. Many of the recommendations of the Kerr Committee were put into effect by the enactment of the Administrative Decisions (Judicial Review) Act 1977 which confers jurisdiction on the Federal Court of Australia to review decisions of an administrative character made or required to be made under any Commonwealth enactment, other than a decision of the Governor-General. Commonwealth legislation cannot, of course, deprive the High Court of its jurisdiction under sec. 75 of the Constitution. If however—as is likely—the new forms of judicial review of administrative action prove more convenient and effective there are likely to be few applications for the present remedies. In any case, as the Attorney-General pointed out when he introduced the legislation, most of the prerogative writs are granted on the discretion of the Court and the High Court, faced with an application for a prerogative writ under sec. 75 (v) would take into account that the application could have been made to the Federal Court of Australia

[199] Minutes of Evidence, p. 786.
[200] ibid.
[201] Commonwealth Administrative Review Committee Report, August 1971, P.P. No. 144, para. 58.

under the Administrative Decisions (Judicial Review) Act.[202]

In a number of cases where the High Court has assumed jurisdiction involving applications to issue writs to a State court, it has not always been clear what is the basis of the High Court's jurisdiction. *Collett v. Loane*[203] was an application for *mandamus* directed to a State stipendiary magistrate who declined jurisdiction in relation to an application for registration as a conscientious objector under the National Service Act. The Minister for Labour and National Service was a respondent to the proceedings. The High Court granted the *mandamus*. The only basis for jurisdiction could be that the Minister was a party and was a person being sued on behalf of the Commonwealth within the meaning of sec. 75 (iii), but jurisdiction was not discussed. In *The Queen v. The District Court of Queensland Northern District; ex parte Thompson*[204] application was made to the High Court for *certiorari* directed to the State Court in relation to an exemption from service under the National Service Act. The Minister for Labour and National Service and the Commonwealth were made respondents. The writ was refused. Barwick C.J., Kitto and Taylor JJ. expressly refrained from determining the question of jurisdiction, preferring to decide on the merits that the writ be refused. McTiernan J., however, held that the Court had jurisdiction under sec. 75 (iii) because the Minister had a right to be represented in the original proceedings under the National Service Regulations and was also given a right of appeal.[205] In *R. v. District Court; ex parte White*,[206] motions for prohibition against the District Court, the Minister for Labour and National Service and the Commonwealth prohibiting them from proceeding further upon an order of the District Court in relation to a similar matter under the National Service Act and for *certiorari* to remove the record of proceedings of the District Court into the High Court, were refused. Barwick C.J. considered that there was 'a serious question' as to the Court's jurisdiction to grant *certiorari* and as to whether the Court in that case should grant prohibition.[207] Menzies J. said that he was not satisfied that there was jurisdiction and Taylor J. found it unnecessary to decide the question.[208] Windeyer J. considered that both the Minister and

[202] Debs. (H. of R.) Weekly Hansards (1977) p. 1396.
[203] (1966) 117 C.L.R. 94.
[204] (1968) 118 C.L.R. 488.
[205] at p. 495; Lane (1969) 43 A.L.J. 21.
[206] (1966) 116 C.L.R. 644.
[207] at p. 648.
[208] at p. 652.

the Commonwealth were proper parties interested in maintaining the order of the Court.[209] If in these cases the matters came within sec. 75 (iii), it is clear, as Mr Katz has said, that a generous interpretation has been given to the word 'party' in sec. 75 (iii).[210] In each case the respondents, other than the Court against which the writ was sought, were what Professor Lane has called 'secondary respondents'.[211]

It is suggested that the tendency disclosed by these cases of rushing into the merits before considering jurisdiction is, as has been stated, 'a most unsatisfactory way of proceeding'.[212] The alacrity with which the Court has in these cases determined the issue despite the expression of doubts (often unexplained) regarding jurisdiction is strangely inconsistent with the expression of view from time to time by the judges that an increase in the Court's jurisdiction impairs its ability to discharge its major role as constitutional interpreter and final court of appeal.[213]

Sec. 75 (v) like sec. 75 (iii) and (iv) on its face appears to confer a *jurisdiction*. Extended reference has already been made to the debate over the question whether sec. 75 (iii) conferred anything more, and particularly whether it gave any *substantive* right to proceed against the Commonwealth. It seems that the better view is that it does not[214] and that sec. 75 (v) should be similarly interpreted.[215] It is clear that this was the intendment of the authors of the clause. At the Melbourne meeting of the Convention of 1898, the proposal to restore the clause was under heavy attack. Mr Kingston asserted that it would give the High Court power to interfere with the executive 'to the very great detriment of constitutional government'.[216] Mr Symon, with Mr Barton's support, energetically denied this: 'The provision does not confer, and is not intended to confer—and I am sure Mr Barton will agree with me in this—any right whatever to interfere in such cases. It merely gives a jurisdiction.'[217] Mr Barton agreed. Mr

---

209 at p. 655.

210 5 U. of Tas. L.R. 188.

211 Lane, *op. cit.*, p. 513. In *White's Case* Mr Katz has pointed out that on any view it should have been held that the Court had jurisdiction under sec. 75 (v) as prohibition was sought, *inter alia*, against the Minister as the applicant's opposing litigant before the Tribunal, so he was one of the primary respondents: 5 U. of Tas. L.R. 188.

212 Katz, *op. cit.*, p. 193.

213 e.g., *Willocks v. Anderson* (1971) 124 C.L.R. 293.

214 See p. 38 ante.

215 See Anderson *ante* note 198 at p. 38.

216 Debs. Melb. (1898) at p. 1877.

217 ibid.

Symon reiterated the point: 'It does not give any right to get *mandamus* or prohibition . . . it merely gives a jurisdiction in certain applications. . . . It is not provided that the right shall exist to get the *mandamus* or prohibition.'[218] And when Sir John Forrest asked: 'It means nothing then?'[219] he was given the answer that it meant that the jurisdiction was given to a federal court. On this basis, Quick and Garran appeared perfectly justified in making the statement that the clause did not confer any right of action against officers of the Commonwealth. The High Court had been given jurisdiction only; and the Court had to determine in each case whether, according to principles of law, an action lay.[220]

Questions have arisen touching the validity and effect of privative clauses which purport to deny power to the High Court to grant the remedies enumerated in sec. 75 (v). An example is sec. 60 of the Conciliation and Arbitration Act 1904 (as amended) which declares that an award of the Commonwealth Conciliation and Arbitration Commission shall be final and conclusive and shall not be challenged, appealed against, reviewed, quashed or called in question in any court and shall not be subject to prohibition, *mandamus* or injunction in any court on any account. There are similar clauses in other Acts[221] which give expression to a policy that the bodies to which they apply shall have conclusive authority to determine all questions arising in the exercise of their functions, including the extent of their own jurisdiction. On the surface these clauses seem like a direct contradiction of the provisions of sec. 75 (v) and on that view would be invalid because Parliament has purported to deprive the Court of jurisdiction with which it is invested under the Constitution. The remedies referred to in sec. 75 (v), however, will not be available where the circumstances are such that no occasion has arisen for the exercise of the jurisdiction. Clearly a privative clause cannot foreclose the grant of remedies mentioned in sec. 75 (v) where the body in question purports to exercise power which the Commonwealth Parliament cannot lawfully confer on it.[222] Outside those limits Parliament may make the jurisdiction of a statutory body as broad or as narrow as it likes. The only duty of the Court in exercising jurisdiction under sec. 75 (v) would, in those circum-

218 ibid. at pp. 1877, 1878.

219 ibid. at p. 1878.

220 *op. cit.*, p. 784.

221 See e.g. Public Service Arbitration Act 1920-1973, sec. 20; Coal Industry Act 1946-1973, sec. 44; Stevedoring Industry Act 1956, sec. 22.

222 *R. v. Portus, ex parte McNeil* (1961) 105 C.L.R. 537, 540-1.

stances, be to ensure that the body keeps within the limits laid down by Parliament. It is possible to argue that the presence of a privative clause indicates an intention by Parliament to give full jurisdiction to the body to determine conclusively all relevant facts and questions of law. It would follow that a privative clause would operate to prevent the issue of the remedies named except where the body is purporting to exercise authority that is beyond the constitutional power of the Commonwealth Parliament to confer.[223]

That is not the way privative clauses have been interpreted. Their operation is somewhat obscure and the High Court has adopted a restrictive view of their scope. There has been an attempt by Dixon C.J. to develop a coherent theory for their application. That theory is to interpret privative clauses as validating any action by the authority concerned, so far as it can validate it constitutionally provided that it is a *bona fide* attempt to exercise its powers, that it relates to the subject matter of the legislation and is reasonably capable of reference to the power given to the authority. This view has been followed by a number of judges of the Court.[224]

It has been aptly observed that, whether appropriately or not, sec. 75 (v) has been largely responsible for the High Court's narrow view of the scope and operation of such privative clauses, just as it has been largely responsible for the extension of the writ of prohibition by the High Court to cover most of the ground of *certiorari*.[225]

# V

The Australian Constitution departed from American precedent in specifying subject-matters in which original jurisdiction might be vested in the High Court by Act of the Commonwealth Parliament. In the United States, all the heads of original jurisdiction and of federal jurisdiction were defined by the Constitution itself. The decision to separate those matters in which original jurisdiction was vested by the Constitution from those

---

[223] This view is favoured by Anderson, *op. cit.*, p. 54 and Sawer: Essays on the Australian Constitution (Ed. Else-Mitchell, 2nd ed., 1961), p. 83.

[224] The cases are collected in the judgment of Kitto J. in *R. v. Commonwealth Industrial Court, ex parte Cocks* (1968) 121 C.L.R. 313, 325. See also *Re Watson, ex parte Australian Workers' Union* (1973) 47 A.L.J.R. 48, 56.

[225] See Anderson, *op. cit., passim*, esp. at p. 55 and Sundberg: Functus Officio and the Prerogative Writ of Prohibition (1970) 7 Melbourne U.L.R. 507, 521 *et. seq.*

in which it might be conferred by Parliament was taken in the Australian Constitution Bill of 1891. Although the form of the provision was somewhat changed in 1897-8, the principle was preserved,[226] and the intendment is clear enough. As Quick and Garran put it: 'the cases mentioned in [sec. 76] are cases in which the Convention did not think it absolutely essential, at the outset, that the High Court should have original jurisdiction; but in which, on the other hand, such jurisdiction was appropriate and might prove to be highly desirable.'[227] Of the four subject-matters of jurisdiction in sec. 76, the first three had counterparts in Art. III, sec. 2 of the United States Constitution, while the fourth—matters relating to the same subject-matter claimed under the laws of different States—was of uncertain meaning and was probably included to deal with matters between States which, in any event, would have been covered by sec. 75 (iv).[228]

It is not at all surprising that the jurisdiction in matters arising under any laws made by the Parliament was consigned to sec. 76. To have set this clause in sec. 75 would have imposed an intolerable burden on the High Court. The case of Admiralty and maritime jurisdiction raises special and difficult problems which will be considered in more detail in the next section. It is rather more surprising, having regard to the matters which were included in sec. 75, that the jurisdiction in matters arising under the Constitution or involving its interpretation was assigned to sec. 76 rather than sec. 75. Although it is by no means necessary for the effective administration of justice that all constitutional cases should be tried in the original jurisdiction of the High Court, it is manifestly convenient that there should be machinery for the prompt disposal of important constitutional questions by bringing them immediately before the High Court.[229] In 1903, by sec. 30 (a) of the Judiciary Act, Parliament exercised its power under sec. 76 to invest the High Court with original jurisdiction in matters arising under the Constitution or involving its interpretation, and special provision was made for dealing with certain constitutional cases by secs. 38A, 40 and 40A of the Judiciary Act.[230]

---

[226] See Quick and Garran, *op. cit.* at pp. 789-90.
[227] *op. cit.* at p. 790.
[228] See p. 23 *ante.*
[229] See Dixon: Minutes of Evidence at p. 784.
[230] See pp. 9-14 Secs. 38A and 40A were repealed by the Judiciary Act Amendment Act 1976.

Sec. 76 (i) and (ii) differ somewhat in their terms. The scope of sec. 76 (ii) fell to be considered by the High Court in *Collins v. Charles Marshall Pty Ltd.*[231] The Court was considering the validity of sec. 31 of the Conciliation and Arbitration Act 1903-1952 which purported to confer on the Commonwealth Arbitration Court an appellate jurisdiction

(a) in proceedings arising under the Arbitration Act or involving the interpretation of the Act;

(b) in proceedings arising under an order or award or involving the interpretation of an order or award.

On the assumption that the Commonwealth Arbitration Court was a federal court within sec. 71 of the Constitution, this was a purported exercise of power under sec. 77 (i) authorizing the Commonwealth Parliament with respect to the matters enumerated in secs. 75 and 76 to make laws defining the jurisdiction of any federal court other than the High Court. It was clear that the only possible source of power was sec. 76 (ii), but the High Court demonstrated that sec. 31 of the Arbitration Act could not be supported by reference to that head of power.

> . . . an order or award of a Conciliation Commissioner or of the Court of Conciliation and Arbitration is not a law of the Commonwealth: *Ex parte McLean* (1930) 43 C.L.R. 472, at pp. 479 and 484. Where is to be found the legislative authority for conferring jurisdiction in matters arising under an order or award, as distinguished from under the Act? Where is the legislative authority for conferring jurisdiction in matters which do not arise under the Act but which do involve the interpretation of the Act or of an order or of an award? It cannot be found in the operation of sec. 76 (ii)—matters arising under any laws made by the Parliament—upon sec. 77 (i)—defining the jurisdiction of any Federal Court with respect (*inter alia*) to such matters.[232]

It follows, as was pointed out by Latham C.J. in *R. v. Commonwealth Court of Conciliation and Arbitration, ex parte Barrett,*[233] that there is a distinction between a matter 'arising under' the Commonwealth law and one involving the interpretation of such a law:

> This variation of language supports the view that, in order to bring a matter within s. 76 (ii) . . . the inquiry to be made is not whether the determination of the matter involves the interpretation of a

---

231 (1955) 92 C.L.R. 529.

232 at p. 540, *per* Dixon C.J., McTiernan, Williams, Webb, Fullagar and Kitto JJ. The Court demonstrated that the legislation under review went beyond the scope of sec. 76 (ii) in other respects: see pp. 540-2.

233 (1945) 70 C.L.R. 141, 154.

Federal law. The relevant inquiry is whether the matter arises under the law. Thus one is compelled to the conclusion that a matter may properly be said to arise under a Federal law if the right or duty in question in the matter owes its existence to Federal law or depends on Federal law for its enforcement, whether or not the determination of the controversy involves the interpretation (or validity) of the law. In either of these cases, the matter arises under the Federal law. If a right claimed is conferred by or under a Federal statute, the claim arises under the statute. . . . The construction of a Federal law, and perhaps a question of the validity of such a law, may be involved in such a matter. But it is not necessary that this should be the case in order that the matter may arise under the law.

This statement seems to refer to the claim being made by the plaintiff or applicant. A similar emphasis was given by the Court in *Collins v. Charles Marshall Pty Ltd*[234] where their Honours said:

Clearly enough a matter or proceeding may involve the interpretation of the Act or of an order or of an award, although the proceeding does not arise under the Act . . . and it may be said that almost always it will be so where the Act order or award is relevant only to some matter of defence to a proceeding based on some cause of action or ground which is prima facie independent of the Act order or award.

It was held, however, in *Felton v. Mulligan*[235] that, if a defence or answer is based on a Commonwealth law and is an issue for decision, the matter arises under that Commonwealth law.

If the High Court were to be granted general jurisdiction over matters falling within sec. 76 (ii), the decision in *Felton v. Mulligan* would give rise to difficulties as it would be necessary to know when proceedings were instituted whether the Court had jurisdiction. However, as Walsh J. remarked, that difficulty in relation to the jurisdiction of the High Court 'is perhaps of theoretical rather than of practical significance'.[236] In any case it is a difficulty always present in relation to jurisdiction under sec. 76 (i) where a question 'involving the interpretation of the Constitution' can arise at any stage in the course of proceedings. As a practical matter, the issue is of more importance in relation to the question whether the State court is exercising State or federal jurisdiction and in the exercise by the High Court of its power to remove a cause under sec. 40 of the Judiciary Act.

The decision in *Felton v. Mulligan* has increased the difficulty

234 (1955) 92 C.L.R. 529 at p. 540.
235 (1971) 124 C.L.R. 367.
236 ibid. at p. 403.

of determining the distinction between a matter arising under a law made by Parliament and one that does not so arise but involves the interpretation of such a law. This difficulty is well illustrated by *Felton v. Mulligan* itself. The plaintiff sought a declaration that, under a deed which provided for payment of periodical maintenance to her by her husband, she was entitled to have those payments continue by the deceased husband's executors. The executors contended that the deed was void on the ground of public policy in that it attempted to oust the jurisdiction of the Court to make orders for maintenance. The Supreme Court of New South Wales upheld the contention and the question of whether the Court was exercising federal or State jurisdiction was relevant to the issue of whether the wife could appeal to the Privy Council. If it was federal jurisdiction, an appeal was prevented under sec. 39 (2) (a) of the Judiciary Act.

While all the judges recognized that, in determining the question raised by the defence of public policy, regard needed to be had to the Matrimonial Causes Act 1959 which provided for the making of maintenance orders, their Honours differed as to whether the Commonwealth Act was, in the words of Windeyer J., 'lurking in the background' or standing 'on the threshold'.[237]

Parliament has made only limited use of its power under sec. 76 (ii) to confer original jurisdiction in the High Court,[238] and this is an area in which restraint is obviously to be commended.

Sec. 76 (i) is wider in purview, and there has been a full grant of original jurisdiction to the High Court. The clause is not free from obscurities and difficulties, and it becomes necessary first to determine when a matter falls within the scope of the clause. A general answer was given in *James v. South Australia*:[239]

> Matters arising under the Constitution or involving its interpretation are those in which the right, title, privilege or immunity is claimed under that instrument, or matters which present necessarily and directly and not incidentally an issue upon its interpretation.

It will be seen that this definition leaves an area of uncertainty and dispute.

In the light of the decision of the majority in *Felton v. Mulligan*, however, there would seem to be very few matters involving the interpretation of the Constitution that do not arise under the Constitution. Dr Wynes has pointed out that, as a result of that

[237] ibid. at p. 391.
[238] See p. 6 *ante*.
[239] (1927) 40 C.L.R. 1, 40 *per* Gavan Duffy, Rich and Starke JJ.

decision 'it is difficult to imagine a case in which mere interpretation of a federal Act is involved and which does not arise thereunder'.[240]

Barwick C. J., who was among the majority in *Felton v. Mulligan*, did state that, for the purposes of sec. 76 (ii), it was not enough that a law made by the Parliament must be construed in the course of the decision of the case:

> There must be a matter arising under a law of the Parliament. The contrast between the language of s. 76 (i) and 76 (ii) is relevant in this connexion. The point at which interpretation of the federal statute, prima facie an apparently incidental consideration, may give rise to a matter arising under the statute is not readily expressed in universally valid terms. But the distinction between the two situations must be maintained.[241]

In the light of this passage and the actual decision in *Felton v. Mulligan*, it would appear that, contrary to the statement in *James v. South Australia* that is referred to above, sec. 76 (i) might include matters in which the issue of constitutional interpretation is raised as an 'incidental consideration'.

In *Hopper v. Egg and Egg Pulp Marketing Board*,[242] it was unsuccessfully argued that a charge imposed by the Board under Victorian legislation imposed an excise contrary to sec. 90 of the Commonwealth Constitution. A challenge was directed to the original jurisdiction of the High Court, but the majority held that the question raised was a matter within sec. 76 (i). Starke J. sharply dissented. The two views may be contrasted. Latham C.J., one of the majority, put it this way:

> The fact that the constitutional objection has failed does not deprive the court of jurisdiction if the facts relied on were *bona fide* raised and were such as to raise the question . . . Although the claim based on the Constitution has failed, I cannot discern a satisfactory reason for saying that it was not a *bona fide* claim so based.[243]

Starke J., on the other hand, said:

> In my opinion an allegation of some contravention of the Constitution which on its face is not such a contravention does not attract or found the original jurisdiction conferred upon this court in matters involving the interpretation of the Constitution. The allegations in the present case are merely colourable: they do not raise any real question involving the interpretation of the Constitution and are in

---

240 Wynes, *op. cit.* (5th ed.) 479.
241 (1971) 124 C.L.R. 367 at p. 374.
242 (1939) 61 C.L.R. 665.
243 at pp. 673-4.

F

truth fictitious. . . . [cases cited] . . . do not, I think, conflict with this view; the questions in those cases were real and not merely pleading allegations as in the present case. The jurisdiction of the court does not rest on the consent of the parties but upon the existence of some matter founding the jurisdiction of the court. . . . I think this case should be dismissed for want of jurisdiction in this court.[244]

In general, it appears that the Court has construed its jurisdiction under this head rather generously, and has on occasion found a basis for the Court's jurisdiction where counsel was apparently unable to detect a problem of constitutional interpretation.[245] On occasion the Court has emphasized that the constitutional point on which jurisdiction was based[246] was raised *bona fide*,[247] but on the cases it would seem that a constitutional issue would have to be extremely far-fetched or remote before the court would treat it as having been raised *mala fide* with the object of attracting jurisdiction. As a matter of practical administration of justice, the question is more serious when a challenge is directed to proceedings in a court of summary jurisdiction, on the ground that the court was improperly constituted to try a case which involved the exercise of federal jurisdiction. Take the case of a court of Petty Sessions constituted by a stipendiary magistrate and justices of the peace. If the thinnest of constitutional defences is raised will this deprive the court so constituted of jurisdiction, or will it render void the decision of the court so constituted, having regard to the terms of sec. 39 (2) (d) of the Judiciary Act? There is very strong support for the answer that

244 at p. 677.

245 See *R. v. Bevan, ex parte Elias and Gordon* (1942) 66 C.L.R. 452, 465, *per* Starke J.: 'Consideration has led me to the conclusion that the matter before us involves the interpretation of the Constitution, which founds the original jurisdiction of this Court, though we heard no argument to that effect from counsel.'

246 The issue does not only arise in founding jurisdiction in the High Court. It is also raised in order to show that a State court is exercising federal jurisdiction, either to establish a right of appeal within sec. 39 of the Judiciary Act, or to challenge the jurisdiction of a court of summary jurisdiction on the ground that it is improperly constituted to exercise federal jurisdiction under sec. 39 (2) (d) of the Judiciary Act. See for example *Hopper v. Egg and Egg Pulp Marketing Board* (1939) 61 C.L.R. 665 (original jurisdiction of High Court); *Troy v. Wigglesworth* (1919) 26 C.L.R. 305 (court of Petty Sessions improperly constituted); *H. V. McKay Pty Ltd v. Hunt* (1926) 38 C.L.R. 308 (right of appeal from courts of Petty Sessions to High Court); *Felton v. Mulligan ante.*

247 *Troy v. Wigglesworth* (1919) 26 C.L.R. 305, 311; *Hopper v. Egg and Egg Pulp Marketing Board* (1939) 61 C.L.R. 665, 673-4.

while 'the objection may be constitutional nonsense . . . (the) . . . case is at once one of federal jurisdiction'.[248]

## VI

In *In re Judiciary and Navigation Acts*,[249] the High Court reviewed the provisions of secs. 75, 76 and 77 of the Constitution and said:

> This express statement of the matters in respect of which and the courts by which the judicial power of the Commonwealth may be exercised is, we think, clearly intended as a delimitation of the whole of the original jurisdiction which may be exercised under the judicial power of the Commonwealth, and as a necessary exclusion of any other exercise of original jurisdiction.

This was in the course of a decision that sec. 88 of the Judiciary Act, which purported to confer jurisdiction on the High Court to give an advisory opinion on the validity of an enactment of the Commonwealth Parliament, was unconstitutional. The passage suggests that secs. 75 and 76 mark out the limits of the original jurisdiction of the High Court. It is clear, however, that so far as Admiralty jurisdiction is concerned, the source of the original jurisdiction of the High Court is the Colonial Courts of Admiralty Act 1890, an enactment of the United Kingdom Parliament and *not* Chapter III of the Commonwealth Constitution. This has been the case since 1939. In *Huddart Parker v. Ship Mill Hill*[250] it was argued that because the Admiralty jurisdiction of the High Court derived from the Colonial Courts of Admiralty Act and not from the Constitution, it was not federal jurisdiction and that therefore sec. 79 of the Judiciary Act, prescribing a choice of law rule for the High Court sitting in its original jurisdiction, did not apply to the particular case of original Admiralty jurisdiction.

---

[248] Dixon: Royal Commission on the Constitution: Minutes of Evidence (1927) at p. 788: 'If a boy is prosecuted before justices of the peace under a municipal by-law for riding a bicycle on the footpath and objects that he did so in the performance of his duties as a messenger of the Post and Telegraph Department and that the by-law cannot affect him, however untenable his objection may be as a defence, yet instantly the justices lose their jurisdiction, because the interpretation of the Constitution is involved. . . . So, if a tramp about to cross the bridge at Swan Hill is arrested for vagrancy and is intelligent enough to object that he is engaged in interstate commerce and cannot be obstructed, a matter arises under the Constitution. His objection may be constitutional nonsense, but his case is at once one of Federal jurisdiction.' See Lane, *op. cit.* at pp. 449-53.

[249] (1921) 29 C.L.R. 257, 265, *per* Knox C.J., Gavan Duffy, Powers, Rich and Starke JJ.

[250] (1950) 81 C.L.R. 502.

The Court acknowledged that its Admiralty jurisdiction depended exclusively upon the Act of 1890, but held nevertheless that sec. 79 of the Judiciary Act applied. The case of original jurisdiction in Admiralty is therefore clear. More difficult problems arise in connection with Commonwealth territories, in which the position cannot be said to be clear, and this case will be considered in a subsequent chapter.

Although it is clear that the High Court now exercises original jurisdiction in Admiralty under the Colonial Courts of Admiralty Act exclusively, this was not always the case. Sec. 76 (iii) of the Constitution authorized the Commonwealth Parliament to invest the High Court with original jurisdiction in matters of Admiralty and maritime jurisdiction. These words were copied directly from Art. III, sec. 2 of the United States Constitution, where the jurisdiction was made *federal* but was not assigned to the original jurisdiction of the Supreme Court of the United States. The historical reasons for conferring federal jurisdiction in Admiralty and maritime cases in the United States are reasonably clear. Admiralty was a separate corpus of law which before the American War of Independence had been administered by British Vice-Admiralty Courts rather than by the ordinary colonial courts, so that general Admiralty jurisdiction covered an area in which the State courts and their predecessors had little experience.[251] Moreover 'Since one of the objectives of the Philadelphia Convention was the promotion of commerce through removal of obstacles occasioned by the diverse local rules of the States, it was only logical that it should contribute to the development of a uniform body of maritime law by establishing a system of federal courts and granting to these tribunals jurisdiction over Admiralty and maritime cases'.[252] The principal commerce of the period was maritime, and it was in this jurisdiction that disputes with foreigners were most likely to arise.

There is a further important point which bears on the scope of Admiralty and maritime jurisdiction in the United States. The struggle between the common law courts and the Admiralty Courts had resulted in the curtailment of Admiralty jurisdiction in England. There was, even at the date of constitution making, a much broader conception of the scope of Admiralty jurisdiction in the United States. It was early ruled by the federal courts that

---

[251] See Hart and Wechsler: The Federal Courts and the Federal System at pp. 20-1.

[252] The Constitution of the United States of America, *op. cit.* at p. 646. See Hart and Wechsler, *loc. cit.*

the extent of Admiralty and maritime jurisdiction was not to be determined by English law, but by principles of maritime law 'as respected by maritime courts of all nations and adopted by most, if not by all of them, on the continent of Europe', and this broader definition was approved by the Supreme Court before 1850 in opinions which asserted that the constitutional grant of the jurisdiction was not to be controlled or limited by English rules of Admiralty law.[253]

English Admiralty jurisdiction, on the other hand, bore the marks of the struggle between the courts, and by 1840 was very narrowly confined. The jurisdiction of the English Courts of Admiralty was extended by statute in that year, and by subsequent legislation. Admiralty jurisdiction was a field in which uniformity and the preservation of Imperial control were regarded as important, and in the colonies the jurisdiction was conferred by Imperial statute on Vice-Admiralty Courts, and special Imperial Acts were passed from time to time extending their jurisdiction. In 1890, the Colonial Courts of Admiralty Act conferred Admiralty jurisdiction on courts in British possessions, while preserving a substantial measure of Imperial control. 'Underlying the Act is the assumption that the matter is essentially of Imperial concern, and that such limited power of local regulation as might for convenience be conceded should be subject to the jealous control of the Imperial authorities.'[254] The Act by sec. 2 vested Admiralty jurisdiction in every court of law in a British possession for the time being declared in pursuance of the Act to be a Court of Admiralty or which, if no such declaration was in force in the possession, had therein original unlimited jurisdiction, which was defined by sec. 15 as civil jurisdiction unlimited as to the value of the subject-matter at issue or as to the amount that could be claimed or recovered. The jurisdiction conferred was that of the Admiralty jurisdiction of the High Court in England. It was provided that colonial laws might declare any court of unlimited civil jurisdiction to be a Colonial Court of Admiralty. Special provision was made for New South Wales and Victoria (among other named British possessions), where the Act came into operation, not in 1891, but by Orders-in-Council in 1911. Two important decisions of the Privy Council limited the jurisdiction of

---

253 *Waring v. Clarke* (1847) 5 How. 441; *New Jersey Steam Navigation Co. v. Merchants Bank* (1848) 6 How 344. See Constitution of the United States of America, *op. cit.* at pp. 647, 653.

254 McGrath: Admiralty Jurisdiction and the Statute of Westminster (1932) 6 A.L.J. 160, 162.

Colonial Courts of Admiralty. In *The Camosun*[255] it was ruled that the Admiralty jurisdiction vested in colonial courts was that of the Admiralty Court in England before its incorporation in the English High Court by the Judicature Acts of 1873 and 1875, so that it was not possible to raise an equitable defence in a Colonial Court of Admiralty even in those British possessions which had adopted the Judicature Acts system. In *The Yuri Maru; the Woron*,[256] it was further held that the jurisdiction conferred by the Act was fixed as of 1890, so that subsequent statutory extensions of the Admiralty jurisdiction of the High Court in England did not extend the jurisdiction of Colonial Courts of Admiralty in British possessions.

In this area, there is reason to doubt whether the Australian Founding Fathers knew what they were doing, when sec. 76 (iii) was written into the Constitution. In view of the Imperial interest in these matters, it is perhaps surprising that this clause was not more carefully scrutinized by the Imperial law officers when the Constitution Bill was submitted to the United Kingdom Parliament, and it is certainly not clear why it was felt that there was any need for a further grant of jurisdiction under the Constitution. No doubt the influence of American precedent was very strong, but it is very uncertain whether the Founding Fathers were aware of the fact that Admiralty and maritime jurisdiction had a significantly wider scope and meaning in the United States—one which differed, as we have seen, from the English jurisdiction. Quick and Garran saw some of the difficulties. 'Under this Constitution, however, the Parliament has power independently of the Colonial Courts of Admiralty Act, to confer Admiralty and maritime jurisdiction on the High Court; and it seems clear that the limitations imposed by that Act on the jurisdiction of "Colonial Courts of Admiralty" within the meaning of that Act . . . cannot be read into the plenary powers conferred by this section. Nevertheless, whatever may be the legal powers of the Commonwealth, it would probably be inexpedient in conferring Admiralty jurisdiction on the High Court or other courts of federal jurisdiction, to go outside the limits defined by that Act,

[255] [1909] A.C. 597.
[256] [1927] A.C. 906. See *F. Kanematsu and Co. Ltd v. Ship 'Shahzada'* (1956) 96 C.L.R. 477, 482-3: 'The Admiralty jurisdiction of the High Court, exercisable by virtue of the provisions of the Colonial Courts of Admiralty Act 1890, is no more extensive than that which was exercisable in the admiralty jurisdiction of the High Court in England "as it existed at the time when the Act was passed".' It was held by Taylor J. that the Court had no jurisdiction in that case.

which may be taken as a guide to the reasonable limits of the jurisdiction.'[257]

In 1914, however, the Commonwealth Parliament enacted two new provisions into the Judiciary Act.[258] Sec. 30 (b) of the Judiciary Act was a purported exercise of power under sec. 76 (iii) of the Constitution and conferred original jurisdiction on the High Court in all matters of Admiralty *or* maritime jurisdiction. It is to be noted that the jurisdiction was conferred in this disjunctive form, while sec. 76 (iii) refers to Admiralty and maritime jurisdiction. Sec. 30A was an exercise of power under the Colonial Courts of Admiralty Act and declared the High Court to be a Colonial Court of Admiralty 'within the meaning of the Imperial Act known as the Colonial Courts of Admiralty Act'. This raised two questions. First, did sec. 30A, by declaring the High Court to be a Colonial Court of Admiralty, deprive the Supreme Courts of the States of their Admiralty jurisdiction under the Colonial Courts of Admiralty Act? Second, what was the relationship between Admiralty or maritime jurisdiction conferred by sec. 30 (b) and the Admiralty jurisdiction of the High Court under the Colonial Courts of Admiralty Act?

The answers to these questions were not clear. Taking first the problem of sec. 30A, it was argued unsuccessfully in *John Sharp and Sons Ltd v. Ship Katherine Mackall*[259] that the Commonwealth was not a British possession for the purposes of the Colonial Courts of Admiralty Act, that the States were British possessions for this purpose, and that the jurisdiction of the High Court in Admiralty matters depended on sec. 76 (iii) and not on the Act of 1890. It was held in the High Court, on the authority of the Imperial Interpretation Act 1889, that the Commonwealth was a British possession for the purposes of the Colonial Courts of Admiralty Act. On this point the case was approved by the High court in *McIlwraith McEacharn Ltd v. Shell Co. of Australia Ltd.*[260] It followed that, if sec. 30A was otherwise validly enacted, the declaration operated to deprive the State Supreme Courts of their Admiralty jurisdiction under the Colonial Courts of Admiralty Act. But whether sec. 30A was otherwise valid was not clear. In *John Sharp and Sons Ltd v. Ship Katherine Mackall*, Isaacs J. was of opinion that it was not valid because as a reserved Bill, it had not satisfied the terms of sec. 60 of the Constitution,

---

257 *op. cit.* at p. 800.
258 Act No. 11 of 1914.
259 (1924) 34 C.L.R. 420.
260 (1945) 70 C.L.R. 175, 202-6.

since the Royal assent had been notified outside the two-year period.[261] This view did not command the assent of the whole Court,[262] but it left the Admiralty jurisdiction of State Supreme Courts uncertain and attention was drawn to this by members of the High Court in later cases.[263] The matter was finally resolved by the enactment of the Judiciary Act 1939 which repealed sec. 30A.

The Attorney-General for the Commonwealth, introducing the Bill, said that there was some doubt, having regard to sec. 60 of the Constitution, whether sec. 30A had been validly enacted. If the section was valid, it probably deprived State Supreme Courts of Admiralty jurisdiction under the Colonial Courts of Admiralty Act. In view of these uncertainties, it was thought desirable to repeal the section to ensure that State Supreme Courts, as well as the High Court, were Colonial Courts of Admiralty, since there would no longer be any declaration in force, and State Supreme Courts were courts of unlimited civil jurisdiction.[264]

There remains the problem of the relationship between 'Admiralty and maritime jurisdiction' under sec. 76 (iii) and Admiralty jurisdiction under the Colonial Courts of Admiralty Act. In *John Sharp and Sons Ltd v. Ship Katherine Mackall*,[265] Isaacs J. drew attention to the very wide scope which had been attributed to this jurisdiction in the United States. He said that it was not conceivable that the framers of the Australian Constitution intended to follow American doctrine on such a subject of common Imperial concern in direct opposition to established English precedent. On the other hand it was not to be supposed that the scope of the jurisdiction under sec. 76 (iii) was merely the stereotyped English common law jurisdiction. For the purposes of the case, it was not necessary to define the scope of the jurisdiction but Isaacs J. observed: 'if it became necessary to determine this case upon sec. 76 (iii) of the Constitution and sec. 30 (b) of the

---

[261] (1924) 34 C.L.R. 420, 429-30. Sec. 60 provides: 'A proposed law reserved for the Queen's pleasure shall not have any force unless and until within two years from the day on which it was presented to the Governor-General for the Queen's assent the Governor-General makes known, by speech or message to each of the Houses of Parliament, or by Proclamation, that it has received the Queen's assent.'

[262] See *per* Starke J. at p. 433. Knox C.J. and Gavan Duffy J. did not find it necessary to deal with the point.

[263] See *McArthur v. Williams* (1936) 55 C.L.R. 324; *Union Steamship Co. of New Zealand Ltd v. The Caradale* (1937) 56 C.L.R. 277; *Nagrint v. Ship 'Regis'* (1939) 61 C.L.R. 688.

[264] Debs. (H. of R.) vol. 161 at p. 162.

[265] (1924) 34 C.L.R. 420.

Judiciary Act there are some very difficult questions to answer . . . were the decision of this case dependent on the provision in sec. 76 (iii) of the Constitution with the statutory exercise of the power, there would be a field of inquiry by no means clear.'[266] It is now clear that original jurisdiction under the Colonial Courts of Admiralty Act is vested in the High Court. It has also been held that the Supreme Courts of the several States also have jurisdiction under that Act.[267]

There seems little doubt that sec. 76 (iii) includes at least all those matters that were within the jurisdiction of Colonial Courts of Admiralty in 1900. On the other hand, there would have been little point to the enactment of sec. 76 (iii) if it were intended to limit jurisdiction to that which already existed. Mr Dixon, in his evidence before the Royal Commission, said that 'no one seems to know what maritime jurisdiction is'.[268] It is nevertheless the task of the judiciary to give meaning to the language used and it is difficult to see why it should be regarded as surplusage or synonymous with 'Admiralty'. In any case, to confine the meaning of a term, such as Admiralty jurisdiction, in the Constitution to those particular objects which it denoted in 1900 would not be consistent with the general approach adopted by the Court.[269] The fact remains, however, that the extent of this head of jurisdiction is extremely uncertain. In *McIlwraith McEacharn Ltd v. Shell Co. of Australia Ltd*[270] Dixon J. said that the jurisdiction of the High Court under the Colonial Courts of Admiralty Act might not be co-extensive with the jurisdiction which sec. 76 (iii) empowered the Commonwealth Parliament to confer on the Court.

The Commonwealth Parliament in 1939 also repealed sec. 30 (b) of the Judiciary Act, and since that date the High Court has not been invested with jurisdiction under sec. 76 (iii). Senator

---

266 at p. 428.

267 *McIlwraith McEacharn Ltd v. Shell Co. of Australia Ltd* (1945) 70 C.L.R. 175, 204 *per* Dixon J.: 'The High Court as well as the Supreme Courts of the States are courts of unlimited civil jurisdiction within this definition. No doubt it is also true of the Supreme Courts of the Territories.'; *Lewmarine Pty Ltd v. The Ship 'Kaptayanni'* [1974] V.R. 465; *Union Steamship Co. of New Zealand Ltd v. Ferguson* (1969) 119 C.L.R. 191.

268 at p. 784.

269 Wynes, *op. cit.*, pp. 25-9; *R. v. Commonwealth Conciliation and Arbitration Commission; ex parte Association of Professional Engineers* (1959) 107 C.L.R. 208, 267 *per* Windeyer J.; *Lansell v. Lansell* (1964) 110 C.L.R. 353, 366-7.

270 (1945) 70 C.L.R. 175, 208-9.

Collett introduced the Judiciary Bill of 1939 in the Senate, and 'explained' the reasons for the repeal of sec. 30 (b) as follows:

> The Commonwealth Constitution also empowers this Parliament to vest original jurisdiction in the High Court in matters of Admiralty and maritime jurisdiction. The amending act of 1914, to which I have already referred, also amended section 30 of the Judiciary Act, which deals with the original jurisdiction of the High Court, by adding paragraph b, which vests in the High Court jurisdiction over matters of Admiralty or maritime jurisdiction. In view of other provisions of the Judiciary Act which remove from State Supreme Courts all matters of federal jurisdiction, and, with certain exceptions, return that jurisdiction to those courts as State courts exercising federal jurisdiction, some doubt also arises whether this amendment does not, to some extent, destroy the full Admiralty jurisdiction which that State Supreme Court would otherwise enjoy. As, by reasons of the decisions of the High Court, it is quite clear that the High Court, as a court of unlimited civil jurisdiction in a British possession, possesses Admiralty jurisdiction, this provision is also unnecessary, and might be repealed in order to remove any semblance of doubt regarding the jurisdiction of the State courts. The bill, therefore, proposes to repeal this paragraph also.[271]

It is not very easy to see what this means. It may be that the point was that while sec. 30 (b) of the Judiciary Act was in force, sec. 39 (1) of the Judiciary Act made the jurisdiction of the High Court exclusive of the jurisdiction of State courts in those matters, and might therefore have possibly deprived State courts of their jurisdiction under the Colonial Courts of Admiralty Act to the extent that the High Court's jurisdiction under sec. 76 (iii) coincided with the jurisdiction conferred by the Colonial Courts of Admiralty Act. While sec. 39 (2) of the Judiciary Act then gave the State courts federal jurisdiction in respect of matters of Admiralty and maritime jurisdiction within the meaning of sec. 76 (iii) of the Constitution, a doubt might remain whether they still had jurisdiction as Colonial Courts of Admiralty.

Another possible reason for the repeal of sec. 30 (b), though it does not emerge from the exposition by Senator Collett, was that it purported to confer on the High Court jurisdiction in matters of Admiralty *or* maritime jurisdiction. It may have been suggested that this went beyond the expression 'Admiralty *and* maritime jurisdiction' in sec. 76 (iii) which was to be read as a composite expression referring to a single and indivisible jurisdiction. If this was so, sec. 30 (b) was misconceived, and it may have been thought that the Colonial Courts of Admiralty Act furnished the

[271] Debs. (Senate) vol. 161 at pp. 271-2.

High Court with adequate Admiralty jurisdiction, so that the better course was to repeal sec. 30 (b) rather than to amend it.

The withdrawal of original jurisdiction from the High Court still leaves the scope of the Admiralty jurisdiction of State courts somewhat obscure. Sec. 39 (2) of the Judiciary Act appears to invest State Courts with Admiralty and maritime jurisdiction. It remains a matter of some doubt whether they also have Admiralty jurisdiction under the Colonial Courts of Admiralty Act. These problems are discussed in Chapter 5. Since 1939, however, the High Court's jurisdiction in Admiralty matters depends exclusively upon the Colonial Courts of Admiralty Act. This jurisdiction is subject to the limitations imposed by the decisions of the Privy Council in *The Camosun*[272] and *The Yuri Maru; the Woron*,[273] so that the Admiralty jurisdiction of the High Court, so long as it depends upon the Colonial Courts of Admiralty Act and so long as there is no investment of jurisdiction under sec. 76 (iii), is fixed by English Admiralty jurisdiction as it existed in 1890.[274] On the other hand, if the original jurisdiction of the High Court depended upon investment under sec. 76 (iii), aided by legislation under secs. 51 (i) and 98 of the Constitution, it appears that it need not be circumscribed in this way. As the law stands, then it appears that the original jurisdiction of State courts in Admiralty matters may be wider than the original jurisdiction of the High Court. Why the High Court should have any original jurisdiction in Admiralty matters is one question— to which it might be found difficult to give a sensible answer. Why that jurisdiction should in any event be controlled by the limitations of the Colonial Courts of Admiralty Act is a matter to which it is still more difficult to give such an answer. Nor is it

---

[272] [1909] A.C. 597.

[273] [1927] A.C. 906. See also *Union Steamship Co. of New Zealand Ltd v. Ferguson* (1969) 119 C.L.R. 191.

[274] Sec. 3 of the Colonial Courts of Admiralty Acts limits the power of any colonial legislature by providing that a colonial law shall not confer any jurisdiction which is not conferred by the Colonial Courts of Admiralty Act. In the absence of any further investment of jurisdiction in the High Court under sec. 76 (iii), it is difficult to see how the Commonwealth Parliament could extend the Admiralty jurisdiction of the High Court beyond the limits of 1890. It is to be noted that sec. 4 of the Colonial Courts of Admiralty Act requiring certain colonial laws to be reserved for Her Majesty's assent was declared by sec. 6 of the Statute of Westminster to cease to have effect in Australia from the coming in to force of the latter Act. Sec. 7 of the Colonial Courts of Admiralty Act, so far as it required the approval of Her Majesty-in-Council for colonial rules of court governing the practice and procedure to be followed in Colonial Courts of Admiralty was likewise dealt with in sec. 6 of the Statute of Westminster.

easy to explain why a State Supreme Court should be in the situation in which it is at least arguable that its original jurisdiction in Admiralty matters is wider than that of the High Court.

## VII

The principle that a party invoking the original jurisdiction of the High Court must show that the subject-matter of his claim is a matter within the original jurisdiction of the Court is clear, but particular applications may give rise to difficulty, and, on occasion, to sharp division within the High Court.[275] If, however, a matter is raised which brings the case within one of the heads of original jurisdiction, the fact that that issue is, so to speak, dissolved by a decision on it adverse to the party raising it, does not, of itself, strip the High Court of jurisdiction to dispose of the case. In *R. v. Carter, ex parte Kisch*[276] an application was made to the High Court for a writ of *habeas corpus*. The jurisdiction of the High Court was invoked because the applicant based his main claim on the ground that Commonwealth legislation under which he was detained was invalid. He also argued that the proper steps had not been taken under the Commonwealth Immigration Act to declare him a prohibited immigrant. Evatt J. rejected the constitutional argument, but upheld the applicant's non-constitutional argument, observing that once the jurisdiction of the High Court was vested it was not lost by the rejection of the constitutional point.[277] This has been affirmed by the High Court on other occasions, and perhaps most picturesquely by Williams J. in terms that 'whenever there is woven across the warp of the facts constituting a cause of action the woof of a constitutional question, this Court has original jurisdiction to determine the whole of that cause of action'.[278] Similarly when a cause was removed into the High Court as an *inter se* question under sec. 40A of the Judiciary Act, the Court had authority to determine the entire cause, since it was the cause and not merely the *inter se* question which was removed.[279]

---

[275] See *Hopper v. Egg and Egg Pulp Marketing Board* (1939) 61 C.L.R. 665. See p. 61 *ante*.

[276] (1934) 52 C.L.R. 221.

[277] at pp. 223-4.

[278] *Carter v. Egg and Egg Pulp Marketing Board (Vic.)* (1942) 66 C.L.R. 557, 602. See also the judgement of Latham C.J. at p. 580.

[279] *O'Neill v. O'Connell* (1946) 72 C.L.R. 101, 116; *Ex parte de Braic* (1971) 124 C.L.R. 162, 165.

This is obviously a practical and desirable result since it enables the High Court to deal expeditiously with a cause which contains elements which lie partly within and partly outside the original jurisdiction of the Court. On the other hand, a statement may allege two or more distinct matters or causes of action, as was the case in *Carter v. Egg and Egg Pulp Marketing Board (Vic.)*.[280] In that case the plaintiff brought an action for a declaration in the original jurisdiction of the High Court in which he challenged the validity of the Victorian Marketing of Primary Products Act and regulations made thereunder. The High Court unanimously held that this raised a matter involving the interpretation of the Constitution which was within the Court's jurisdiction. The plaintiff also claimed an account on the footing that the State Act and regulations were valid and that the defendant board had not discharged its obligations thereunder. The Court unanimously held that it had no jurisdiction to entertain this matter. The principle was stated in the judgement of Latham C.J.:

> There are decisions . . . which . . . support the view that the Court can adjudicate in a case from which all questions of constitutional significance have been eliminated by the rejection of contentions based upon the Constitution, the whole cause, and not merely the cause so far as its decision depends upon such contentions. . . . But in each of these cases a single claim or charge or a defence thereto was supported upon several grounds, one or more of which involved the interpretation of the Constitution. None of the cases mentioned presented the feature which is to be found in this case, namely an entirely severable claim having no relation whatever to another claim or claims made in the same proceeding which other claim or claims alone involved the interpretation of the Constitution.[281]

This means that if a plaintiff desires to invoke the original jurisdiction of the High Court in such a case as this, he must separate his causes of action, bringing the action in part in the High Court, and in part in a State court. If he brings his action wholly in a State court and the High Court exercises its power under sec. 40 of the Judiciary Act to remove the cause into the High Court, part of the case (being a separate cause) must remain behind in a State court. This is hardly a convenient or expeditious method of disposing of litigation. Moreover it is not always clear whether a particular claim is severable. In *Parton v. Milk Board (Victoria)*[282] it was argued by the plaintiff that sec. 30 of

280 (1942) 66 C.L.R. 557.
281 *per* Latham C.J. at p. 580.
282 (1949) 80 C.L.R. 229.

the Milk Board Acts, and regulations and determinations made thereunder, were invalid since they purported to impose a duty of excise contrary to sec. 90 of the Constitution. It was also argued that the levy had not been properly made under the authority of the Act since it covered a class of persons excepted under the Act. It was clear that the first contention raised a matter arising under the Constitution or involving its interpretation, but the defendant board argued on the footing of *Carter's Case* that other submissions based upon the construction of the State legislation did not raise a matter within the original jurisdiction of the Court. Three members of the Court dealt with this argument, Latham C.J. and Dixon J. holding the whole cause was within jurisdiction, McTiernan J. *contra.* Latham C.J. pointed to the distinction drawn in *Carter's Case* between a claim completely separate in all its characteristics from the claim raising a constitutional issue, and a single claim which was supported on several grounds, one or more of which involved the interpretation of the Constitution. 'The present is a case of the latter description, and in my opinion the Court has jurisdiction to deal with it.'[283] McTiernan J. disagreed. He observed that the non-constitutional claim 'involves only the interpretation of the Milk Board Acts. Such a question is not within the original jurisdiction of this Court. No declaration should therefore be made as to the validity of the regulations and the determination: *Carter v. The Egg Board.*'[284]

Similarly, in *Airlines of New South Wales Pty Ltd v. New South Wales* (No. 1)[285] a matter was referred to the Full Court under sec. 18 of the Judiciary Act. Four questions were put to the Court. Two of them asked whether various provisions of the State Transport (Co-ordination) Act 1931 (N.S.W.) were inconsistent with the Air Navigation Act 1920-1961 (Cth) and instruments made under that Act. The third question was whether, if the plaintiff complied with the Commonwealth legislation, it was entitled to carry on its business without being required to be the holder of a licence under the State Act. The fourth question related solely to the construction of the State Act and concerned the power of the Commissioner under that Act to vary licences so as to re-allocate routes in the manner in which he had purported to do. The Court answered the first three questions but refused to answer the fourth except to the extent of saying that no provisions of

283 at p. 249. See also *per* Dixon J. at pp. 257-8.
284 at p. 268.
285 (1964) 113 C.L.R. 1.

the Constitution or federal law prevented the Commissioner from exercising any power he had under State law to vary the licences in question. Dixon C.J. said of the fourth question[286] 'As framed this question may be treated as one directed only to the interpretation of State law without regard to federal law at all'. All the other judges except Menzies J. agreed with this approach.[287]

These inconveniences and uncertainties will no doubt survive so long as the High Court retains an original jurisdiction. They reinforce the argument that the original jurisdiction should be confined as narrowly as possible.[288]

## VIII

It is clear law that Parliament cannot shut out the original jurisdiction of the High Court so far as it has been conferred by sec. 75 of the Constitution.[289] It is not altogether clear, however, whether the High Court may decline to exercise jurisdiction conferred on it directly by sec. 75, or by Parliament under sec. 76. It may be argued that jurisdiction is the grant of authority to adjudicate, and does not necessarily require a court to exercise that authority. But there are many judicial statements in England, Australia and the United States to the effect that a grant of jurisdiction carries with it a duty to exercise that jurisdiction.[290] The writ of *mandamus* lies to compel lower courts to exercise their jurisdiction. This assumes the existence of a duty. While *mandamus* does not lie to so compel the High Court, the absence of the remedy is no reason for distinguishing superior and inferior courts so far as the question whether there is a duty is concerned.[291]

---

286 ibid. 30.

287 See Lane, *op. cit.*, pp. 454-6.

288 Cf. sec. 32 of the Federal Court of Australia Act 1976 which provides: '32(1) To the extent that the Constitution permits, jurisdiction is conferred on the Court [i.e. the Federal Court of Australia] in respect of matters not otherwise within its jurisdiction that are associated with matters in which the jurisdiction of the Court is invoked.' It is doubtful whether this provision has any valid operation.

289 *Bank of New South Wales v. Commonwealth* (1948) 76 C.L.R. 1 at p. 357.

290 Lindell: 'Duty to Exercise Judicial Review' in: Commentaries on the Australian Constitution (Ed. Zines, 1977).

291 *Ah Yick v. Lehmert* (1905) 2 C.L.R. 593; *The King v. Commonwealth Court of Conciliation and Arbitration, ex parte Ozone Theatre (Aust.) Ltd* (1949) 78 C.L.R. 389, 398.

The same general view as to judicial duty has been taken in the United States since Marshall C.J. said in *Cohens v. Virginia*[292] 'We have no more right to decline the exercise of jurisdiction which is given, than to usurp that which is not given'. It has been emphasized on a number of occasions that this duty is subject to exceptions, one of which allows the Supreme Court to decline jurisdiction on the ground that it is a *forum non conveniens*,[293] but it has been observed that the authority on which the Court relied to reach this conclusion was not strong,[294] and the Court's invocation of the doctrine of *forum non conveniens* has been subjected to criticism.[295]

There is little authority on the matter in Australia. In *Fausset v. Carroll*,[296] which was a matter between residents of different States tried in the original jurisdiction of the High Court, the short cover note report states that, while the Court has jurisdiction in such cases, it is important to note that the practice of bringing actions in the High Court merely because the plaintiff resides in one State and the defendant in another is not encouraged. In *Fausset v. Carroll*, where the issue was one of fact and the sum at stake small, Gavan Duffy J. said that he had consulted his colleagues, and that in future plaintiffs would not be allowed costs in such actions. On other occasions the Court has indicated that it will make a special order for reduced costs where a plaintiff brings a diversity action in the High Court where the case 'is one normally and more appropriately' brought in the Supreme Court of a State and the action in the High Court has resulted in a material increase in costs,[297] or where an action was one which could have been brought in a district or county court.[298] This is a curious and rather backhand way of invoking the doctrine of *forum non conveniens*. The Court did not directly

[292] (1871) 6 Wheat. 264, 404.
[293] *Georgia v. Pennsylvania Rly* 340 U.S. 439.
[294] Hart and Wechsler: The Federal Courts and the Federal System at pp. 258-9.
[295] ibid. at p. 259.
[296] (1917) 15 W.N. (N.S.W.) No. 12 Cover Note (14 August 1917).
[297] *Marlow v. Tatlow* noted in (1965) 39 A.L.J. 140.
[298] *Cadet v. Stevens* noted in (1967) 40 A.L.J. 361; *Morrison v. Thwaites* (1969) 43 A.L.J.R. 452. A similar approach was taken in relation to the appellate jurisdiction of the court. In *Ritter v. North Side Enterprises Pty Ltd* (1975) 49 A.L.J.R. 202 an appeal was brought from a judge of the Queensland Supreme Court to the High Court against an order for specific performance of a covenant. The appeal was allowed but the Court expressed the opinion that, as the appeal was a minor matter, the appellant should have gone to the Full Court of the Supreme Court and Gibbs J. (with whom Stephen and Murphy JJ. agreed) said: 'I would in future be inclined to

question its obligation to provide a forum, but effectively denied it by a general prospective declaration that it would refuse or reduce costs. It is easy to sympathize with the Court's impatience with this time-wasting and purposeless jurisdiction, but the Constitution specifically confers the jurisdiction without any prescription of the amount in issue. In the United States, original diversity jurisdiction is exercisable by federal district courts, and then only if the amount in issue is not less than $10,000. If a smaller sum is involved, the parties must seek relief in State courts. But if, as is the case in Australia, the Constitution confers this original jurisdiction on the High Court without any such limit, it is difficult to see what can justify the Court in ruling that the jurisdiction is available, but that a party may be deprived of costs simply because he exercises his constitutional right to invoke it.

In *Queen v. Langdon*[299] an application was made to the High Court in its original diversity jurisdiction for a writ of *habeas corpus* in child custody proceedings. The application had originally been made in the Sydney registry of the Court and was transferred to Melbourne. The plaintiff husband was a Victorian resident, and the wife resided in Tasmania. Taylor J. had some doubt whether such a case fell within the diversity jurisdiction, but on the assumption that it did, proceeded to consider what law should be applied. This he held to be Tasmanian law as set out in the Guardianship and Custody of Infants Act 1934. After examining the provisions of this Act, Taylor J. said:

> The 'Court' in each case is defined by the Act to mean the Supreme Court of Tasmania, and the jurisdiction which is conferred by these sections is a special statutory jurisdiction with respect to infants. I very much doubt whether the jurisdiction conferred by (sec. 10) is exercisable by this Court in its original jurisdiction merely because the husband and wife are residents of different States and I have no doubt that the jurisdiction of this Court to issue a prerogative writ should not be exercised on the husband's application unless it is open to the Court to refuse the application in the exercise of a discretion similar to that reposed in the Supreme Court. The writ, although grantable ex debito justitiæ, does not issue as of course . . . and it may be sufficient to say that the husband's application should be refused on the ground that it would be more appropriate for this and similar applications to be made to the Court to whom the appropriate special

---

entertain the view that appellants who bring appeals of this kind to this court rather than to the Full Court of the Supreme Court ought to be visited with consequences in costs': at p. 204.

[299] (1953) 88 C.L.R. 158.

G

jurisdiction has been committed. But it is quite clear that it should be refused unless it is open to this Court to exercise such a discretion as that given by the statute to the Supreme Court.

The proposition that, where parties are residents of different States, this Court may exercise powers conferred upon particular courts for special purposes involves such far reaching consequences that I think the question, if and when it arises in an appropriate case, should be determined by the Full Court. . . . It would, I think, be most inappropriate for this Court to make an order for custody and maintenance where there exist courts specially constituted for this purpose and which may, if and as occasion requires, review the matter from time to time.[300]

Leaving aside any question as to the propriety of the choice of Tasmanian law to govern the case, the judgement raises a variety of problems posed by the availability of original jurisdiction in the High Court in diversity cases. It is apparent that the Tasmanian draftsman did not consider the possibility of such original jurisdiction in drafting the Guardianship and Custody of Infants Act, and other State Acts which ascribe special jurisdiction to particular courts have likewise been drawn without regard to the original jurisdiction of the High Court. Taylor J., in the passages cited, appears to suggest that in such a case, where relief is not available as of right, the High Court may refuse to make an order on the ground that a State court is, in the circumstances, a more appropriate forum. If this is a correct reading of *Queen v. Langdon* it lends support to the view that it is open to the High Court to refuse a remedy, on the ground that it is *forum non conveniens*.

It has been argued that this case is not merely one where the Court chose not to deal with a matter because the case was minor and the time of the High Court should not be taken up with such questions. Rather it might be seen as a case where the High Court was not able to provide an appropriate remedy. It is said that 'section 75 (iv) jurisdiction exists to provide a different forum not to provide a different remedy'.[301] This argument suggests that a principle of the conflict of laws should be adopted, namely that English courts will not determine a claim if the machinery by way of remedies is so different as to make the right sought to be enforced a different right.[302]

So in *Queen v. Langdon* while the High Court could have granted a writ of *habeas corpus*, it was assumed it could not have

---

[300] at pp. 161-3.
[301] Lane, *op. cit.* at p. 492; Pryles and Hanks: Federal Conflict of Laws (1974) at p. 135.
[302] *Phrantzes v. Argenti* [1960] 2 Q.B. 19; Pryles and Hanks, *op. cit.* at p. 136.

done so subject to the conditions and limitations that were laid down in the Tasmanian Act with respect to the jurisdiction of the State Supreme Court. It is clearly undesirable that the High Court adjudicate on a case governed by State law where that Court is unable adequately to administer that law. It should be noted, however, that this argument is based largely on the administration of justice as between the parties. The doctrine of *forum non conveniens* in the conflict of laws is confined to those considerations.[303] The American doctrine goes further and includes considerations of whether the assumption of jurisdiction would constitute a 'burden' on the federal Supreme Court and interfere with the discharge of its duties in deciding cases that are thought to be more important.[304]

Sir Garfield Barwick, before he became Chief Justice, considered that this American doctrine might apply in Australia, at any rate, where another federal court was available to deal with the matter.[305] It has also been pointed out[306] that the view that the High Court cannot refuse to exercise its jurisdiction gives an undue advantage to the plaintiff to choose the forum that suits him best. Under sec. 40 of the Judiciary Act a cause within federal jurisdiction may be removed from a State, federal or Territory court into the High Court. So, in those situations, the defendant is given an opportunity of arguing that the forum chosen by the plaintiff is not the most appropriate. As a matter of policy it would seem desirable that the defendant have a similar opportunity when the plaintiff commences his suit in the High Court.

It remains to consider sec. 44 of the Judiciary Act, which provides:

44. Any matter that is at any time pending in the High Court, whether originally commenced in the High Court or not, may, upon the application of a party or of the High Court's own motion, be remitted by the High Court to any federal court, court of a State or court of a Territory that has jurisdiction with respect to the subject-matter and the parties, and, subject to any directions of the High Court, further proceedings in the matter shall be as directed by the court to which it is remitted.

This provision was enacted in 1976. (Before that date a similar provision (sec. 45) enacted in 1903 authorized the High Court to

---

303 *Re Kernot* [1965] Ch. 217.
304 *Massachusetts v. Missouri* (1939) 308 U.S. 1.
305 (1964) 1 F.L. Rev. 1, pp. 10-15.
306 Howard: Australian Federal Constitutional Law (2nd ed., 1972) at p. 196.

remit matters for trial to any court of a State which had federal jurisdiction.) On its face sec. 44 appears to give statutory authority to the High Court, on the application of a party, to invoke what is in effect a doctrine of *forum non conveniens*, and to transfer the trial of the matter to an appropriate State, federal or Territory court as defined in the section, and it impliedly enables the proceedings to be continued in that court as if they had been commenced there. The question arises whether the section is constitutionally valid. If, as Quick and Garran state, a plaintiff has a *right* to bring an action in a matter falling within sec. 75 of the Constitution in the original jurisdiction of the High Court, there appears to be a corresponding obligation on that Court to try the cause itself and give judgement. If the High Court may remit the matter for trial in a State court, the theory of federal jurisdiction allowing the party a choice between a national and a State court (in cases of concurrent jurisdiction) is altogether defeated. On this view, there is a strong case for arguing that in respect of matters falling within sec. 75 of the Constitution, sec. 44 of the Judiciary Act is unconstitutional. A further question arises as to the original jurisdiction of the High Court under sec. 76. It may be argued that once Parliament has conferred jurisdiction on the High Court under sec. 76, the Court's position is the same as in a case arising under sec. 75, so that sec. 44 of the Judiciary Act can have no operation at all. But it is possible to argue that Parliament may validly provide that the High Court shall have jurisdiction in respect of defined matters within sec. 76, not being matters which in the opinion of the High Court should be dealt with by a lower court, and that secs. 30 and 44 of the Judiciary Act are to be read together as an exercise of power under sec. 76. This may be put in terms that it is incidental to the exercise of power under sec. 76 to provide for the exercise of the jurisdiction conferred only where the High Court thinks it appropriate that it should exercise the jurisdiction.

Sir Garfield Barwick, as Chief Justice, has indicated that he adheres to his earlier view expressed while Attorney-General that the High Court may under statutory provision remit to other courts matters that come within the High Court's original jurisdiction conferred by sec. 75 of the Constitution. In an address to the Nineteenth Australian Legal Convention he said that the Court had begun the practice of remitting accident cases arising in the diversity jurisdiction of the Court to a State court for disposal.[307]

[307] Barwick: The State of the Australian Judicature (1977) 51 A.L.J. 480, 489.

There can be little doubt that, as a matter of policy, the doctrine of *forum non conveniens* is desirable both from the point of view of doing justice to the parties and of the public interest in ensuring that the High Court is able to deal properly with its important constitutional functions.

It is submitted, however, that sec. 75 should be read as requiring the High Court to exercise its original jurisdiction, so that the Court, like the Parliament, has no constitutional power to tamper with or in any way modify the jurisdiction conferred by sec. 75. If this is so, the Court may not invoke the doctrine of *forum non conveniens* either under the authority of statute or of its own volition. Nor is it proper for the Court to refuse to exercise a discretion or to refuse costs *merely* because a party has exercised his constitutional right to bring his action in the High Court. In respect of jurisdiction conferred on the Court by Parliament under sec. 76, it may be that Parliament may authorize the High Court to invoke the doctrine of *forum non conveniens* as it has done in sec. 44 of the Judiciary Act, but apart from statutory authority there is no inherent power in the Court to decline to exercise jurisdiction once it has been conferred under sec. 76.

This reasoning, however, assumes that the High Court has the machinery and remedies to administer the law properly and adequately. As *Queen v. Langdon* shows, that may not be the case in certain circumstances where State law providing administrative machinery and judicial discretions is concerned. In those circumstances the High Court could well adopt the view that the purpose of the grant of jurisdiction is to give the plaintiff a choice of going to the High Court to determine the suit and, when that Court cannot properly determine it but another court can, the High Court's jurisdiction should not be invoked.[308] It is submitted that the principles applied by the courts in the area of conflict of laws in this respect can, by analogy, be applied to the exercise by the High Court of its original jurisdiction.[309]

308 Cf. Lane, *op. cit.* at p. 492.

309 In *Queen v. Langdon* itself it would have been preferable for the High Court to have regarded itself as subject to the statutory fetters imposed by State legislation on the Supreme Court. 'Such a result would appear to reconcile as far as possible the constitutional right to bring suit in the original jurisdiction of the High Court with the obligation under section 79 of the Judiciary Act to apply State statute law': Cowen (1955) 7 Res. Jud. 1 at p. 27.

# = 2 =

## *Jurisdiction between Residents of Different States*

### I

In the course of the debates on the Judicature Chapter of the Commonwealth Constitution in the Federal Convention of 1897-8, references to the American Constitution came thick and fast. One member could not restrain his impatience:

> We have heard too much about the example of the United States all through the meetings of this Convention. If the Constitutions of the United States and Canada had been burned before the Convention met we should have done more practical work, and we should probably have evolved a Constitution quite as suitable, if not more suitable to the people we represent.[1]

It is interesting to note that these words were spoken by a South Australian delegate, by name Mr Solomon. We have already noted that there were some significant departures from the American model.[2] The High Court of Australia was designed as a general court of appeal, and federal jurisdiction might be vested in State courts. The method of appointment and removal of justices of the High Court followed British rather than American patterns,[3] and the provisions with respect to the appellate jurisdiction of the Privy Council obviously had no counterpart in the American Constitution.[4] In conferring federal jurisdiction, the Australian draftsmen omitted some matters which appeared in the American instrument[5] and incorporated others which were novel.[6]

But there was heavy reliance on American precedent. This is certainly true in the case of diversity jurisdiction which appears in the American Constitution, Art. III, sec. 2: 'The judicial

---

1 Debs. Melb. (1898), p. 303.
2 See pp. 1-2 *ante*.
3 See Constitution, secs. 71 and 72.
4 Secs. 73, 74.
5 For example in matters of land grants under Art. III, s. 2.
6 e.g. sec. 75 (v) ; see pp. 22-3 *ante*.

power shall extend . . . to Controversies . . . between Citizens of different States.' In the 1890 meeting at Melbourne, Alfred Deakin had drawn attention to the pattern of federal jurisdiction in the United States, including diversity jurisdiction, and said that this exactly fitted the needs of Australia.[7] At the 1891 Convention in Sydney, a committee on the Judiciary was appointed under the chairmanship of Inglis Clark.[8] The committee reported in favour of a provision that 'the Judicial power of the Union shall extend—to disputes between residents of different States'.[9] It is clear that Inglis Clark intended to reproduce the American diversity provision.[10] At the 1898 meeting in Melbourne, Barton moved to add the words of diversity jurisdiction 'or between residents of different States', and this was adopted without discussion.[11] This was the history of the provision which appeared in sec. 75 (iv) of the Commonwealth of Australia Constitution Act. 'In all matters—(iv) between residents of different States . . . the High Court shall have original jurisdiction.'

It is appropriate to ask why this clause was incorporated into the Constitution apparently without expressed doubt or hesitation on the part of anyone. This in turn leads us to an enquiry into the origins and purpose of the American diversity clause. The classic statement is in the opinion of Marshall C.J. in *Bank of the United States v. Deveaux*:[12]

> . . . However true the fact may be, that the tribunals of the States will administer justice as impartially as those of the nation, to parties of every description, it is not less true that the constitution itself either entertains apprehensions on this subject, or views with such indulgence the possible fears and apprehensions of suitors, that it has established national tribunals for the decision of controversies . . . between the citizens of different States.

The traditional explanation of diversity jurisdiction emphasizes the necessity for protection of out-of-State litigants against local prejudice in State courts. Whether this danger was real at

[7] Debs. Melb. (1890), pp. 89 *et. seq.*
[8] See Reynolds: A. Inglis Clark and His Influence on Australian Federation (1958) 32 A.L.J. 62; La Nauze: Making of the Australian Constitution (1972) p. 12.
[9] Text printed in Hunt: American Precedents in Australian Federation (1930) p. 261.
[10] See Inglis Clark: Australian Constitutional Law (1901) p. 164, speaking of American diversity jurisdiction as being conferred 'in the same words as those by which the like jurisdiction is conferred upon the federal courts of the Commonwealth by the Constitution of the Commonwealth'.
[11] Debs. Melb. (1898), p. 1885. See Hunt, *op. cit.*, p. 198.
[12] (1809) 5 Cranch 61, 87.

the date of constitution-making in the United States, is a matter of some doubt.[13] It has been argued that diversity jurisdiction stemmed rather from fears of State legislatures than of State courts; it was felt that the new federal courts would provide more adequate protection for the interests of creditors and commercial enterprise.[14]

If there is some doubt about the original justification of diversity jurisdiction in the United States, the doubt about the Australian clause is much stronger. Quick and Garran, driven no doubt to find some explanation for the enactment of the provision, followed the classic American statement.[15] But it is perfectly clear that there was no fear of partiality or bias on the part of State tribunals in 1900; nor was there any felt necessity for protection of out-of-State commerce against legislative depredation enforced by State courts. The inappropriateness of carrying over the American provision into the Australian Constitution was the subject of judicial comment in the High Court in *Australasian Temperance and General Mutual Life Assurance Society Ltd v. Howe*[16] where it was held by a majority that a corporation was not a resident for the purposes of diversity jurisdiction. Higgins J. (who had been a member of the Constitutional Convention which had adopted the clause) said:

> We might think that the jurisdiction given in matters 'between residents of different States' is a piece of pedantic imitation of the Constitution of the United States, and absurd in the circumstances of Australia, with its State Courts of high character and impartiality.[17]

Starke J. likewise observed that the fear of bias on the part of State tribunals was 'little grounded in point of fact in Australia'.[18] Mr Dixon stated in evidence before the Royal Commission on the Constitution in 1927, that there was no better reason for transcribing diversity jurisdiction into the Australian Constitution

---

[13] See Friendly: The Historic Basis of Diversity Jurisdiction (1928) 41 Harvard Law Review 483. His conclusion is that the diversity jurisdiction 'had its origin in fears of local hostilities which had only a speculative existence in 1789, and are still less real today' (at 510). But see Yntema and Jaffin: Preliminary Analysis of Concurrent Jurisdiction (1930-31) 79 University of Pennsylvania Law Review 869; Frank: Historical Bases of the Federal Judicial System (1948) 13 Law and Contemporary Problems 3; Hart and Wechsler: The Federal Courts and the Federal System (1953) 892-3.

[14] See esp. Friendly, *op. cit.*; Frank, *op. cit.*

[15] The Annotated Constitution of the Commonwealth (1901) at p. 776.

[16] (1922) 31 C.L.R. 290.

[17] at p. 330.

[18] at p. 339.

than the desire to imitate an American model.[19] Even if it could plausibly be argued that there might be bias in State courts against out-of-State litigants, the general appellate jurisdiction of the High Court might have been thought to provide an adequate safeguard—lacking in this respect in the United States where there was no single general appellate jurisdiction—without recourse to a special diversity jurisdiction.[20] At lowest it can be put as an oddity that the Founding Fathers, who were on occasion prepared to jettison American precedents where they were thought to be inapplicable to Australian conditions and needs, let this particular provision slip in without proper analysis or consideration.

A further reason for conferring this jurisdiction on the High Court has been suggested. In *Howe's Case* Starke J.[21] pointed to the fact that at the time of federation the service of process and the enforcement of judgements beyond the limits of a State were somewhat technical proceedings and he considered that sec. 75 (iv) was, in part, designed to cure those defects, by conferring jurisdiction on a court, the process and judgements of which ran throughout the Commonwealth. This was the reason given for this head of jurisdiction by Inglis Clark who, as has been mentioned above, in 1891, had been chairman of the Judiciary Committee which had recommended its inclusion in the Constitution.[22] Similarly, Quick and Groom, writing in 1904, were able to say:

> The reason which influenced the framers of the American Constitution to federalise inter-State litigation never existed to any extent in Australia. . . . Considerations of convenience, facilitation of legal proceedings and the avoidance of circuity of procedure, were the

---

19 'We can see no better reason for this provision in the Australian Constitution than the desire to imitate an American model. The courts of no State were ever, so far as we are aware, accused of partiality towards their own citizens, nor does there seem any reason for suspecting them of it.' Royal Commission on the Constitution, Minutes of Evidence, p. 785.

20 See Moore: The Commonwealth of Australia (2nd ed., 1910) at p. 492: 'Cases between residents of different States are of so common occurrence, and are so much in the ordinary experience of the courts that there seems no particular reason for giving the High Court original jurisdiction over them, or even for making them matters of federal jurisdiction at all, especially as the appellate jurisdiction of the High Court and the King-in-Council offers a sufficient protection.'

21 (1922) 31 C.L.R. 290, 339-40.

22 Inglis Clark: Studies in Australian Constitutional Law (2nd ed., 1905) at pp. 157-8; Pryles and Hanks: Federal Conflict of Laws (1974) p. 114.

main justification of the inclusion of this sub-section in the new Constitution.[23]

The provisions of the Service and Execution of Process Act 1901 have provided for a nation-wide system for the service of process and the execution of judgements and State laws also have provisions for service out of the jurisdiction. It has been pointed out that original suit in the High Court is nevertheless simpler.[24] It is suggested, however, that such advantage as remains from this point of view in suing in the High Court rather than in a State court is not sufficient to justify this head of jurisdiction.

## II

Taken a step further, the story becomes stranger. The classical justification for the existence of diversity jurisdiction in the United States puts it upon the basis of possible bias in State courts. An out-of-State party could opt to have his case tried in the federal court. But failing the exercise of such an option, the case might be tried in a *State* court in the exercise of the normal State jurisdiction. Diversity jurisdiction therefore assumes a choice between the two jurisdictions. More than that, it was only in certain cases that a party was entitled to bring a diversity suit in a federal court. The first congressional enactment with respect to diversity jurisdiction provided that the federal circuit courts should have concurrent jurisdiction with the State courts in civil suits at law or equity where the amount in dispute exceeded $500 in value.[25] The present minimum jurisdictional requirement in the federal district courts is $10,000.[26] Moreover, it has been held that federal courts will not grant probate of wills, nor administer deceased estates, nor grant divorces, nor interfere in other matters of intimate domestic relations, such as the custody of children.[27] This means that a litigant in a diversity case may opt for a federal court and federal jurisdiction *only* if the matter in issue is not one upon which the federal courts have declined to adjudicate. In any event, he clearly has no right to invoke the original juris-

[23] Quick and Groom: The Judicial Power of the Commonwealth (1904) pp. 112-3.

[24] Pryles and Hanks, *op. cit.*, p. 115.

[25] Judiciary Act 1789, sec. 25.

[26] Sec. 1. Title 28 U.S.C., sec. 1332 (1958). See Ilsen and Sardell: The Monetary Minimum in Federal Court Jurisdiction (1954) 29 St John's Law Review 1.

[27] Hart: The Relations between State and Federal Law (1954) 54 Columbia Law Review 489, 509. See also Hart and Wechsler, *op. cit.* at pp. 1001-18.

diction of the Supreme Court of the United States: he must go to a federal district court.

The Australian situation is different. For purposes of diversity jurisdiction, the only existing federal court is the High Court of Australia, which is invested with diversity jurisdiction in general terms by sec. 75 (iv). It appears that a party may bring an action under sec. 75 (iv) in the High Court without any restriction fixed by the amount in issue. *Fausset v. Carroll*,[28] *Marlow v. Tatlow*[29] and other cases which have already been discussed,[30] suggest that a party invoking the diversity jurisdiction of the High Court may be penalized in costs, but it is doubtful whether this is good doctrine. It also appears that the American gloss on the subject-matter of diversity suits has not been carried over into Australian law. It appears to be the view of the High Court that child custody suits are within the diversity jurisdiction of the Court.[31]

What is peculiar in the Australian situation is that there is no *State* jurisdiction in diversity actions at all. This follows from sec. 39 of the Judiciary Act, the operation of which has already been described.[32] Apart from that legislation, a litigant's choice of forum in a diversity suit would be between the High Court and a State court exercising jurisdiction by authority of State law. But sec. 39 (1) of the Judiciary Act operates to deprive State courts of all jurisdiction in matters in which the High Court has original jurisdiction, and sec. 39 (2) confers federal jurisdiction on State courts in respect, *inter alia*, of those matters. In the context of diversity jurisdiction, this means that the *content* of the jurisdiction of State courts remains the same, but the *source* is different and the conditions and regulations imposed by sec. 39 (2) (a) (c) and (d) are attached.

No doubt the draftsmen of the Judiciary Act had no special concern for diversity jurisdiction which fell into the scheme along with the other subject-matters of original High Court jurisdiction under sec. 75, but the consequence is that diversity jurisdiction, whether exercised by the High Court or by any other tribunal, can only be an exercise of federal jurisdiction. There cannot be any State jurisdiction in such cases. So, for Australia, the classical *raison d'être* of diversity jurisdiction so far as it postulates a choice for litigants as between State and federal jurisdiction has

---

[28] (1917) 15 W.N. (N.S.W.) No. 12, Cover Note. See p. 76 *ante*.

[29] Noted in (1965) 39 A.L.J. 140.

[30] See p. 76 *ante*.

[31] *Queen v. Langdon* (1953) 88 C.L.R. 158; *Queen v. Macdonald* (1953) 88 C.L.R. 197; *Queen v. Oregan* (1957) 97 C.L.R. 323, 333.

[32] See pp. 11-12 *ante*. See also pp. 199 ff.

no meaning. In Australia, the mere fact that a case has diversity elements inexorably makes it a matter of federal jurisdiction. The litigant's choice is between the High Court and a State court, both exercising federal jurisdiction.

As a practical matter, the exercise of federal jurisdiction by a State court in a diversity action may give rise to difficulties and inconveniences. As the famous Monsieur Jourdain is reported to have talked prose without knowing it, so too a State court may exercise federal jurisdiction without knowing it. It is possible, as Mr Dixon told the Royal Commission on the Constitution, at least in the case of a matter between residents of different States, that neither the court nor the parties may know of the facts which render the jurisdiction federal.[33] In *Sanderson and Co. v. Crawford*,[34] a Victorian plaintiff sued a New South Wales defendant for a small sum in a Victorian court of Petty Sessions which was constituted by a police magistrate *and* two honorary justices. On appeal, the Supreme Court of Victoria held that the court had no jurisdiction. As Hood J. put it:

> The Court of Petty Sessions has only jurisdiction over matters be-
> tween residents in different States by virtue of the legislation I have
> referred to,[35] and must exercise that jurisdiction subject to the con-
> ditions imposed. One of those conditions is that such jurisdiction shall
> not be judicially exercised except by a police magistrate, so in this case
> the Court which sat had no power to hear the matter.[36]

Compare with this *Alba Petroleum Co. of Australia Pty Ltd v. Griffiths*[37] in which one of the interstate parties was a company. Corporations, as we shall see, have been held not to be residents for the purpose of diversity jurisdiction. The Court pointed out that *Sanderson and Co. v. Crawford* concerned diversity jurisdiction and was not therefore applicable to the instant case which fell outside that jurisdiction and was a simple exercise of State jurisdiction by an inferior State tribunal constituted in accordance with State law. The same issue has arisen in other cases.[38]

This is a very unsatisfactory situation. If a case happens to involve diversity, the decision of an inferior State court may be upset on the ground that it was improperly constituted. If a case is heard in a State court, and happens to involve diversity, the

[33] Minutes of Evidence, p. 788.
[34] [1915] V.L.R. 568.
[35] Judiciary Act, sec. 39.
[36] [1915] V.L.R. 568, 579.
[37] [1951] V.L.R. 185.
[38] See e.g. *City and Suburban Parcel Delivery (Bryce) Ltd v. Gourlay Bros Ltd* [1932] St.R.Qd. 213.

special provisions for appeal set out in sec. 39 (2) of the Judiciary Act apply; if, on the other hand, no diversity element is present, the appeal provisions may be substantially different.

So far as State courts are concerned, many of these defects might be resolved by amendment of the Judiciary Act. It is clear that a State court may not be aware that the parties before it are residents of different States and it may be improperly constituted. Parliament, however, has the power to repeal the condition relating to the composition of the Bench in so far as it affects diversity suits if it considers that the inconvenience that can arise outweighs the policy of not having lay justices of the peace on the Bench in those cases. It could go further and repeal the investiture of federal jurisdiction in relation to diversity cases. This would leave the State court to exercise its State jurisdiction free of the conditions set out in sec. 39 (2) of the Judiciary Act. The main effect of such a move would be to enable appeals to the Privy Council from decisions of State courts in such cases. Appeals to the Privy Council in diversity suits cannot be brought under present law because the jurisdiction of the State courts is federal and para. (a) of sec. 39 (2) forbids appeals to the Privy Council.

The question whether diversity suits should remain within federal jurisdiction is a matter that should be considered apart from the wider issue of appeals to the Privy Council from State courts in all matters arising under State law. The wider issue is not going to be affected very much either way by preserving federal diversity jurisdiction.

It has been suggested that, apart from the general question of appeals to the Privy Council, there might be some reason for preventing appeals where diversity jurisdiction is exercised. Pryles and Hanks said:

> Suits between residents of different States will often involve questions of conflict of laws and it seems desirable to have appeals in cases involving conflicts problems within the federation determined by the High Court rather than the Privy Council.[39]

The policy behind these views is no doubt sound but as the writers themselves admit, many conflict of laws cases can arise when there is no diversity jurisdiction and many diversity suits will involve no conflict of laws problems. It seems therefore that diversity cases do not have any special features so far as Privy Council appeals are concerned. It is suggested that the Act should be amended to exclude diversity suits from the federal jurisdiction of State courts. From the point of view of the work of the

39 *op. cit.* at p. 117.

High Court, the best solution would be a constitutional amendment deleting from sec. 75 (iv) all the words after 'Between States'. This was recommended in 1974 by Standing Committee D of the Australian Constitutional Convention.[40]

## III

The words of the American diversity clause are 'controversies between citizens of different States'. The Australian provision speaks of 'matters . . . between residents of different States'. A question was raised in the High Court in *Queen v. Langdon*[41] and *Queen v. Macdonald*[42] as to whether *habeas corpus* applications in child custody proceedings were 'matters' so as to attract the original diversity jurisdiction of the court. In *Queen v. Macdonald* counsel informed the Court that the parties had reached agreement and desired that an order be made, and Fullagar J., who had raised this jurisdictional point, made the order. In *Queen v. Langdon*, Taylor J. referred to *Queen v. Macdonald* on this point, but refused to make an order on other grounds. It has been noted that federal courts in the United States decline to assume jurisdiction in such cases. In custody cases, the reason appears to be that although they were originally entertained in Chancery proceedings, the Chancellor assumed jurisdiction not in a judicial capacity, but by virtue of the royal prerogative as *parens patriae*, to which the States and not the United States fell heir.[43] No such doctrine appears to have troubled the Australian law of federal jurisdiction.

It has been suggested that there is some uncertainty in the word 'between' (residents). If a trust is created in favour of a number of persons, some living in one State and some in another, and a controversy arises as to the proportion in which they are entitled to share the trust property, it may be that this is a matter 'among' but not 'between' residents.[44] Again, it has been held that there is no diversity jurisdiction if there are residents of the same State on each side. In *Watson and Godfrey v. Cameron*[45] an action was

---

40 Report of the Executive Committee, p. 38.

41 (1953) 88 C.L.R. 158.

42 (1953) 88 C.L.R. 197.

43 See *Fountain v. Ravenal* (1855) 17 How. 369. See Hart and Wechsler, *op. cit.*, p. 1018. See also Jurisdiction of the Federal Courts over Domestic Relations (1948) 48 Columbia Law Review, 154.

44 Mentioned by Dixon K.C. in Evidence before the Royal Commission, p. 786.

45 (1928) 40 C.L.R. 446.

instituted in the original diversity jurisdiction of the High Court. The plaintiffs were a Victorian and a New South Wales resident and the defendant was a resident of New South Wales. It was held that there was no jurisdiction, since diversity was not shown. Where there was a resident of New South Wales on each side it was impossible to say that there was a matter between residents of different States. Isaacs J. suggested that a contrary conclusion would lead to an alarming increase in the original jurisdiction of the High Court by resort to the device of adding an out-of-State party.[46] In *Union Steamship Co. of New Zealand Ltd v. Ferguson*[47] the plaintiff commenced an action in the original jurisdiction of the High Court claiming damages for injuries received while working as a crew member of a ship owned by the defendant. The statement of claim alleged that the action was in the original jurisdiction of the Court on the ground that the parties were residents of different States. The plaintiff was a resident of South Australia and it was alleged that the defendant resided in Victoria. It had, however, been held some years earlier that a corporation could not be a resident within the meaning of sec. 75 (iv).[48] This issue is discussed below. The plaintiff then made an application asking that the winchman of the ship, a resident of New South Wales, be added as a defendant. Windeyer J., however, said

> . . . it was apparently thought that by making him an additional defendant, the action would be saved and could proceed with the defendant company still a party, although not a 'resident'. This was a mistaken view: cf. *Watson and Godfrey v. Cameron.*[49]

This statement of Windeyer J. has been criticized on the ground that *Watson and Godfrey v. Cameron*[50] had nothing to do with the issue. That case, it is said, merely held that if there were residents of the same State on both sides there was no diversity jurisdiction.[51] This aspect of *Ferguson*, however, conforms to the reasons of policy given by Isaacs J. in *Watson and Godfrey v. Cameron* that an interpretation of sec. 75 (iv) should be avoided that would enable a plaintiff to resort to the court, where he otherwise could not, by the device of adding an out-of-State

[46] Cf. *Strawbridge v. Curtiss* (1806) 3 Cranch 267.
[47] (1969) 119 C.L.R. 191.
[48] *Australasian Temperance and General Mutual Life Assurance Society Ltd v. Howe* (1922) 31 C.L.R. 290.
[49] at p. 196. It was held that the High Courts nevertheless had jurisdiction under the Colonial Courts of Admiralty Act.
[50] (1928) 40 C.L.R. 446.
[51] Pryles and Hanks, *op. cit.* 127.

party. Accepting that a suit against a corporation cannot come within the diversity jurisdiction, the danger that Isaacs J. saw of 'an alarming increase' in the original jurisdiction of the High Court would certainly be present if the involvement of a corporation in the suit was regarded as not excluding the diversity jurisdiction where the other parties on either side of the suit otherwise conformed to the requirements of sec. 75 (iv).

The view expressed by Windeyer J. conforms to the decision of Dixon J. in *Cox v. Journeaux*.[52] In that case action was brought by a Queensland resident against natural persons resident in Victoria and two companies incorporated in Victoria. The order of Dixon J. was that the suit should be dismissed as not being within sec. 75 (iv) unless the plaintiff elected to proceed only against the defendants who were individuals.

The onus of showing diversity is on the party seeking to establish jurisdiction. In *Dahms v. Brandsch*[53] there was a motion for judgement in the High Court in a foreclosure suit on an equitable mortgage by deposit of title deeds in Western Australia. The mortgagee was a resident of South Australia and the mortgagor's residence was unknown. It was stated that when last heard of, his residence was in Victoria. Griffiths C.J. dismissed the suit for lack of jurisdiction. The Court must be satisfied that the parties were residents of different States and here it was impossible to establish affirmatively that such was the case.

The most interesting problem in this area is the meaning to be assigned to 'resident'. This is a departure from the American phraseology which speaks of 'citizens'. In *Australasian Temperance and General Mutual Life Assurance Society Ltd v. Howe*,[54] Higgins J. dwelt on this difference. He observed that 'citizen' was a republican word, not appropriate to subjects of a prince, and drew the conclusion (in the context of the question whether a corporation was a resident) that the difference of terminology produced a significant difference in result. In the report of Inglis Clark's Judiciary Committee of 1891 the word 'resident' was used in this context, but Clark did not regard the change as possessing any significance.[55] In 1899 there had been a protracted debate on a clause which finally emerged as sec. 117 of the Constitution, which provides that 'a subject of the Queen, resident in any State,

52 (1934) 52 C.L.R. 282.
53 (1911) 13 C.L.R. 336. See also *Watson v. Marshall and Cade* (1971) 124 C.L.R. 621.
54 (1922) 31 C.L.R. 290.
55 See p. 83 *ante*.

shall not be subject in any other State to any disability or dis-crimination which would not be equally applicable to him if he were a subject of the Queen resident in such other State'. The earlier draft was in quite different form: 'A State shall not make or enforce any law abridging any privilege or immunity of citizens of other States of the Commonwealth nor shall a State deny to any person within its jurisdiction the equal protection of the laws.' In the course of the debate on this clause, a great deal of difficulty was found in the definition of citizenship[56] and this word finally disappeared from the clause. It may be that the form in which Barton subsequently introduced the diversity jurisdiction clause was influenced by this involved debate on citizenship, and that the substitution of residence here, as in sec. 117, was designed to avoid these difficulties. This may suggest that the distinctions later elaborated by Higgins J. in *Howe* were not very convincing, but there is insufficient evidence on which a certain conclusion on the matter may be reached.

For natural persons, the American law is clear. Citizenship for purposes of diversity jurisdiction means domicile. In *Messick v. Southern Pennsylvania Bus Co.*[57] it was said that:

'Citizenship' signifies the identification of a person with a State and a participation in its functions. . . . It implies a person possessing social and political rights and bearing social, political, and moral obligations to a particular state. Citizenship and domicile are sub-stantially synonymous terms and, with respect to the jurisdiction of federal courts, domicile is the test of citizenship.

So far as diversity jurisdiction within the Australian framework of residence is concerned, it is equally clear that diversity of residence may be established without reference to domicile. This is supported by a group of cases involving suits between husband and wife. It is settled law for Australia that a wife takes the domicile of her husband throughout the marriage, even though the parties are separated by court order. This was laid down in the Privy Council in *A.-G. for Alberta v. Cook.*[58] In *Renton v. Renton,*[59] the Supreme Court of South Australia had to consider

---

[56] For an account, see Quick and Garran, *op. cit.*, p. 776.

[57] 59 F.Supp. 799, 800. See also Hart and Wechsler, *op. cit.*, p. 898: 'From the beginning the Court has steadily insisted that state citizenship for the pur-poses of the diversity jurisdiction is dependent upon two elements: first, United States citizenship; and second, domicile in the State, in the traditional sense of the conflict of laws.' See also Reese and Green (1953) 6 Vanderbilt L.R. 571.

[58] [1926] A.C. 444.

[59] [1917] S.A.L.R. 277. Reversed on other grounds by the High Court (1918) 25 C.L.R. 291.

H

the validity of a summons issued from a court of summary jurisdiction which was not properly constituted if it were exercising
federal diversity jurisdiction. The summons was issued under the
Interstate Destitute Persons Relief Act at the suit of a deserted
wife. The Court concluded that there was diversity, as the wife
was a resident of South Australia and the husband a resident of
Queensland. It was specifically stated that the husband had never
been domiciled in South Australia. It followed that the wife's
South Australian residence depended on criteria other than those
necessary to establish domicile. In *Coates v. Coates*,[60] a similar
case, a Victorian court held that diversity of residence had not
been established, but it was implicit in the judgement that it was
possible to establish such diversity as between husband and wife.
Both these cases were decided before *A.-G. for Alberta v. Cook*,
but the two decisions in *Queen v. Langdon* and *Queen v. Macdonald* which were *habeas corpus* applications in child custody
proceedings as between husband and wife, were decided without
any apparent doubt that husband and wife might be proper
parties in diversity suits.[61] So, too, in *Cohen v. Cohen*,[62] the High
Court assumed jurisdiction in a money claim between spouses.

Apart from the cases of husband and wife, Higgins J. in
*Howe's Case*[63] contrasted the notions of domicile and residence on
the footing that 'residence is a mere question of fact; . . . domicile
is an idea of law'. Residence appears as a requirement in various
places in the Constitution. Sec. 34 requires as a qualification for
membership in the House of Representatives three years' residence within the limits of the Commonwealth; sec. 100 deals with
the rights of residents of a State to river waters for conservation
or irrigation[64] and sec. 117, as we have seen,[65] is concerned with
discrimination against subjects of the Queen resident in one
State, in other States. In *Howe's Case*, there were suggestions that
residence does not necessarily have the same meaning in all these
sections, and specifically that a decision that a corporation was
not a resident for the purposes of diversity jurisdiction did not

---

60 [1925] V.L.R. 231.
61 See also *Queen v. Oregan, ex parte Oregan* (1957) 97 C.L.R. 323, 332-3.
62 (1929) 42 C.L.R. 91.
63 (1922) 31 C.L.R. 290, 329.
64 'The Commonwealth shall not, by any law or regulation of trade or
commerce, abridge the right of a State or of the residents therein to the
reasonable use of the waters of rivers for conservation or irrigation.'
65 See pp. 92-3 *ante*.

necessarily mean that it was not a resident within the terms of sec. 100.[66]

There has been little general discussion of the residence requirement for diversity jurisdiction. Quick and Garran considered that 'it should be of a character to identify the resident to some extent with the corporate entity of the State'.[67] This statement was approved by Isaacs J. in *Howe's Case*.[68] After citing the passage, Isaacs J. said:

> I would add . . . that the identification by reason of residence of the litigants with one State connotes his exclusion from similar identification by reason of residence with any other State. If I were to express it in a word, it is 'status'. Every Australian is, when all the facts are known, residentially identifiable pre-eminently with some one State and he is therefore a resident of that State and of that State alone, for the purposes of s. 75 (iv).

The judge stressed the *singleness* of residence and instanced the example of a man who had his family, home, and chief place of business in Melbourne and had branch establishments in Adelaide and Perth in which he spent a week every month for the purposes of conducting the branch business. While in one sense he was resident in Adelaide and Perth, his *status* as a resident for the purposes of diversity jurisdiction was fixed in Victoria.

Such a notion of residence would seem to bring it very close to domicile, and it is to be noted that in the same case Higgins J. expressly distinguished domicile as a matter of law from residence as a matter of fact. The view of Isaacs J. was considered in *Coates v. Coates*[69] by Irvine C.J. of Victoria. The parties were husband and wife. The wife depended upon Victorian residence and the evidence of the husband's residence in New South Wales was very thin. Irvine C.J. did not commit himself to full adoption of the views of Isaacs J. in *Howe*, but indicated that residence involved 'more than the mere fact of residing temporarily in that State for purposes of business or pleasure'. In his evidence before the Royal Commission Mr Dixon said: 'Residence seems to be a

---

[66] (1922) 31 C.L.R. 290, 299.
[67] 'Residence in a State, for the purposes of [diversity jurisdiction] should . . . be interpreted as involving a suggestion of State membership and perhaps even of domicile . . . such residence as, if combined with British nationality, would constitute citizenship of the State in the general sense of the term. It is not meant by this that the residence should be such as is required by the laws of the particular State for the exercise of any particular franchise, but merely that it should be of such a character to identify the resident to some extent with the corporate entity of the State.' *op. cit.*, p. 776.
[68] (1922) 31 C.L.R. 290, 307-8.
[69] [1925] V.L.R. 231, 235.

strange criterion, moreover, to adopt. Some persons have no residence, and some have several.'[70] This suggests some doubt as to the correctness of Isaacs J.'s insistence on the single and exclusive character of residence for diversity jurisdiction. However Mr Dixon was not expressing a settled view of the meaning of residence, but was concerned to point out the ineptitude of the constitutional provision for diversity jurisdiction and the ambiguities and uncertainties in its language.

In *Watson v. Marshall and Cade*[71] the defendant was a resident of Victoria but there was some doubt and argument as to whether the plaintiff was a resident of New South Wales or of Victoria. Walsh J. followed *Dahms v. Brandsch*[72] which held that the plaintiff was required to establish the facts that gave the court jurisdiction. In examining the facts, his Honour applied the reasoning of Isaacs J. in *Howe's Case* that it was not permissible to treat the plaintiff as a resident, within the meaning of sec. 75 (iv), of both States and that a choice had to be made.

The state of authority makes it clear that to establish residence for diversity purposes, proof of domicile is not required, at least in the case of persons whose domicile is governed by dependence. The cases show that a wife may sue a husband in the diversity jurisdiction, and presumably the same argument would apply to other persons of dependent domicile, such as infants. Apart from such cases, it may be suggested that the courts will continue to follow Isaacs J.'s view of the singleness of residence for the purpose of this jurisdiction, so that at any given time a person will be held to be resident in one State. Such residence would in most cases be in the State of domicile, although it seems likely that the strict requirements of domicile would not be invoked. For example, it would very probably be held that a person who had lived for a number of years in Victoria would be held to be resident in that State for the purposes of diversity jurisdiction, although under the technical rules relating to domicile, for want of sufficient proof of *animus*, he would be held to retain an English or other domicile of origin.[73] It would hardly be sensible to reject the strict requirements of domicile in suits between spouses and other dependent persons, and to insist upon them to establish residence in all other cases.

---

70 *op. cit.*, p. 785.
71 (1971) 124 C.L.R. 621.
72 (1911) 13 C.L.R. 336.
73 See *Winans v. A.-G.* [1904] A.C. 287; *Ramsay v. Liverpool Royal Infirmary* [1930] A.C. 588.

A further point was posed by Mr Dixon as to the time at which residence must attach. He asked whether a Victorian resident who was sued in the High Court by a New South Wales resident might defeat the action by instantly changing his residence to New South Wales.[74] This reveals another drafting uncertainty. Similar problems are encountered in other areas of the law, for example in divorce jurisdiction based on domicile. It seems to be established that the decisive date should be the institution of proceedings. This view has been adopted in a number of cases.[75] Thereafter jurisdiction should not be defeated by reason of a subsequent change of residence by a defendant.[76]

Thus far the discussion of the meaning to be given to 'residents' for the purposes of diversity jurisdiction has been directed to the case of natural persons. The question next arises as to the position of corporations. It is settled law in the United States that diversity jurisdiction may be invoked by or against a corporation, and suits involving corporations account for a very substantial part of diversity litigation.[77] This American doctrine was well settled at the date of the drafting and enactment of the Australian Constitution, and Quick and Garran in 1901 stated explicitly that 'a corporation may clearly be a "resident" within the meaning of this section'.[78] In 1922, however, the High Court by a majority held in *Australasian Temperance and General Mutual Life Assurance Society Ltd v. Howe*[79] that a corporation was not a resident for the purposes of diversity jurisdiction, and unanimously refused to reverse this decision when it was challenged some twelve years later in *Cox v. Journeaux*.[80]

---

74 *op. cit.*, p. 786.

75 *R. v. Oregan, ex parte Oregan* (1957) 97 C.L.R. 323 at 332-3; *Parente v. Bell* (1967) 116 C.L.R. 528, 529; *Dzikowski v. Mazgay* noted (1967) 40 A.L.J. 361; *Watson v. Marshall and Cade* (1971) 124 C.L.R. 621, 623.

76 Pryles and Hanks, *op. cit.*, p. 132 and Lane: The Australian Federal System (1972) pp. 496-7.

77 See Frankfurter: Judicial Power of Federal and State Courts (1928) 13 Cornell Law Quarterly 499, 523: 'An examination of ten recent volumes of the Federal Reporter shows that out of 3,618 full opinions, 959 or 27 per cent were written in cases arising solely out of diversity of citizenship. In 716 of these cases, or 80 per cent, a corporation was a party. Corporate litigation, then, is the key to diversity problems.' See also McGovney: A Supreme Court Fiction (1943) 56 Harvard Law Review 853, 1090, 1225; Wechsler: Federal Jurisdiction and the Revision of the Judicial Code (1948) 13 Law and Contemporary Problems 216, 234-40.

78 *op. cit.*, p. 777.

79 (1922) 31 C.L.R. 290.

80 (1934) 52 C.L.R. 282.

The American doctrine has a somewhat extraordinary history. The constitutional provision for diversity jurisdiction speaks of 'citizens' of different States. In *Bank of United States v. Deveaux*[81] Marshall C.J. stated that 'that invisible, intangible and artificial being, that mere legal entity, a corporation aggregate, is certainly not a citizen; and consequently cannot sue or be sued in the courts of the United States, unless the rights of the members in this respect can be exercised in their corporate name.' In this case it was held that the qualification rather than the general rule applied, and the bank was permitted to bring suit in the federal courts on a showing that all of its members were citizens of one State and Deveaux was a citizen of another State.

Had this been the only class of case in which the diversity jurisdiction was open to a corporate party, it would have been of relatively little significance with the growth of corporations with shareholders in many States. It would then have been in comparatively rare cases that the requisite diversity could be shown. However, in *Louisville, Cincinnati and Charleston Railroad Co. v. Letson*,[82] the Supreme Court of the United States ruled: 'a corporation created by and doing business in a particular State, is to be deemed at all intents and purposes as a person, although an artificial person, an inhabitant of the same State, for the purposes of its incorporation, capable of being treated as a citizen of that State, as much as a natural person'. This gave rise to a conclusive and irrebuttable jurisdictional fiction that for purposes of establishing diversity all the shareholders were to be deemed citizens of the State of incorporation.[83] It was upon this decision, which has been subjected to trenchant criticism,[84] that the inclusion of corporations within the scope of diversity jurisdiction depended. The fiction did not purport to treat a cor-

---

[81] (1809) 5 Cranch 61, 86.

[82] (1844) 2 How. 497, 558.

[83] Constitution of the United States of America: Analysis and Interpretation (Eds Small and Jayson, 1964) at pp. 683-6.

[84] It was called a 'malignant decision' by Warren in his famous article, New Light on the History of the Federal Judiciary Act of 1789 (1923) 37 Harvard L.R. 49, 90. Warren observed further of the right of a foreign incorporated company to remove a case arising in a State in which it actually does business into a federal court that 'no single factor has given rise to more friction and jealousy between State and Federal Courts or to more State legislation conflicting with and repugnant to Federal jurisdiction than has the doctrine of citizenship for corporations'. See also Frankfurter, *op. cit.* at p. 523, Mc-Govney, *op. cit.* esp. at p. 1258. But see Green: Corporations as Persons, Citizens and Possessors of Liberty (1946) 94 University of Pennsylvania L.R. 202, especially 217, 218, 227-8. See also Hart and Wechsler, *op. cit.* at pp. 914-6.

poration as a citizen; it achieved the same result by shutting out evidence that its members, for purposes of diversity jurisdiction involving the corporation, were citizens of States other than that of incorporation. The results were quite remarkable.

The absurdity of the fiction is patent with respect to any large corporation whose shares are sold throughout the United States. The American Telephone and Telegraph Co. had 630,902 shareholders of record, December 31, 1940, holding 18,686,794 shares. It is incorporated under the laws of New York. The Company's records show that it has some shareholders residing in every one of the forty-eight States. In taking jurisdiction of suits by or against this corporation, the judges of the lower federal courts are required by the Supreme Court to regard all shareholders as citizens of New York. The records of the corporation show that about one fourth of the shares are held in New York.

Suppose, as is probably true, that one of the shareholders of this New York corporation is a Delaware corporation. In suits to which the Delaware corporation is a party all of its shareholders are regarded as citizens of Delaware to give it a fictitious Delaware citizenship, but in a suit to which the New York corporation is a party, this Delaware corporation is deemed to be a citizen of New York, or all of its shareholders are deemed to be citizens of New York.[85]

Bills were introduced from time to time to strike at the use of federal courts by corporations under shelter of this fiction and were strongly opposed by representatives of corporate interests.[86] In 1958 Congress amended sec. 1332 of the United States Code by providing that, for this purpose, a corporation should be deemed a citizen of any State by which it has been incorporated and of the State where it has its principal place of business. This prevents corporations engaging in local business with a foreign charter from entering the federal courts on a showing of diversity; though it does not affect the position of a corporation doing business in a large number of States, except in the State in which it has its principal place of business. A further amendment in 1964 was designed to deal with the case where under a statute a plaintiff was empowered to sue directly a tortfeasor's insurance company. Under the amendment the insurance company is deemed to be a citizen of the State in which the insured was a citizen as well as of the State of its incorporation and of its principal business.

In Australia, this question has arisen in the context of corporate

85 McGovney, *op. cit.* at p. 1097.
86 See McGovney, *op. cit.* at pp. 1225 *et seq.*; Hart and Wechsler, *op. cit.* at pp. 893-4.

claims to invoke the original diversity jurisdiction of the High Court. In *Australasian Temperance and General Mutual Life Assurance Society Ltd v. Howe,* the case for the plaintiff company was argued by Dixon K.C., and there was no appearance for the defendant. The Court by a bare majority[87] held, however, that a corporation could not be a 'resident' for the purposes of diversity jurisdiction under sec. 75 (iv) of the Constitution.

The majority opinion of Knox C.J. and Gavan Duffy J. and the dissenting judgement of Isaacs J. paid little attention to American authority. Consideration was directed primarily to matters of general principle and to a review of authorities, principally English, in which the question whether a corporation could be held to be a 'resident' had been before the courts. Knox C.J. and Gavan Duffy J. took as a starting point the proposition that the ordinary connotation of 'resident' was 'living' and that this was the attribute of a natural person. The onus was therefore upon the party seeking to establish jurisdiction to show an affirmative legislative intent to vary the normal meaning of the word. The authorities gave no general assistance; those which ascribed residence to corporations did so under the compulsion of specific statutes. Furthermore, it did not follow that 'resident' necessarily had the same meaning in every place in which it appeared in the Constitution; it might be (though no settled answer need be given) that a corporation was a resident for the purposes of sec. 100.[88] Isaacs J. took precisely opposite ground. There was no justification for any presumption that residence could be ascribed only to natural persons; indeed the presumption operated the other way. The cases which ascribed residence to corporations were not to be treated as of such limited operation, but demonstrated that it was proper in the present context to treat a corporation as a resident. The original jurisdiction of the High Court in diversity cases conferred 'a right as valuable to a corporation as an individual'.[89] The general conclusion which Isaacs J. reached was that a corporation might clearly and properly be a resident for the purposes of diversity jurisdiction. In the instant case the plaintiff company, on this reasoning, was a Victorian resident: it was incorporated in Victoria, and the head office and central management of its Australia-wide business was in that State. The defendant was a New South Wales resident

---

[87] Knox C.J., Higgins and Gavan Duffy JJ.; Isaacs and Starke JJ. dissenting.
[88] See note 66 *ante.*
[89] (1922) 31 C.L.R. 290, 307.

and, upon this showing, Isaacs J. held that the suit was properly brought in the original diversity jurisdiction of the High Court.

Higgins and Starke JJ. looked more closely at the American diversity provision and its interpretation. Higgins J. laid stress on the differences between the two diversity clauses; one spoke of 'citizens', the other of 'residents', and American decisions which were concerned with the status of corporations as citizens did not assist in the resolution of questions relating to residence. From this point he followed Knox C.J. and Gavan Duffy J. in regarding residence as presumptively attributable to natural persons only, and in treating the decisions ascribing residence to corporations as inapplicable to the case of diversity jurisdiction. Starke J. after referring to the 'somewhat similar provision in the Constitution of the United States'[90] and to the views of Quick and Garran on the question of corporate standing under the diversity clause, found no apparent difficulty in holding that a corporation might be a 'resident' for such purposes. He stated further that it had been the practice of the High Court to assume jurisdiction in cases involving corporations, although the point of jurisdiction had not been argued.[91]

In *Cox v. Journeaux*[92] action was brought in the High Court by a Queensland resident against, *inter alios*, two companies incorporated in and carrying on business in Victoria, and managed and controlled there. On an application by the companies for an order dismissing them from the action, the plaintiff argued that the decision in *Howe's Case* was wrong. Dixon J. refused an application to refer this question to the Full High Court and on application for leave to appeal, the Full Court (Gavan Duffy C.J., Starke, Evatt and McTiernan JJ.) refused to reconsider *Howe's Case*.

It must therefore be taken as settled law for Australia that a corporation is not a resident for purposes of diversity jurisdiction, and in view of the peremptory rejection of the plaintiff's argument in *Cox v. Journeaux* it is most unlikely that the decision in *Howe's Case* will be reversed. In this light, extended examination of the differing views expressed in the Court in *Howe's Case* would not be very profitable. It may be thought that on the level

90 at p. 339.

91 'Even this Court has entered judgements both in favour of and against corporations. True, the question of jurisdiction was not argued in connection with these judgements, and I refer to them, not as authorities, but in support of the statement that the received view was heretofore in favour of the jurisdiction of this Court' (p. 340).

92 (1934) 52 C.L.R. 282.

at which the argument was conducted, Isaacs J.'s dissent was very persuasive. There is a substantial body of English case law ascribing residence to corporations and the showing of the majority that these had no general application, and specifically no application to the case of diversity jurisdiction, does not carry conviction. The argument *ad absurdum* of Knox C.J. and Gavan Duffy J. that if a corporation had standing to sue, it would follow that a corporation resident and conducting operations within a State would be entitled to invoke the diversity jurisdiction, while a corporation not so resident but conducting similar operations within the State would not,[93] carries no real conviction, because it applies equally to individuals whose right to invoke the diversity jurisdiction is beyond question. Again, it may be thought that the differences between the American and Australian diversity provisions which were emphasized by Higgins J. would assist a conclusion that there is less difficulty in assigning residence than citizenship to a corporation, particularly in view of the substantial body of British authority on the point of residence of corporations which Isaacs J. reviewed so convincingly.

Even if the dissenters had the better of the logic and the authority, it may nonetheless be suggested that the exclusion of corporations from the scope of diversity jurisdiction is to be welcomed. A distinguished American commentator, noting *Howe's Case*, observed:

> The Australian High Court, confronted with similar difficulties, avoided our pitfalls. . . . The phrasing of two Constitutions varies. But the real difference between our doctrines and the Australian decision is a difference of 100 years. The underlying assumption in Australia is that an Australian corporation no matter where registered, can obtain justice in every State court.[94]

Diversity jurisdiction has thrown a heavy burden on American federal courts, the greater part of which derives from cases involving corporate litigants. And there is a powerful argument that the *raison d'être* of federal diversity jurisdiction in the United States has disappeared, if indeed it ever existed.

It has been argued that there never was any justification for writing a diversity jurisdiction clause into the Australian Constitution and that this was a piece of blind and unintelligent copying. It permitted a litigant to come into the High Court of Australia on a simple showing of diversity. Our Constitution placed a potentially great burden of original jurisdiction upon a

[93] at p. 300.
[94] Frankfurter, *op. cit.* at p. 524.

court invested not only with special constitutional and other important federal functions, but also with a general appellate jurisdiction from State courts on matters of State law. Whereas in the United States, original jurisdiction in diversity suits is vested not in the Supreme Court, but in district courts and even there is restricted to suits involving specified minimum amounts, and is further restricted by judicial gloss as to the subject-matter of actions, any Tom, Dick or Harry on a showing of diversity may take up the time of the High Court of Australia without restriction of amount in issue, and without restriction of subject-matter of litigation. A decision that corporations cannot be 'residents' for the purposes of diversity jurisdiction helps to reduce this unwarranted strain upon the time and energies of the High Court. If the result looks illogical, it is not unreasonable to say that the less we have of a bad thing, the better. Nevertheless, because of the situation in which the jurisdiction of Australian State courts in diversity suits is *federal*, and because that jurisdiction is to be exercised subject to the terms of sec. 39 (2) of the Judiciary Act, different results follow from the presence or absence of corporate parties in suits. Thus we have seen[95] that in *Sanderson and Co. v. Crawford*[96] a decision of a court of Petty Sessions was upset on appeal because the court was not constituted in accordance with the terms of sec. 39 (2) (d) of the Judiciary Act and the parties were residents of different States. Had one or both parties been incorporated, the appeal could not have succeeded.[97] For such results there can be no conceivable justification, but the proper cure does not lie in a general holding that corporations should be held to be residents for purposes of diversity jurisdiction, but rather in the disappearance of the diversity jurisdiction altogether.[97A]

---

95 See p. 88 *ante*.

96 [1915] V.L.R. 568.

97 *Alba Petroleum Co. of Australia Pty Ltd v. Griffiths* [1951] V.L.R. 185; see also *City and Suburban Parcel Delivery (Bryce) Ltd v. Gourlay Bros Ltd* [1932] St.R.Qd. 213.

97A A Bill to abolish federal jurisdiction in respect of disputes between citizens of different States (H.R. 9622) was passed by the United States House of Representatives on 28 February 1978. At the time of writing it was still pending in the Senate. The Bill seeks to amend section 1332 (a) of 28 U.S.C. by removing diversity jurisdiction involving citizens of different States. It would retain diversity jurisdiction involving aliens but would raise the jurisdictional amount to $25,000.

# = 3 =

## *The Federal Courts*

'Neither from the point of view of juristic principle nor from
that of the practical and efficient administration of justice can
the division of the courts into State and federal be regarded
as sound.'[1]

'The Supreme Court is the ultimate judicial exponent of
federal rights; the lower federal courts are their vindicators . . .
It hardly seems open to doubt that a full system of independent
federal courts plays a valuable part in furthering the rapid,
widespread, yet uniform and accurate interpretation of federal
law.'[2]

### I

THE establishment of federal courts, other than the High Court
of Australia, is contemplated by the Commonwealth Constitution.
Sec. 71 authorizes the vesting of the judicial power of the Commonwealth in such federal courts as the Parliament creates, sec.
77 (i) empowers the Parliament, with respect to the matters
enumerated in secs. 75 and 76, to make laws defining the jurisdiction of any federal court other than the High Court, and sec.
77 (ii) authorizes the making of such laws defining the extent to
which the jurisdiction of any federal court shall be exclusive of
that which belongs to or is invested in the courts of States. The
authority to create federal courts is implied;[3] nowhere in the
Constitution is there any express power to establish them. In
this respect, the Australian Constitution differs from the Constitution of the United States which specifically authorizes the constitution of tribunals inferior to the Supreme Court as one of
the enumerated powers of Congress under Art. I, sec. 8. It is surprising that such an important power should have been left to
implication in the Australian Constitution, although it has

---

[1] Dixon: The Law and the Constitution (1935) 51 L.Q.R. 590, 606.

[2] Mishkin: The Federal 'Question' in the District Courts (1953) 53 Columbia L.R. 157, 170-1.

[3] Quick and Garran: The Annotated Constitution of the Australian Commonwealth (1900) 726.

been suggested by the High Court that the Australian Founding
Fathers 'who adopted so definitely the general pattern of Art. III
but in their variations and departures from its detailed provisions
evidenced a discriminating appreciation of American experience'[4]
may have thought it unnecessary to spell out a power to create
federal courts in express terms.

The major departure from American precedent was the adoption of the 'autochthonous expedient'[5] of conferring federal
jurisdiction on State courts, and this has made for a significant
difference in the judicial organizations of the two federations. In
the United States, the decision to authorize the establishment of
inferior federal courts was taken only after sharp debate in the
Constitutional Convention. It was argued on the one side that
'the State tribunals might and ought to be left in all cases to
decide in the first instance, the right of appeal to the supreme
national tribunal being sufficient to secure the national rights and
uniformity of judgments; that it was making an unnecessary
encroachment on the jurisdiction of the States, and creating
unnecessary obstacles to their adoption of the new system' and
to the contrary by Madison that 'a government without a proper
executive and judiciary would be the mere trunk of a body,
without arms or legs to act or move'. It was also argued that the
establishment of a body of federal courts would be a burdensome
expense. The original proposal to create a body of inferior federal courts by force of the Constitution itself was lost, but a compromise was finally reached which permitted the establishment
of federal courts by act of Congress.[6] The opponents of the federal
courts did not even then wholly give up the fight; a resolution was
introduced into the Senate in 1793 to amend the Constitution by
authorizing Congress to vest the judicial power of the United
States in such of the State courts as it should deem fit.[7] This
failed to carry, and the establishment of the federal courts was
authorized without any alternative or complementary legislative
authority to vest federal jurisdiction in State courts.

Congress took early action to constitute federal courts. The
Judiciary Act 1789 established a system of federal courts throughout the country which was divided into thirteen districts, each

[4] *Queen v. Kirby, ex parte Boilermakers' Society of Australia* (1956) 94
C.L.R. 254, 268.
[5] ibid.
[6] See Prescott: Drafting the Federal Constitution (1941). See also *National
Insurance Co. v. Tidewater Co.* (1949) 337 U.S. 582, 647.
[7] Frankfurter and Landis: The Business of the Supreme Court (1927).

with a federal district court. A second tier of federal courts was created by forming three circuits, each with two justices of the Supreme Court of the United States and one district judge within the circuit sitting twice a year in the various districts comprised within the circuit. The Supreme Court of the United States with a Chief Justice and five associate justices crowned the system.[8] Since 1789, the organization of the federal court system has undergone some changes, but the United States has since that date possessed a self-contained structure of federal courts of original and appellate jurisdiction. The jurisdiction of the federal courts has grown and the broad grant of jurisdiction to the district courts over federal questions by the Judiciary Act 1875 'in a very real sense revolutionized the concept of the federal judiciary'[9] by vastly increasing their jurisdiction. Congress has not only exercised its powers to create federal courts exercising what may be described as *general* federal jurisdiction; it has also from time to time created *specialized* federal courts such as the Commerce Court, established in 1910 and abolished in 1913, and the Emergency Court of Appeals organized by the Emergency Price Control Act 1942.[10]

The Australian story has been quite different. Quick and Garran's prediction in 1900 that 'it is probable that for some time there will be no necessity for the creation of any inferior federal courts, but that all the cases in which the original jurisdiction of the Commonwealth is invoked can be dealt with either by the High Court itself or by the Courts of the States'[11] has proved substantially accurate. The Parliament has made liberal use of the State courts as repositories of federal jurisdiction, and also until recently made regrettably liberal use of the High Court as a court of original jurisdiction. Unlike the United States, the Commonwealth did not proceed to create a hierarchy of federal courts.

For many years the only federal courts were the Australian Industrial Court and the Federal Court of Bankruptcy. The Federal Court of Bankruptcy, which exercised jurisdiction only in New South Wales and Victoria, was created in 1930 by the insertion of sec. 18A into the Bankruptcy Act 1924 and continued in existence by sec. 21 of the Bankruptcy Act 1966. It was de-

---

8 In 1863 the Supreme Court had its largest membership, ten. In 1869 the number became nine and it has since remained at that number.

9 Hart and Wechsler: The Federal Courts and the Federal System (1953) 729.

10 See *Yakus v. United States* (1944) 321 U.S. 414.

11 *op. cit.*, p. 726.

clared to be a superior court of record. In 1976 its jurisdiction was transferred to the Federal Court of Australia.[12] The jurisdiction of that Court will be discussed later. The Bankruptcy Act also confers jurisdiction in bankruptcy on the Northern Territory Supreme Court and invests the Supreme Courts of New South Wales, Queensland, Western Australia and Tasmania and the Insolvency Courts of Victoria and South Australia with jurisdiction in bankruptcy (sec. 27). Each Court has jurisdiction in bankruptcy throughout Australia.

The Commonwealth Electoral Act 1918, Part XVIII, constitutes a Court of Disputed Returns, but this, as defined in sec. 184, is the High Court of Australia.

The Commonwealth Industrial Court was created in 1956 by sec. 98 of the Conciliation and Arbitration Act 1904-1956. Its name was changed to the Australian Industrial Court in 1973.[13] The Court, which was given original and appellate jurisdiction, was established together with the Australian Conciliation and Arbitration Commission,[14] and the legislation was framed in light of the High Court's decision,[15] subsequently affirmed by the Privy Council,[16] in the *Boilermakers' Case*, that the Commonwealth Court of Conciliation and Arbitration which had been constituted on the assumption that it was a federal court constituted under the authority of secs. 71 and 77 (i) was not such a court and was not competent to exercise the judicial power of the Commonwealth. In *Seamen's Union v. Matthews*[17] prohibition was sought against the Industrial Court on the ground that it was not validly constituted as a federal court. It was argued that a conglomerate mass of powers and functions had been conferred upon the Court, so that it could not lawfully exercise the judicial power of the Commonwealth within the rule of the *Boilermakers' Case*. The High Court unanimously rejected this argument. It pointed to the propriety of considering the history of the legislation, that it was passed after and in light of the High Court's decision in the *Boilermakers' Case*, that the legislative scheme of the Conciliation and Arbitration Act 1956 separated those powers of dealing with industrial matters falling within the main purpose of sec. 51 (xxxv) of the Constitution from those conferred upon the

12 Bankruptcy Amendment Act 1976.

13 No. 138 of 1973, sec. 41.

14 No. 44 of 1956.

15 *Queen v. Kirby, ex parte Boilermakers' Society of Australia* (1956) 94 C.L.R. 254.

16 *Attorney-General for Australia v. Queen* [1957] A.C. 288.

17 (1956) 96 C.L.R. 529.

Industrial Court, and that the Court had been constituted with due regard to sec. 72 of the Constitution so far as the tenure of the judges was concerned.

> When you look at the powers of the Commonwealth Industrial Court which, it is said, go beyond the judicial power of the Commonwealth it will be seen that they are of a kind which the legislature might well have thought appropriate to a judicial tribunal and are not manifestly of an industrial or arbitral character. We think that it is quite plain that in the light of the decision of the Court in *The Queen v. Kirby, ex parte the Boilermakers' Society of Australia*, the legislature attempted to set up a new court for the judicial enforcement of the provisions of the Act and of the award and for the exercise of other judicial functions arising out of the Conciliation and Arbitration Act. On the assumption that provisions conferring authority upon the Court are found which do go outside Chapter III of the Constitution we think it is quite clear that the only result is that they must be severed as bad and that the Commonwealth Industrial Court is validly established and remains in possession of the judicial powers conferred on it by the Act.[18]

In 1976 the jurisdiction of the Australian Industrial Court was transferred to the Federal Court of Australia.[19]

The Banking Act 1947 made provision for the establishment of a Court of Claims which was constituted as a federal court. It was given exclusive jurisdiction to hear and determine claims and entitlements to compensation under the Act. In the *Bank Nationalization Case*[20] it was held that the grant of exclusive jurisdiction to the Court was unconstitutional and the Court was never in fact constituted.

The Family Court of Australia was created by the Family Law Act 1975. It is a superior court of record with wide jurisdiction in family law matters including divorce, nullity, guardianship and custody of children, maintenance and the declaration and alteration of property interests. It has both original and appellate jurisdiction (secs. 28, 35). Provision is made for investing State Family Courts with federal jurisdiction to deal with matters under the Act in certain circumstances (sec. 41). The only State court that has been proclaimed for this purpose is the Family Court of Western Australia. Jurisdiction was also vested in the State and Territory Supreme Courts and, in the case of matrimonial causes not being proceedings for principal relief, in courts of summary jurisdiction of the States and Territories (sec. 39). However, the

---

[18] at p. 535.
[19] Conciliation and Arbitration Amendment Act (No. 3) 1976.
[20] (1948) 76 C.L.R. 1; see pp. 39-40 *ante*.

Governor-General is authorized by Proclamation to fix a date on which proceedings under the Act may not be instituted or transferred to those courts (secs. 39 (7) and 40 (3)). The first day of June 1976 was fixed by Proclamation as the date on which proceedings were not to be instituted in the Supreme Courts of the States or Territories in relation to specified proceedings.[21] In relation to courts of summary jurisdiction, the only Proclamation made relates to courts of summary jurisdiction in the metropolitan region of Perth.[22]

Much of the jurisdiction that the Act purported to confer was upheld as valid by a majority of the High Court in *Russell v. Russell*.[23]

The Federal Court of Australia was created by the Federal Court of Australia Act 1976. It is a superior court of record and consists of a Chief Judge and such other judges as are appointed. The Court has two Divisions, namely, an Industrial and a General Division. The reason for this relates primarily to the transfer of jurisdiction from the Australian Industrial Court and the appointment of most of the judges of that Court to the Federal Court of Australia. In his second reading speech, the Attorney-General, Mr Ellicott, said:

> The primary purpose of these proposals is that a special character of the industrial jurisdiction under the Conciliation and Arbitration Act will be preserved and will be exercised in the Industrial Division of the Court.[24]

The original jurisdiction of the Court is described in the Federal Court of Australia Act as being 'such original jurisdiction as is vested in it by laws made by the Parliament, being jurisdiction in respect of matters arising under laws made by the Parliament'.[25] The other Acts which actually invest the jurisdiction are the Conciliation and Arbitration Act 1904 (as amended in 1976), secs. 118A-118B (which transfers the industrial jurisdiction of the Australian Industrial Court), the Bankruptcy Act 1966 (as amended in 1976), sec. 28 (under which the Federal Court of Australia is substituted for the former Federal Court of Bankruptcy

---

[21] Australian Government Gazette, 27 May 1976.

[22] ibid.

[23] (1976) 9 A.L.R. 103. The issues in that case involve the operation of sec. 51 (xxi) and (xxii) of the Constitution—the powers of the Commonwealth with respect to 'marriage' and 'divorce and matrimonial causes; and in relation thereto, parental rights and the custody and guardianship of infants'. These questions are beyond the scope of this book.

[24] Debs. (H. of R.) Weekly Hansards (1976) p. 2112.

[25] sec. 19.

J

in exercising bankruptcy jurisdiction) and the Federal Court of Australia (Consequential Provisions) Act 1976 which transfers from the Australian Industrial Court to the Federal Court of Australia jurisdiction under 11 other Acts including the Trade Practices Act 1974, the Prices Justification Act 1973, the Financial Corporations Act 1974 and the Administrative Appeals Tribunal Act 1975. The Administrative Decisions (Judicial Review) Act 1977 confers jurisdiction on the Federal Court of Australia to review administrative decisions made or proposed to be made under any enactment of the Commonwealth, other than a decision of the Governor-General.

The creation of the new Court and its two Divisions has resulted in a more appropriate court for dealing with those specialized matters which it has been thought should be determined by a federal tribunal rather than a court of general jurisdiction, such as a State Supreme Court. For a number of years the Australian Industrial Court had been invested with jurisdiction under a wide range of Acts relating to such matters as restrictive trade practices, consumer protection, insurance law, administrative appeals and so on. These matters were far removed from the chief functions of the Court, namely, industrial matters. The judges of the Court were, one assumes, appointed primarily for their ability and aptitude in the industrial relations area. For appointment as a judge of the Industrial Division of the Federal Court of Australia, similar qualities will still be required. The General Division is responsible for all other jurisdiction, i.e. which does not arise under the Conciliation and Arbitration Act. In order to preserve the separateness of the industrial Bench, the Act provides for all judges, other than the Chief Judge, to be attached to a Division of the Court to hear and determine cases in that Division except in special circumstances and then only with the consent of the judge concerned (sec. 13). As the Attorney-General put it:

> The Australian Industrial Court, created under the Conciliation and Arbitration Act, had had added to it in a piecemeal fashion jurisdiction in a diverse variety of matters. That Court is neither appropriately named nor structured to serve federal judicial administration in an adequate matter. As presently structured under the Conciliation and Arbitration Act, it is not really suitable for more general work.[26]

The Federal Court of Australia is given appellate jurisdiction to determine appeals from

26 Debs. (H. of R.) Weekly Hansards (1976) p. 2110.

(a) judgements of the Court constituted by a single judge,
(b) judgements of the Supreme Court of a Territory and
(c) 'in such cases as are provided by any other Act', appeals
    from judgements of a court of a State, other than a Full
    Court of the Supreme Court of a State, exercising federal
    jurisdiction (sec. 24).

Jurisdiction to hear appeals from State courts exercising federal jurisdiction has been provided for by the Patents Act 1952, sec. 148; the Income Tax Assessment Act 1936, sec. 196; and the Trade Marks Act 1955, sec. 114, as a result of amendments made to those Acts in 1976. In each of these cases the matter in original jurisdiction is determined by the Supreme Court of a State. There is no appeal from a single judge of a State Supreme Court to the Full Court of that Court in any of those matters. A court from which an appeal lies to the Federal Court of Australia may state a case or reserve any question for consideration by the Federal Court of Australia concerning a matter with respect to which such an appeal would lie.[27]

The jurisdiction of the Federal Court of Australia and the role envisaged for it by the Government is very different from other schemes for a federal court that were presented in the form of Bills to the Parliament by both Labor and non-Labor Governments in previous years.

A Bill introduced into the House of Representatives in November 1968 proposed a court to be known as the Commonwealth Superior Court. Its jurisdiction as set out in clause 19 included all the matters referred to in secs. 75 and 76 of the Constitution with the exception of certain specific matters, many of which had been made fully or partly exclusive to the High Court under secs. 38, 38A and 40A of the Judiciary Act. Its appellate jurisdiction was extended to appeals from a single judge of that Court, the Supreme Courts of the Territories and State course, other than Supreme Courts, exercising federal jurisdiction. The Bill was not proceeded with.

Bills to establish a Superior Court of Australia were introduced in 1973, 1974 and 1975 by the Whitlam Government but were rejected by the Senate. These Bills similarly gave very broad federal jurisdiction to the proposed new court.

There has been much argument and discussion as to the merits of creating a federal court with wide federal jurisdiction, as envisaged in the Bills referred to above, as distinct from relying chiefly on State courts as has been the Australian practice.

27 Federal Court of Australia Act 1976, sec. 26.

The arguments in favour of a court of broad federal jurisdiction are that it would help to relieve the High Court of a great deal of its original jurisdiction;[28] that it would permit uniformity of interpretation of federal laws; that it would relieve State courts of an increasingly heavy burden and State Governments of the cost of maintaining State courts for federal purposes and that it would ensure that the Commonwealth Government had proper control of the organization and administration of the courts to ensure that federal matters were dealt with efficiently and with reasonable speed.[29]

The main attack on the idea of such a federal court has been made by Mr Justice Else-Mitchell,[30] Professor Sawer[31] and Mr Ellicott as a member of the Opposition in the Commonwealth Parliament.[32] A basic argument against adopting a division of courts for State and federal matters is that of Sir Owen Dixon given in his submissions to the Royal Commission on the Constitution in 1927. Sir Owen urged a move in the opposite direction, namely, a constitutional structure under which all superior courts would derive their existence not from the Commonwealth or the States but from the Constitution itself. There are many difficulties in establishing such a system and it would require constitutional amendment. The ideal of a single national system of courts is best approached under the present constitutional structure by placing the State courts in the position of having full jurisdiction, subject to express exceptions, to determine all matters, with the High Court as a final court of appeal.

The alleviation of the burdens on the High Court can be achieved by using State Courts in cases where legislation confers original jurisdiction on the High Court and by limiting the occasions on which a litigant has an appeal as of right to the High Court. Steps to achieve this have, to some extent, been taken as to original jurisdiction by the transfer to State courts of jurisdiction previously exercised exclusively by the High Court under income tax, patents and trade marks legislation[33] and as to

[28] Barwick: The Australian Judicial System: The Proposed New Federal Superior Court (1964) 1 F.L. Rev. 1.

[29] Byers and Toose: The Necessity for a New Federal Court (1963) 36 A.L.J. 308.

[30] (1969) 3 F.L. Rev. 187.

[31] (1964-5) VIII Journal of Society of Public Teachers of Law.

[32] Debs. (H. of R.) 1974, vol. 89 p. 594ff.

[33] Income Tax Assessment Act (No. 3) 1973, Patents Amendment Act 1976 and Trade Marks Amendment Act 1976.

appellate jurisdiction by the amendment made in 1976 to sec. 35 of the Judiciary Act 1903.[34]

Other arguments against the creation of a court with general federal jurisdiction relate to more practical matters. Federal courts can only be given jurisdiction that comes within secs. 75 and 76 of the Constitution (apart from the possibility of jurisdiction in relation to the Territories under sec. 122 which will be considered in chapter 4). As has been seen, this is a complex and highly technical area. A litigant might be faced with many arguments relating to jurisdiction before the court has any chance of considering the merits of his claim. This possibility or even likelihood has been compared with the absurd expensive and time consuming problems of jurisdiction that faced litigants before the great reforms of the 19th century. The aim of those reforms was to ensure that attention 'can be directed to the real problems of what are the rights between man and man, what is the substantive law'.[35]

There is the further problem of 'split proceedings'.[36] Some aspects of a plaintiff's claim might be within federal jurisdiction and some not. A suit for breach of a trade mark arises under a federal law, namely, the Trade Marks Act 1955 and is therefore within sec. 76 (ii) of the Constitution and such jurisdiction can therefore be conferred on a federal court; but a companion claim for passing off is not within federal jurisdiction unless, for example, the suit is between residents of different States or otherwise comes within one of the other heads of jurisdiction under secs. 75 and 76 of the Constitution. Similar considerations arise in respect of a claim on a cheque (which is within sec. 76 (ii)) and one for simple contract debt (which would not normally come within federal jurisdiction).

A further problem has arisen to bedevil this area and raise jurisdictional arguments. As mentioned earlier, the High Court has held that a matter can 'arise under' a law made by Parliament within the meaning of sec. 76 (ii) even though the Commonwealth Act is first raised in defence or in a later stage of proceedings.[37] Thus a matter might commence in a State court which has all the hallmarks of State jurisdiction and it might be discovered later that, as a result of matters raised, the case is

[34] Judiciary Amendment Act 1976.

[35] Else-Mitchell, *op. cit.*, 191 quoting Maitland: Equity and Forms of Action at Common Law (1910) 375.

[36] Lane: The Commonwealth Superior Court (1969) 43 A.L.J. 148, 150.

[37] *Felton v. Mulligan* (1971) 124 C.L.R. 367.

now one of federal jurisdiction which would, if the proponents of a general federal court had their way, have to be transferred to a federal court. While secs. 38A and 40A of the Judiciary Act were in operation, that happened from time to time in State Supreme Courts in relation to the raising of *inter se* questions. However, then the problem was of comparatively small dimensions, relating not to all federal jurisdiction but only to constitutional questions.

It is clear that litigants are best served and justice done where a court can determine all the issues arising between them and concentrate on the substance of the case. This is well summed up by Mr Justice Else-Mitchell:

> The function, nay the duty, of every one of the Queen's Courts of Justice, manifested by the judicial oath which every incumbent of judicial office takes, is to apply the law and to do so 'without fear or favour, affection or ill-will'. This duty can be performed so as to do complete justice between the parties only if the Court is able to apply all relevant law, whether it arise from a Commonwealth, State, or local enactment, regulation, or ordinance, or has its origin in the common law or the rules of equity: anything less than a comprehensive power to determine and apply the law regardless of its origin or constitutional or statutory force will necessarily result in the imperfect and incomplete resolution of claims and matters, not to mention the institution of abortive proceedings for which a proper jurisdictional basis cannot be found. A judicial system which limits the jurisdiction of a court by criteria other than the traditional and simple ones of *quantum* such as are found in the legislation constituting the County and District Courts of the States cannot fail to produce frustrations for the litigants who are encouraged to resort to it.[38]

It is suggested that this factor far outweighs the alleged benefits to be derived from a federal court of general jurisdiction.

This does not mean, however, that there is not a case for courts of special jurisdiction. Even unitary countries without problems of federal and State jurisdiction find the need to create specialized tribunals. The policy behind the Federal Court of Australia Act would appear to be to treat that Court as a repository for jurisdiction of that type.[39]

[38] *op. cit.*, 190-1.
[39] Sir Garfield Barwick has recently expressed the hope that the jurisdiction of the Federal Court of Australia will be extended to the hearing of all appeals in matters of invested federal jurisdiction. He further advocates State legislation to confer appellate jurisdiction on the Federal Court of Australia in all appellate matters of a major kind in State jurisdiction; but he admits that at present 'such a course is, to say the least, more than unlikely' ((1977) 51 A.L.J. 480, 491).

## II

The first paragraph of sec. 72 of the Commonwealth Constitution provides:

> The Justices of the High Court and of the other courts created by the Parliament—
>   (i) Shall be appointed by the Governor-General in Council:
>  (ii) Shall not be removed except by the Governor-General in Council, on an address from both Houses of the Parliament in the same session, praying for such removal on the ground of proved misbehaviour or incapacity:
> (iii) Shall receive such remuneration as the Parliament may fix; but the remuneration shall not be diminished during their continuance in office.

Until its amendment in 1977, this was all that sec. 72 contained. Art. III, sec. 1 of the United States Constitution is differently phrased; it confers tenure during good behaviour on the judges of the Supreme Court and inferior federal courts. A constitutional requirement of tenure during good behaviour necessarily excludes an appointment of a federal judge for a term of years, but it was at least arguable that an appointment for a fixed term of years was not inconsistent with the rather different text of the first paragraph of sec. 72 of the Australian Constitution. In *Waterside Workers' Federation of Australia v. J. W. Alexander Ltd*,[40] it was held, however, by a majority in the High Court that a court within the meaning of sec. 71 must be staffed by judges appointed for life, subject to the powers of removal set out in sec. 72. The matter for determination was the validity of the constitution of the Commonwealth Court of Conciliation and Arbitration whose president was at that time appointed for a term of years. Dogmatic views were expressed on either side. Barton J., one of the majority judges, stated flatly that the argument that federal judges might be appointed for a term of years was 'untenable'[41] and said that he did not think that the argument necessitated extended discussion. On the other side, Higgins J. has flatly stated that there was 'not one word'[42] in the Constitution to justify a decision that a life tenure for federal judges was obligatory. Sec. 72 in providing that judges should not be removed except in stated circumstances meant only that a term of years could not otherwise be cut short by removal. In argument before the Privy Council in *Shell Co. of Australia Ltd. v. Federal*

[40] (1918) 25 C.L.R. 434.
[41] at p. 457.
[42] at p. 472.

*Commissioner of Taxation*,[43] an attack was made on the majority view in *Alexander's Case*, but the Board, without expressly deciding the point, stated that it was not prepared, as then advised, to dissent from the view that life tenure was required for federal judges. The ruling in *Alexander's Case* has been followed by the High Court.[44]

In 1977, sec. 72 of the Constitution was amended following a referendum held in accordance with sec. 128. The following paragraphs were added to sec. 72:

> The appointment of a Justice of the High Court shall be for a term expiring upon his attaining the age of seventy years, and a person shall not be appointed as a Justice of the High Court if he has attained that age.
>
> The appointment of a Justice of a court created by the Parliament shall be for a term expiring upon his attaining the age that is, at the time of his appointment, the maximum age for Justices of that court and a person shall not be appointed as a Justice of such a court if he has attained the age that is for the time being the maximum age for Justices of that court.
>
> Subject to this section, the maximum age for Justices of any court created by the Parliament is seventy years.
>
> The Parliament may make a law fixing an age that is less than seventy years as the maximum age for Justices of a court created by the Parliament and may at any time repeal or amend such a law, but any such repeal or amendment does not affect the term of office of a Justice under an appointment made before the repeal or amendment.
>
> A Justice of the High Court or of a court created by the Parliament may resign his office by writing under his hand delivered to the Governor-General.
>
> Nothing in the provisions added to this section by the *Constitution Alteration (Retirement of Judges)* 1977 affects the continuance of a person in office as a Justice of a court under an appointment made before the commencement of those provisions.
>
> A reference in this section to the appointment of a Justice of the High Court or of a court created by the Parliament shall be read as including a reference to the appointment of a person who holds office as a Justice of the High Court or of a court created by the Parliament to another office of Justice of the same court having a different status or designation.

The result of the amendment is that any appointment to the High Court after the date of the amendment is for a term expiring when the judge attains seventy years of age. The

[43] [1931] A.C. 275, 280 by Simon K.C.
[44] *Silk Bros Pty Ltd v. State Electricity Commission* (1943) 67 C.L.R. 1; *Peacock v. Newtown etc. Building Society* (1943) 67 C.L.R. 25.

position is the same for the appointment of a judge of any other federal court unless Parliament, before the appointment of that judge, fixes an age for retirement at less than seventy years.

The Commonwealth Conciliation and Arbitration Act was amended in 1926 to provide life tenure for the judges of the Conciliation and Arbitration Court.[45] The assumption in the Act of 1926 was that it was permissible to commingle functions which were primarily non-judicial with others that were judicial in a federal body assumed to be a court whose members satisfied the tenure requirements of sec. 72. In the *Boilermakers' Case*[46] it was held that the Court of Conciliation and Arbitration whose functions were construed as primarily arbitral could not conjointly exercise judicial power. The Court stated the broad principle that the exercise of judicial power could not constitutionally be combined with the exercise of non-judicial power. This was stated by the High Court as follows:

> Chap. III does not allow the exercise of a jurisdiction which of its very nature belongs to the judicial power of the Commonwealth by a body established for purposes foreign to the judicial power, notwithstanding that it is organized as a court and in a manner which might otherwise satisfy ss. 71 and 72, and Chap. III does not allow a combination with judicial power of functions which are not ancillary or incidental to its exercise but are foreign to it.[47]

The *Boilermakers' Case* imposes an important constitutional restraint on the grant of power to a federal court in so far as powers cannot validly be conferred upon it which go outside the conception of judicial power and what is incidental to it in the sense explained in that case and elsewhere.[48] The High Court in *Seamen's Union v. Matthews*[49] indicated that while the Commonwealth Industrial Court was validly constituted as a federal court under secs. 71 and 77 (i), some of the powers conferred upon it might, within the rule of the *Boilermakers' Case*, be construed as non-judicial and therefore *ultra vires,* though severable. In *Queen v. Spicer, ex parte Australian Builders' Labourers' Federation,*[50] the High Court unanimously held that sec. 140 of the Con-

---

[45] For the history of the legislation, see *Queen v. Kirby, ex parte Boilermakers' Society of Australia* (1956) 94 C.L.R. 254, 284 *et seq.*

[46] (1956) 94 C.L.R. 254 (H.C.); [1957] A.C. 288 (P.C.)

[47] (1956) 94 C.L.R. 254, 296. See also *per* Lord Simonds [1957] A.C. 288, 318-9.

[48] Lane: The Australian Federal System (1972) pp. 311-54.

[49] (1956) 96 C.L.R. 529. See Merralls: Judicial Power Since the Boilermakers' Case: Statutory Discretion and the Quest for Legal Standards (1959) 32 A.L.J. 283, 303.

[50] (1957) 100 C.L.R. 277.

ciliation and Arbitration Act attempted to confer non-judicial power on the Commonwealth Industrial Court and, therefore, in accordance with the doctrine in the *Boilermakers' Case*, the section was held to be invalid. Section 140 purported to authorize the Industrial Court to disallow any rule of an industrial organization on wide discretionary grounds, and had been copied from earlier versions of the Conciliation and Arbitration Act. When this power had been conferred on the former Commonwealth Conciliation and Arbitration Court, it had been held in *Consolidated Press Ltd v. Australian Journalists' Association*[51] to be non-judicial, so that no appeal lay to the High Court under sec. 73 (ii) of the Constitution. As Dixon C.J. observed in *Queen v. Spicer*: 'sec. 140 was framed as one of the industrial powers of the Commonwealth Court of Conciliation and Arbitration to be exercised at the instance of the Court or a member of the organization independently of any consideration which must govern a judicial determination within Chapter III, except that the Court should have assured itself that there was a compliance with one or other of the paragraphs (a), (b), (c) or (d) of subsec. (1) of sec. 140. In effect that is what was decided in *Consolidated Press Ltd v. Australian Journalists' Association* and there is no sufficient reason for refusing to apply that decision.'[52]

Again in *Queen v. Spicer, ex parte Waterside Workers' Federation*,[53] the High Court unanimously held that sec. 37 of the Stevedoring Industry Act 1954-1956, which purported to confer appellate jurisdiction on the Commonwealth Industrial Court in respect of the cancellation or suspension of the registration of a waterside worker, was invalid for the same reason. In *Queen v. Commonwealth Court of Conciliation and Arbitration, ex parte Ellis*,[54] it had been held that a like power conferred on the Commonwealth Court of Conciliation and Arbitration by the Stevedoring Industry Act 1949 was, in effect, an authority to make an administrative review of an administrative decision, and that its re-enactment in like terms in 1956 as a grant of power to the Commonwealth Industrial Court must be read as an intention to confer a power to be governed by what might broadly be called administrative and industrial considerations, and therefore outside the permissible limits of the exercise of federal judicial power.

[51] (1947) 73 C.L.R. 549.
[52] (1957) 100 C.L.R. 277, 291.
[53] (1957) 100 C.L.R. 312.
[54] (1954) 90 C.L.R. 55.

Sec. 140 was repealed and a new section inserted by sec. 24 of the Conciliation and Arbitration Act 1958, which empowered the Industrial Court to declare the rules of an organization to be void on newly defined grounds. The new sec. 140 (1) provided that a rule of an organization 'shall not', among other things, be contrary to the Act, the regulations or an award, or otherwise be contrary to law or impose on applicants for membership or members conditions, obligations or restrictions which, having regard to the objects of the Act and the purposes of the registration of organizations under the Act, are oppressive, unreasonable or unjust. A member of an organization could apply to the Court for an order declaring that a rule contravened the section. Sub-sec. (5) provided that, if the Court made an order declaring that a rule contravened the Act, the rule 'shall be deemed to be void from the date of the order'. The Court was further given power to adjourn proceedings for the purpose of giving the organization an opportunity to alter its rules.

In *R. v. Commonwealth Industrial Court, ex parte Amalgamated Engineering Union, Australian Section*[55] the Court unanimously held that the new sec. 140 conferred part of the judicial power of the Commonwealth on the Commonwealth Industrial Court, and was therefore valid.

The earlier provision had been declared invalid having regard to the total effect of a number of factors, including an earlier decision, the fact that the Court could act on its own motion, the use of the word 'may' in conferring the power (which was said to be apt for a complete discretion based on industrial or administrative considerations), and the vagueness and generality of the criteria which seemed to refer to an industrial discretion rather than a legal standard.

The revamped section had deleted the provision allowing the Court to act on its own motion and the discretion given to the Court as to whether an order should be made. The Court was not given power 'to disallow' a rule but merely to declare that it contravened the Act. However, the criteria was just as general, and sub-sec. (5) indicated that the Court's declaration operated only 'in futurum' and therefore resembled a quasi-legislative order rather than a judicial one.

A majority of the judges (McTiernan, Fullagar, Taylor and Menzies JJ.) considered that an infringement of sec. 140 (1) resulted in invalidity from the time that the sub-section operated. They regarded sub-sec. (5) as merely extending the operation of

55 (1960) 103 C.L.R. 368.

an order made under the section. Dixon C.J., Kitto and Windeyer JJ., however, were prepared to hold the provisions consistent with the exercise of judicial power even if a contravention of sec. 140 (1) was not *per se* a cause of invalidity.

From the point of view of a government anxious to give a judicial body authority to deal with trade union rules, the differences between the old and new provisions were comparatively minor. From an analytical aspect the Court examined the cumulative effect of various factors without indicating that the absence or presence of any one of them was essential to the judgement. One could reply to each of the separate reasons given for holding that the old section conferred non-judicial power by pointing to courts that had traditionally exercised power in the form expressed; for example, a court acts on its own motion in dealing with a contempt of court and there are many areas in which courts have a discretion in making orders. The new provisions still left the Court a lot of discretion by virtue of the vagueness of the criteria and the fact that it could adjourn proceedings to enable an amendment of the rules.

Generally the High Court has in recent years been loathe to strike down powers given to federal courts on the grounds that they amount to an exertion of non-judicial power. Quite large discretions and very vague criteria have been held to come within the notion of the judicial power of the Commonwealth.[56] A discretion given to a judge to make an order if he considers it 'just and equitable' or 'proper' to do so has been upheld on many occasions as coming properly within the concept of the judicial power of the Commonwealth and therefore validly conferred on a federal court or a State court exercising federal jurisdiction.[57]

In *R. v. Joske, ex parte Australian Building Construction Employees and Builders Labourers Federation*[58] a challenge was made to sec. 143 of the Conciliation and Arbitration Act. That provision enabled a person or organization or the Registrar to apply to the Industrial Court directing the cancellation of the registration of an organization on various grounds. The Court, however, was required to make the order directing the Registrar

---

[56] *Cominos v. Cominos* (1972) 127 C.L.R. 588. See Zines: The Australian Constitution 1951-1976 (1976) 7 F.L. Rev. 89 at pp. 123-131.

[57] *Lansell v. Lansell* (1964) 110 C.L.R. 353; *Sanders v. Sanders* (1967) 116 C.L.R. 366; *Peacock v. Newtown, Marrickville and General Co-operative Building Society (No. 4) Ltd* (1943) 67 C.L.R. 25; *Talga Ltd v. MBC International Ltd* (1976) 9 A.L.R. 359.

[58] (1974) 130 C.L.R. 87.

to cancel registration only if it did not consider that 'having regard to the degree of gravity' of the matter, it would be unjust to do so. The High Court unanimously held that sec. 143 conferred judicial power on the Court. However, the Chief Justice questioned the whole doctrine of the *Boilermakers' Case.* He said:

> The principal conclusion of the *Boilermakers' Case* was unnecessary, in my opinion, for the effective working of the Australian Constitution or for the maintenance of the separation of the judicial power of the Commonwealth or for the protection of the independence of courts exercising that power. The decision leads to excessive subtlety and technicality in the operation of the Constitution without, in my opinion, any compensating benefit. But none the less, and notwithstanding the unprofitable inconveniences it entails, it may be proper that it should continue to be followed. On the other hand, it may be thought so unsuited to the working of the Constitution in the circumstances of the nation that there should now be a departure from some or all of its conclusions.[59]

Mason J. also agreed that a 'serious question' had arisen as to the course the High Court should adopt in relation to the *Boilermakers' Case.*[60] However, it was unnecessary for the Court to consider whether that case should be overruled.

As a result of these comments, an attempt to get the Court to depart from the *Boilermakers' Case* was made in *R. v. Joske, ex parte Shop Distributive and Allied Employees Association.*[61] That case involved *inter alia* secs. 171C and 171D of the Conciliation and Arbitration Act which empowered the Industrial Court to make orders in respect of the consequences of invalidity in the management or administration of an industrial organization and to approve schemes for reconstitution of an organization or part of an organization which had ceased to exist or function effectively. The Court held that those provisions conferred judicial power and therefore found it unnecessary to consider the correctness of the *Boilermakers' Case.*

These cases illustrate that the High Court is prepared to allow a fairly wide range of powers to be given to federal courts even under the existing restraint imposed by the *Boilermakers' Case.*

## III

There is a further important limitation on the power to create federal courts and to define their jurisdiction. 'The constitutional

[59] at p. 90.
[60] at p. 102.
[61] (1976) 10 A.L.R. 385.

authority to create new federal courts is limited; the extent of the jurisdiction which Parliament may confer on any such court is determined solely by reference to the matters enumerated in secs. 75 and 76.'[62] This arises from the form of the power, sec. 77 (i), which authorizes the legislative definition of the jurisdiction of federal courts. The matters which may be the subject of such definition are those in secs. 75 and 76, the matters of original or potential original jurisdiction of the High Court. Sec. 77 (i) authorizes the definition of jurisdiction with respect to all or any of these matters irrespective of any action by the Parliament under sec. 76 to invest the High Court with original jurisdiction. For example: if a matter falls within the description of sec. 76 (ii), that is to say, arises under any law made by the Parliament, jurisdiction with respect to it may be conferred on an inferior federal court, even though there has been no grant of original jurisdiction to the High Court under sec. 76 (ii).

Beyond the limits marked out by the matters in secs. 75 and 76, it is not possible to confer jurisdiction on federal courts. A grant may therefore fail because it is not defined by reference to a 'matter'. In *Collins v. Charles Marshall Pty Ltd*[63] the High Court elaborately considered the validity of sec. 31 of the Conciliation and Arbitration Act 1904-1952 which purported to confer jurisdiction on the Commonwealth Court of Conciliation and Arbitration[64] by providing that:

(1) There shall be an appeal to the Court from a judgment or order of any other court—
> (a) in proceedings arising under this Act (including proceedings under section 59 of this Act or proceedings for an offence against this Act) or involving the interpretation of this Act; and
> (b) in proceedings arising under an order or award or involving the interpretation of an order or award, and the Court shall have jurisdiction to hear and determine any such appeal.

(2) Except as provided in the last preceding sub-section, there shall be no appeal from a judgment or order from which an appeal may be brought to the Court under this order.

The section refers to 'proceedings', not matters. On this point the Court observed:

[62] *Collins v. Charles Marshall Pty Ltd* (1955) 92 C.L.R. 529, 562, *per* Taylor J.

[63] (1955) 92 C.L.R. 529, 537-8.

[64] Counsel raised in argument the broader constitutional questions which were subsequently decided in the *Boilermakers' Case*, but the High Court disposed of the case without dealing with this question (1955) 92 C.L.R. 529, 546-7.

It is a distinction which s. 31 (1) fails to make and it may be that if pursued to its logical consequences this failure might prove in itself fatal. It is enough to quote the following passage from the joint judgment in *Re Judiciary and Navigation Acts:* [65] It was suggested in argument that 'matter' meant no more than legal proceeding, and that Parliament might at its discretion create or invent a legal proceeding in which this Court might be called on to interpret the Constitution by a declaration at large. We do not accept this contention; we do not think that the word 'matter' in sec. 76 means a legal proceeding, but rather the subject-matter for determination in a legal proceeding. In our opinion there can be no matter within the meaning of the section unless there is some immediate right, duty or liability to be established by the determination of the Court. If the matter exists, the Legislature may no doubt prescribe the means by which the determination of the Court is to be obtained, and for that purpose may, we think, adopt any existing method of legal procedure or invent a new one.[66]

Apart from the non-correspondence between 'matters' and 'proceedings', sec. 31 was held bad—assuming, or in any event not passing on the question of, the validity of the constitution of the Arbitration Court under secs. 71 and 77 (i)—on the ground that the grant of jurisdiction was not referable to any of the heads of secs. 75 and 76. The reasons were stated concisely by Taylor J.:

Unless they are matters which are mentioned in s. 75 or s. 76 there is no constitutional foundation for the provisions of s. 31. The four categories specified by the last-mentioned section are: (1) proceedings under the Act; (2) proceedings involving the interpretation of the Act; (3) proceedings arising under an order or award; and (4) proceedings involving the interpretation of an order or award. Quite apart from the difficulties which arise from the use of the word 'proceedings' it is clear that neither matters involving the interpretation of the Act nor matters involving the interpretation of an order or award, by virtue of that character alone, fall within the specification of matters contained in ss. 75 and 76. Nor, I should think, do matters 'arising under an order or award'. Matters of these descriptions may on occasions, of course, present other features which may bring them within the purview of those sections as they would, for example, if they arose between residents of different States, or if any such matter should also involve the interpretation of the Con-stitution or if it arose under any laws made by Parliament, but the descriptions which have been selected by s. 31 are quite inappropriate, in the main, to describe matters in respect of which the High Court is given original jurisdiction under s. 75 or in respect of which it may be conferred upon it by s. 76. This being so, they are not matters with

65 (1921) 29 C.L.R. 257.
66 (1955) 92 C.L.R. 529, 542.

respect to which Parliament may make laws either defining the jurisdiction of the Arbitration Court or defining the extent to which the
jurisdiction of that court shall be exclusive of that which belongs to or
is invested in the courts of the State.[67]

In such a case the excess of jurisdiction is clear on the face of
the definition itself, but the problem may arise in a less obvious
form. A grant of jurisdiction may be made to a federal court over
matters which on their face are within the legislative competence
of the Parliament so as to be referable to sec. 76 (ii). But it may
be argued that the vice in the grant is that Parliament has been
too sparing in the exercise of its powers and has made only a
bare grant of jurisdiction without enacting a substantive law to
which the exercise of jurisdiction is referable. In the United
States, this problem has been discussed by reference to such an
enactment as sec. 301 (a) of the Labor Management Relations
Act 1947, which provides that

> . . . suits for violation of contracts between an employer and a labor
> organization representing employees in an industry affecting com-
> merce as defined in this Act or between any such labor organizations
> may be brought in any district court of the United States having
> jurisdiction of the parties without respect to the amount in con-
> troversy or without regard to the citizenship of the parties.

On what basis can such a grant of jurisdiction be supported?
The argument against validity is that, absent diversity of citizenship, the judicial power of the United States attaches to a private
party's case only if it arises under the Constitution of the United
States, an Act of Congress or a treaty, and a case arises under an
Act of Congress only if the Act itself supplies part of the basis
of the party's claim. While the Labor Management Relations Act
requires parties to bargain, it does not of itself give legal force to
their agreement; that depends on State law and a suit for viola-
tion of such a contract does not arise under federal law. On this
argument, sec. 301 (a), as a bare grant of jurisdiction, is constitutionally defective.

To this two possible answers may be given. The first is that a
substantive federal law to be applied in suits under sec. 301 (a)
may be spelled out of the section itself. The second is that the
grant of jurisdiction may be supported by reference to a doctrine
of protective jurisdiction.

> The power of the Congress to confer the federal judicial power . . .
> should extend . . . to all cases in which Congress has authority to
> make the rule to govern disposition of the controversy, but is content

instead to let the States provide the rule so long as jurisdiction to
enforce it has been vested in a federal court. Where, for example,
Congress by the commerce power can declare as federal law that
contracts of a given kind are valid and enforceable, it must be free
to take the lesser step of drawing suits upon such contracts to the
district courts without displacement of the States as sources of the
operative, substantial law. A grant of jurisdiction is, in short, one
mode by which the Congress may assert its regulatory powers.[68]

It is clear under the Commerce Clause that Congress could have
enacted a substantive law to which the exercise of jurisdiction
under sec. 301 (a) could have been referable and, so supported,
the grant of jurisdiction would have been valid, and 'it would be
most regrettable if a federal constitution forbade the general
government to exercise its regulatory powers in this forbearing,
sanguine and initially perhaps experimental manner which turns
to account the genius of a federal system. It would be regrettable
for Congress to be forced instead to exert its authority to the full
in order to employ it at all.'[69]

In *Textile Workers' Union of America v. Lincoln Mills of
Alabama*,[70] an action for specific enforcement of an arbitration
clause in a collective bargaining contract, the Supreme Court of
the United States upheld the validity of sec. 301 (a). Douglas J.,
speaking for five members of the court, discovered in the section
a congressional direction to treat grievance arbitration agreements as enforceable and to apply federal law which the courts
must fashion from the policy of the national labor laws. Burton
and Harlan JJ. concurred in the result, on the ground that the
section was supportable as a grant of protective jurisdiction, but
rejected the view that any obligation to apply federal law could
be spelled out of sec. 301 (a).

The High Court of Australia has been concerned with broadly
similar problems both in the contexts of the definition of federal
jurisdiction under sec. 77 (i) and the investment of State courts
with federal jurisdiction under sec. 77 (iii). In *R. v. Commonwealth Court of Conciliation and Arbitration, ex parte Barrett*[71]

---

[68] Wechsler: Federal Jurisdiction and the Revision of the Judicial Code
(1948) 13 Law and Contemporary Problems, 216, 224-5.
[69] Bickel and Wellington: Legislative Purpose and the Judicial Process: The
Lincoln Mills Case (1957) 71 Harvard L.R. 1, 20-1.
[70] (1957) 353 U.S. 448; 1 L.Ed. 2d. 972. See *McCarroll v. Los Angeles County
District Council of Carpenters* (1957) 315 P. 2d. 322; (1957) 71 Harvard L.R. 1;
Bunn: Lincoln Mills and the Jurisdiction to Enforce Collective Bargaining
Agreements (1957) 43 Virginia L.R. 1247. Note: Lincoln Mills: Labour Arbitration and Federal-State Relations (1957) 57 Columbia L.R. 1123.
[71] (1945) 70 C.L.R. 141.

K

there was a challenge to the validity of sec. 58E of the Conciliation and Arbitration Act 1904-1934 which authorized the Court,
on complaint by a member of an organization, to make an order
giving directions for the performance or observance of any of the
rules of an organization by any person who is under an obligation
to perform or observe those rules. On the assumption that this
was a grant of judicial power,[72] it was argued that there was no
support to be derived from sec. 76 (ii) for this grant of jurisdiction—this being the only possible head to which the jurisdiction might be attributed—because the substantive rights and
obligations arising under the rules of the organization arose
not under any law of the Parliament, but as a matter of State
law. The High Court rejected this argument, and discovered in
sec. 58E a body of substantive law to which the grant of jurisdiction was referable, so that it was supportable as a grant of
jurisdiction under sec. 76 (ii). Dixon J. said:

> It appears to me, that, on the footing that sec. 58E includes
> judicial power, it must be taken to perform a double function, namely
> to deal with substantive liabilities or substantive legal relations and
> to give jurisdiction with reference to them. It is not unusual to find
> that statutes impose liabilities, create obligations or otherwise affect
> substantive rights, although they are expressed only to give jurisdic-
> tion or authority, whether of a judicial or administrative kind.[73]

Dixon J. observed that under the general law, the rules of a
voluntary association did not always confer enforceable rights on
members. He referred to various Commonwealth Acts in which
the High Court or the Supreme Courts of the States were given
jurisdiction to make discretionary orders touching patents, trade
marks and a wide variety of other matters. The legislature had
preferred to arm the courts with a broad discretion, rather than
to legislate specifically or to prescribe fixed rules of substantive
law by reference to which the courts should be required to
act in exercise of their jurisdiction.[74] It lay within parliamentary
competence under sec. 51 (xxxv) and (xxxix) to deal with the
rules of organizations and, in appropriate circumstances, to prescribe the conditions of their enforcement. Parliament might have
chosen to define the circumstances in which actions for the enforcement of rules might be brought; but it preferred to give the
Court a discretionary power to intervene on the complaint of a

---

[72] *Jacka v. Lewis* (1944) 68 C.L.R. 455; see also *R. v. Commonwealth Court
of Conciliation and Arbitration, ex parte Barrett* (1945) 70 C.L.R. 141, 164, *per*
Dixon J.
[73] at pp. 165-6.
[74] at pp. 167-9.

member. 'The grant of that discretionary power appears to me to involve an exercise of the legislative power under s. 51, and, on the assumption that it is a judicial matter, either in whole or in part, an exercise of that power *uno ictu* with a use of the legislative power under s. 77 (i).'[75]

This conclusion does not depend on a doctrine of protective jurisdiction; it rests, like the reasoning of Douglas J. in the *Lincoln Mills Case*, on the discovery within the text of the section conferring jurisdiction of a substantive rule of federal law, couched in discretionary terms, which the federal court is called on to apply. In *Hooper v. Hooper*,[76] the High Court, this time in the context of the investment of State Supreme Courts with federal jurisdiction under sec. 77 (iii), and in face of a similar argument, discovered a federal substantive law which the State courts, exercising federal jurisdiction, were required to apply. By the Commonwealth Matrimonial Causes Act 1945, sec. 10, jurisdiction in matrimonial causes, based on the residence of the petitioner, was conferred on State Supreme Courts invested with federal jurisdiction under sec. 77 (iii). Sec. 11 of the Act was a choice of law rule directing the application of the *lex domicilii*. It was argued that as the Commonwealth Parliament had not exercised its powers under sec. 51 (xxii) to enact a federal substantive law of matrimonial causes, sec. 10 was bad as a bare grant of jurisdiction not referable to sec. 76 (ii), since the only applicable law was State law. The High Court had little difficulty in disposing of this argument. Sec. 10, read with sec. 11, gave a party a *federally created right* to have his case tried by the court according to the *lex domicilii*.

> What the Act does is to give the force of federal law to the State law. The relevant law is administered in a suit instituted under the Act not because it has the authority of a State, but because it is part of the law of the Commonwealth.[77]

*Hooper v. Hooper*, as the High Court remarked, was an easier case than *R. v. Commonwealth Court of Conciliation and Arbitration, ex parte Barrett*, because the Matrimonial Causes Act, in sec. 11, provided an express choice of law rule. A more difficult question would have arisen had sec. 10 of the Act stood alone, unsupported by sec. 11. There is a possibility that the Court would have spelled out a grant of jurisdiction coupled with an implied direction to the Court to discover some federal choice

[75] at p. 169.
[76] (1955) 91 C.L.R. 529.
[77] at p. 536.

of law rule, whether the *lex fori* or the *lex domicilii*. This is the sort of approach that was taken by Windeyer J. in *Suehle v. Commonwealth*[78] in relation to sec. 56 of the Judiciary Act. That section provides that 'A person making a claim against the Commonwealth, whether in contract or in tort' may bring a suit against the Commonwealth in various specified courts. A Commonwealth employee brought a suit against the Commonwealth for injuries that were sustained in South Australia. The case was heard in the High Court in Sydney by Windeyer J. His honour applied the law of South Australia on the ground that sec. 56 contained within itself an implication that the law to be applied was the law of the State where the tort was committed or the cause of action arose.[79]

In that case, of course, there clearly was federal jurisdiction under sec. 75 (iii) of the Constitution as the Commonwealth was a party. The fact is, however, that as a matter of construction a rule of substantive law, namely a choice of law rule, was deduced from a grant of jurisdiction. Whether the High Court would be prepared to support a grant of jurisdiction by reference to a doctrine of protective jurisdiction can only be a matter for conjecture. If a guess may be hazarded, it is very doubtful whether the Court would do so; faced with arguments touching the validity of grants of federal jurisdiction, the Court has been concerned to discover a body of substantive law (even though framed in wide discretionary terms) which, on the face of the legislation, it is directed to apply.

It may be that in substance there will be little difference in the two approaches depending on how far the High Court is prepared to go in implying rules of substantive law. There would be no practical difference if the rule that is implied is an ambulatory provision incorporating State statutory or common law. Assume, for example, a provision conferring on a federal court jurisdiction relating to contracts between inter-State traders or exporters and their customers. Under the protective jurisdiction doctrine the grant of jurisdiction would be valid, as the transactions which provide the criterion for jurisdiction are within the legislative power of the Commonwealth under sec. 51 (i) of the Constitution to control. Under the approach adopted in *R. v. Commonwealth Court of Conciliation and Arbitration, ex parte Barrett* and *Hooper v. Hooper* it would be necessary to argue that the law of contract to be applied by the Court is derived from

[78] (1967) 116 C.L.R. 353.
[79] at p. 355.

common law and State statutory law and that that law is incorporated by reference as federal law i.e., that there is to be implied a federal choice of law rule. (It is doubtful if it could be argued in these cases that sec. 79 of the Judiciary Act, which directs the application of State law by courts exercising federal jurisdiction, provides the rule of substance, namely a choice of law rule, as that section operates only if the court is antecedently exercising federal jurisdiction.)

It would, however, obviously be wise for the draftsmen to provide expressly for the application of the common law or statutory law of a particular State. If that is done, it would appear that an object similar to that of 'protective jurisdiction' can be achieved. It is for this purpose, of course, necessary that the matter in respect of which jurisdiction is granted is one that can be controlled under Commonwealth law.

An example of a provision expressly providing for a federal choice of law rule is sec. 42 (2) of the Family Law Act 1975 which provides:

> (2) Where it would be in accordance with the common law rules of private international law to apply the laws of any country or place (including a State or Territory), the court shall apply the laws of that country or place.

The limits of the approach suggested above are illustrated by *Carter Bros. v. Renouf*.[80] Sec. 105 of the Life Insurance Act 1945 enabled a life insurance company to pay into Court any moneys payable by the Company in respect of a policy for which, in the opinion of the company, no sufficient discharge could be obtained. Sec. 89 allowed payment into the Court where the company had received written notice of a trust or other specified interest in the policy. Dixon C.J.[81] stated that those provisions operated as a discharge of the company's liability and a jurisdiction was by necessary implication given to the Court. His Honour regarded the jurisdiction as limited to determining a matter involving conflicting claims against the insurance company or which might affect its liability. All provisions of the Act relating to assignments, mortgages and trusts of policies dealt with them from the point of view of the company: 'But, when once what was initially the company's problem has been solved, the rights and duties of the payee with respect to the policy moneys in his hands are not—

---

[80] (1962) 111 C.L.R. 140.
[81] Dixon C.J. in that case delivered a judgement with the consent of the parties that had been prepared by Fullagar J. who died before he could deliver it.

or normally will not be—the concern of Commonwealth law'.[82] As they fall for determination under State law, they are not capable of being determined by the High Court under sec. 76 (ii).


## IV

It is settled law that the power to create federal courts and to define their jurisdiction pursuant to secs. 71 and 77 (i) authorizes the creation of federal *appellate* courts. There can have been no doubt about *original* jurisdiction, but the authority to establish appellate courts was not so clear on the face of the Constitution. In the first place, the matters in secs. 75 and 76, by reference to which the jurisdiction of federal courts may be defined, are all matters of original jurisdiction, actual or potential, of the High Court. This might have been found persuasive in fixing the character of the jurisdiction (as original or appellate) of any inferior federal courts created by the Parliament.[83] Moreover, as Taylor J. observed in *Collins v. Charles Marshall Pty Ltd*,[84] the organization of appeals to the High Court under sec. 73 of the Constitution suggests an intention to restrict inferior federal courts to original jurisdiction. Sec. 73 (ii) authorizes appeals to the High Court from judgements, decrees, orders and sentences of any other federal court, or court exercising federal jurisdiction; or of the Supreme Court of any State or any other court of any State from which at the establishment of the Commonwealth an appeal lay to the Queen-in-Council. This grouping of the various courts from which an appeal lies to the High Court suggests that the federal courts created by the Parliament should be courts of original jurisdiction, though the argument is not compelling.

The authorities, however, establish that it is within the power of Parliament to create federal appellate courts. This was the opinion of Quick and Garran[85] and it was affirmed in the broadest

---

[82] at p. 148.

[83] See *Cockle v. Isaksen* (1957) 99 C.L.R. 155, 163 where the Court also draws attention to sec. 78 which provides that the Parliament may make laws conferring rights to proceed against the Commonwealth or a State in respect of matters within the limits of the judicial power.

[84] (1955) 92 C.L.R. 529, 559.

[85] *op. cit.*, at p. 802: 'There may be established not only courts of original jurisdiction corresponding to the District Courts of the United States, but also courts of appellate as well as original jurisdiction, corresponding to the Circuit Courts of the United States.'

terms by the High Court in *Ah Yick v. Lehmert*,[86] where it was held that in investing State courts with federal jurisdiction under sec. 77 (iii), sec. 39 of the Judiciary Act 1903 conferred jurisdiction on the courts of general sessions in Victoria to hear and determine an appeal from a conviction by a magistrate in respect of an offence against the Immigration Restriction Act 1901. Griffith C.J. said:

> The term 'federal jurisdiction' means authority to exercise the judicial power of the Commonwealth, and again that must be within limits prescribed. Then 'federal jurisdiction' must include appellate jurisdiction as well as original jurisdiction. The whole scheme of the Constitution assumes that the judicial power includes both in the case of the High Court, and from the history of the Constitution and the practice in English-speaking countries, it must be taken for granted that the judicial power was known by the framers of the Constitution to include both, and that those framers intended that the judicial power might be exercised by courts of original jurisdiction or by Courts of appellate jurisdiction. . . . Taking sec. 71 into consideration, sec. 77 (i) means that the Parliament may establish any Court to be called a federal Court, and may give it jurisdiction to exercise any judicial power of the Commonwealth, which the Parliament may think fit to confer upon it, either by way of appellate or original jurisdiction. Sub-sec. (iii) must receive a precisely similar interpretation. Parliament may invest any Court of a State with authority to exercise federal judicial power, again to the extent prescribed by the Statute. There is nothing to restrict that judicial power to original jurisdiction any more than to appellate jurisdiction, and there is no reason why there should be a restriction. There can be no doubt that Parliament might think fit to invest one Court exclusively with original jurisdiction, another with appellate jurisdiction, and another with both. There is nothing to limit that power.[87]

In this case, the Court was concerned with one paragraph of sec. 77—sec. 77 (iii), but the conclusion must be equally applicable to the whole section.[88] Though there have been doubts expressed as to the soundness of the reasoning which allows the grant of appellate jurisdiction to federal courts and State courts invested with federal jurisdiction, the High Court has refused to disturb the authority of *Ah Yick v. Lehmert* and subsequent decisions[89]

---

[86] (1905) 2 C.L.R. 593.
[87] at pp. 603-4.
[88] *Cockle v. Isaksen* (1957) 99 C.L.R. 155.
[89] *Collins v. Charles Marshall Pty Ltd* (1955) 92 C.L.R. 529, 559, *per* Taylor J.; *Cockle v. Isaksen* (1957) 99 C.L.R. 155.

and has held that federal courts may exercise appellate jurisdiction.[90]

In *Cockle v. Isaksen*[91] the High Court sustained the validity of sec. 113 of the Conciliation and Arbitration Act which conferred appellate jurisdiction on the Commonwealth Industrial Court. That section provided (1) that the Court had jurisdiction to hear and determine an appeal from a judgement, decree, order or sentence of a State court (not being a Supreme Court) or a court of a Territory of the Commonwealth made, given or pronounced in a matter arising under this Act or under the Public Service Arbitration Act 1920-1956; (2) that it was not necessary to obtain the leave either of the Industrial Court or the court appealed from in respect of appeals under sub-sec. (1); (3) that an appeal did not lie to the High Court from a judgement, decree, order or sentence from which an appeal might be brought to the court under sub-sec. (1); (4) that the jurisdiction of the Court under sub-sec. (1) was exclusive of the jurisdiction of a State court or court of a Territory to hear and determine an appeal from a judgement, decree, order or sentence from which an appeal might be brought to the Court under that sub-section.

The policy of the section was to make the Industrial Court the exclusive court of appeal for the matters described.[92] So far as it purported to authorize appeals from State courts, it was an exercise of power under secs. 71 and 77 (i); so far as it purported to define the extent to which the jurisdiction of the Industrial Court should be exclusive of the jurisdiction of State courts, it was an exercise of power under sec. 77 (ii). *Cockle v. Isaksen* squarely raised the validity of sec. 113 (3) which was held to be a legislative exception from the appellate jurisdiction of the High Court as defined in sec. 73. So far as it provided for appeals from territorial courts it appeared to be an exercise of power under sec. 122 of the Constitution as interpreted in the cases, which are discussed in the following chapter.[93] On the authority of those cases, the Privy Council in *Attorney-General for Australia v. Queen*[94] stated that 'there appears to be no reason why the Parliament, having

90 See *New South Wales v. Commonwealth* (1915) 20 C.L.R. 54, 90, *per* Isaacs J.; *Commonwealth v. Limerick Steamship Co. Ltd and Kidman* (1924) 35 C.L.R. 69, 114, *per* Starke J.; *Collins v. Charles Marshall Pty Ltd* (1955) 92 C.L.R. 529, 557; *Queen v. Spicer* (1957) 98 C.L.R. 48; *Cockle v. Isaksen* (1957) 99 C.L.R. 155.

91 (1957) 99 C.L.R. 155.

92 *Queen v. Spicer* (1957) 98 C.L.R. 48.

93 See pp. 152 ff.

94 [1957] A.C. 288, 320.

plenary power under section 122, should not invest the High Court or any other court with appellate jurisdiction from the courts of the territories. The legislative power in respect of the territories is a disparate non-federal matter.'

Putting aside the thicket of problems which affect jurisdiction with respect to territorial courts, it should be noted that there are qualifications upon the power to create federal appellate courts and to define their jurisdiction. In the first place that jurisdiction is subject to the limits imposed by secs. 75 and 76. In determining whether a grant of appellate jurisdiction to a federal court (or to a State court invested with federal jurisdiction) is validly made, it is the matter arising on the *appeal* and not the matter arising in the *original proceedings* that must fall within the heads of secs. 75 and 76. This was pointed out by the High Court in *Collins v. Charles Marshall Pty Ltd.*[95]

> If s. 77 (i) would suffice to empower the Parliament to confer appellate jurisdiction over State courts in matters arising under a law made by the Parliament, it is the appeal and not the original proceeding that must answer the description. It may often be a distinction without a difference. But it need not always be so. In a 'proceeding under the Act' in the primary court the whole matter so far as it rests on the Act may be confessed and reliance may be placed wholly on matter in avoidance which has nothing to do with the Act or an order or award and to that alone the appeal may be addressed. Yet it seems certain that the court, the jurisdiction of which is defined in terms of s. 73 (ii) [*sic*: should be s. 76 (ii)?] can receive jurisdiction only in respect of what, when that court becomes seised of it, is a matter arising under the law of the Parliament. The same distinction between the character of the original cause and of an appeal from the decision thereof sometimes arises in connection with s. 76 (i) and s. 39 (2) of the Judiciary Act. An ordinary proceeding in a court of petty sessions under State law may be decided without the intrusion of the federal Constitution or any other federal element. Thus there is no federal jurisdiction. On an appeal to general sessions or on an order nisi to review, an argument may be raised, for example, under one or other of ss. 90, 92, 109, 117 or 118 of the Constitution. At once the appeal becomes one in federal jurisdiction with all the consequences under ss. 39 (2), 40, 79 and 80 of the Judiciary Act.

These difficulties were briefly mentioned in the context of sec. 113 of the Conciliation and Arbitration Act, in *Queen v. Spicer*,[96] and in *Cockle v. Isaksen* they were considered at length. The Court 'with some misgiving'[97] concluded that the provision for

---

[95] (1955) 92 C.L.R. 529, 541.
[96] (1957) 98 C.L.R. 48, 53.
[97] (1957) 99 C.L.R. 155, 164.

appellate jurisdiction in sec. 113 (1) could be sustained 'as a law substantially with respect to matters arising under a federal law', namely the Conciliation and Arbitration Act, conferring jurisdiction in respect of such matters. It warned that there might still be an excess of power within sec. 113 (1).

> At the same time it cannot be denied that the law is one going, or possibly going, beyond that category. The provision, however, is distributable and s. 15A of the Acts Interpretation Act will operate to confine its operation to appeals which themselves come within s. 77 (i) of the Constitution. The central point is whether the section sufficiently manifests an intention to legislate with respect to a matter within s. 76 (ii) and, on the whole, we think that it does so, although owing to the form in which the sub-section is cast, it may include cases outside the required description.[98]

There are two further limitations on the power to create and to define the jurisdiction of federal appellate courts. The first is quite simple; judgements, decrees or orders of the High Court cannot be made subject to review by or appeal to any federal court. The Constitution envisages the High Court as the apex of the Australian judicial structure, an appeal from other federal courts lies to the High Court under sec. 73 (ii), and under sec. 75 (v) it may award *mandamus*, prohibition or injunction against officers of the Commonwealth who, for this purpose, include judges of other federal courts.[99] The second qualification is that it is not possible to provide for appeals from State courts exercising *State* jurisdiction to a federal court other than the High Court.[100] This arises by implication from the terms of the Constitution itself and as a matter of general federal implication. As the High Court in *Collins v. Charles Marshall Pty Ltd* observed:

> The Commonwealth Constitution is unlike the Constitution of the United States in the manner in which the relation of Federal judicial power to State courts is dealt with specifically. Sec. 73 (ii) is very specific in defining the jurisdiction of this Court to hear and determine appeals from State courts. Section 77 (iii) gives a specific power to invest State courts with federal jurisdiction and s. 77 (ii) a specific power to define the extent of the jurisdiction of a Federal court which

[98] at p. 165.

[99] (1955) 92 C.L.R. 529, 538. This is so even though the federal court is declared to be a superior court of record: *R. v. Mr Justice R. S. Watson; ex p. Armstrong* (1976) 9 A.L.R. 551.

[100] In an address to the Nineteenth Australian Legal Convention, Sir Garfield Barwick suggested that it would be possible for *State* legislation to invest the Federal Court of Australia with State jurisdiction: The State of the Australian Judicature (1977) 51 A.L.J. 480, 491.

shall be exclusive of the jurisdiction belonging to the courts of the States. On the face of the provisions they amount to an express statement of the Federal legislative and judicial powers affecting State courts which, with the addition of the ancillary power contained in s. 51 (xxxix), one would take to be exhaustive. To construe the very general words of s. 71 relating to the definition of their jurisdiction as containing a power to establish a further appellate control of State courts exercising State functions would seem to be opposed to the principles of interpretation, particularly those applying to a strictly federal instrument of government.[101]

Taylor J. said: 'to conclude otherwise would be to permit direct interference with the exercise by the courts of the States of State judicial functions, and such a notion is, as I have already said, inconsistent with the maintenance of Federal and State judicial authority under the Federal system erected by the Constitution.'[102] Though Australia has an integrated judicial structure in the sense that appeals lie from State courts on matters of State jurisdiction to the federal High Court; though State courts may be repositories of federal jurisdiction, so that an appeal from a State court exercising federal jurisdiction may be taken to a federal appellate court (as sec. 113 of the Conciliation and Arbitration Act contemplates), the courses of State jurisdiction and the jurisdiction of federal courts established pursuant to secs. 71 and 77 (i) run separately.

It has been suggested that there is another limitation on the power to define federal appellate jurisdiction. Sec. 113 of the Conciliation and Arbitration Act excluded a judgement or order of the State Supreme Court from the ambit of the appellate jurisdiction of the Industrial Court. Kitto J. considered that this exclusion was a matter of constitutional necessity and in *R. v. Spicer, ex parte Truth and Sportsman Ltd*[103] he said that 'the exception in sub-sec. (1) of the judgement of a Supreme Court is attributable to the fact that the Constitution does not enable the Commonwealth Parliament to create any appellate tribunal over the Supreme Courts of the States'.[104] Interestingly, the Bills introduced to establish first a Commonwealth Superior Court and then a Superior Court of Australia of broad federal jurisdiction would have also excluded judgements of the Supreme Courts of the States from the appellate jurisdiction of those Courts.[105] In

[101] at p. 543.
[102] at p. 563.
[103] (1957) 98 C.L.R. 48.
[104] at p. 61.
[105] Commonwealth Superior Court Bill 1968, cl. 20(1) (c), Superior Court of Australia Bill 1974, cl. 21(1)(c).

the case of the Federal Court of Australia, however, sec. 24 of the Act merely excludes from the appellate jurisdiction that other Acts might confer on the Court, judgements of 'a Full Court of the Supreme Court'. The Income Tax Assessment Amendment (Jurisdiction of Courts) Act 1976, the Patents Amendment Act 1976 and the Trade Marks Amendment Act 1976 all invest the Federal Court of Australia with jurisdiction to hear appeals from orders of a single judge of a State Supreme Court.

Assuming that sec. 77 (i) extends to appellate jurisdiction—and that is now established doctrine—any argument that a federal court cannot be invested with federal jurisdiction to hear an appeal from a judgement of a State Supreme Court exercising federal jurisdiction must rest on implication. It may be that such a view can be deduced from sec. 73 of the Constitution. That section gives the High Court jurisdiction 'with such exceptions and subject to such regulations as the Parliament prescribes' to determine an appeal from a judgement or order of *inter alia* a federal court, a State court exercising federal jurisdiction and the Supreme Court of any State. The second last paragraph of sec. 73 provides:

> But no exception or regulation prescribed by the Parliament shall prevent the High Court from hearing and determining any appeal from the Supreme Court of a State in any matter in which at the establishment of the Commonwealth an appeal lies from such Supreme Court to the Queen in Council.

It has been held that a judgement of a judge of a Supreme Court exercising original jurisdiction is a judgement of the Supreme Court of a State for purposes of sec. 73.[106] It follows from sec. 73 that legislation cannot abolish appeals from a judgement of the Supreme Court in original jurisdiction to the High Court where an appeal lay in 1900 to the Privy Council.[107] The Judiciary Act provides for an appeal from a single judge of the Supreme Court of a State to the High Court by special leave of the High Court only (sec. 35). It is difficult to see how there could be any further limitation or restriction on appeals from judgements of the Supreme Court of a State in its original jurisdiction to the

---

[106] *Parkin v. James* (1905) 2 C.L.R. 315.

[107] This means where the appeal lay as of right: *Collins v. Charles Marshall Pty Ltd* (1955) 92 C.L.R. 529, 538, 543-4. Such an appeal lay in the case of judgements involving £500 or more except in the case of the Supreme Court of Tasmania where the amount was £1,000: Quick and Garran, *op. cit.*, 739, 740. For a list of the instruments governing appeals as of right to the Privy Council at 1900 see Barwick: The State of the Australian Judicature (1977) 51 A.L.J. 480, 500 (Appendix C).

High Court in the face of sec. 73 where the judgement is one from which an appeal lay to the Privy Council in 1900.

In *Collins v. Charles Marshall Pty Ltd* a joint judgement of six judges (including Kitto J.) briefly discussed the position that would exist if a federal court had appellate jurisdiction in respect of a State Supreme Court. Their Honours said:

> In the first place a new Federal court of appeal if brought into existence would clearly be a Federal court from which an appeal would lie to the High Court under s. 73 (ii). It may be assumed that when that provision speaks of a court from which an appeal lies to the Privy Council that means lies as of right. If the court subject to the appeal to the supposed new Federal court of appeal was a Supreme Court of the State or a court whence an appeal lay as of right at the establishment of the Commonwealth, there would be a parallel right of appeal to the High Court. This would be true too if the primary court were exercising Federal jurisdiction. That would mean that alternative rights of appeal would exist from State courts to different Federal courts of appeal, one being subject to appeal in its turn to the other. It is true that the Parliament has a power of making exceptions from the subject matter of the appellate jurisdiction of the High Court, but the power is limited in the case of Supreme Courts in the manner already described and moreover after all it is only a power of making exceptions. Such a power is not susceptible of any very precise definition but it would be surprising if it extended to excluding altogether one of the heads specifically mentioned by s. 73.

This passage, however, occurred in the course of reasoning that a federal court could not be given jurisdiction over State courts exercising *State* jurisdiction even though the matter on appeal came within sec. 75 or sec. 76 of the Constitution. The judges went on to say:

> In the second place it is apparent from s. 73 (ii) that the principle or policy which it embodies was to place the court that is supreme in the State judicial hierarchy under the appellate jurisdiction of the High Court and no other State courts, unless they were invested under s. 77 (iii) with Federal jurisdiction.

It would be unfortunate if the Constitution prevented the implementation of the policy behind the Federal Court of Australia Act, which is to use the State Supreme Courts as trial courts in relation to many federal matters allowing an appeal to a special federal court. It is true that an alternative appeal must lie to the High Court but the fact that that appeal can be had only by special leave ensures that the High Court can have regard to the purpose of the legislation establishing the new federal court in determining whether to grant leave.

It would seem that there is no authority to support the statement of Kitto J. in *R. v. Spicer* and it is suggested that the Court
should not imply this further limitation on Commonwealth
power to create federal appellate jurisdiction.

## V

The quotations which prefaced this chapter reveal sharply
differing views of the functions and merits of federal courts as
repositories of federal jurisdiction. Sir Owen Dixon's arguments
against the Australian construction of federal jurisdiction are
cogent and practical; and many of the difficulties in the practical
administration of justice in this area arise, in part at least, from
foolish and ill-conceived copying. But with the very general statement that 'neither from the point of view of juristic principle
nor from that of the practical and efficient administration of
justice can the division of the courts into State and federal be
regarded as sound',[108] there is room for disagreement and the
other passage quoted from a study by an American scholar, Professor Paul Mishkin, expresses complete disagreement. No doubt
both writers would agree that there is absurdity in a notion of
separate channels of State and federal jurisdiction within the same
single court system. It may, of course, be perfectly sensible and
desirable to use State courts as *general* trial and inferior appellate
courts, subject to the ultimate control of a federal High or Supreme Court, and it may be necessary with the establishment of
new entities such as the Commonwealth of Australia or the
United States to extend the competence of such State courts to
take proper account of these new parties who may appear in
litigation before them. But there is no good sense in constructing
two levels of jurisdiction, State and federal, for such purposes and
in conferring authority to exercise both on the very same body
of courts.

If, however, two separate court structures are created, the argument is not so clear. Sir Owen Dixon believes that it is improper
to carry the federal division of power and functions into the
field of adjudication, and that it is for the courts in the ordinary
course of ascertaining and enforcing the law to pass on the validity of governmental action. He observes further that the natural
course is to establish the courts as independent organs which are
neither Commonwealth nor State in character. If it were possible
to establish the courts in this way by agreement between the

108 (1935) 51 L.Q.R. at 606.

federal partners it would obviously be a more satisfactory solution than the multiplication of federal and State courts and jurisdictions. But failing such agreement, the question resolves itself into a practical enquiry into the operation of courts which are appointed by different elements within a given federal structure. It may be that the pattern of historical development, the method of selection of State judges and the operation of local pressures and prejudices, and the character of the constitutional problems which arise for decision make it undesirable, in a particular federation, to vest jurisdiction in respect of the broad range of federal matters exclusively in State courts, even with the control of a final appeal to a federal Supreme or High Court. This is the broad assumption which underlies Mishkin's argument in favour of the federal trial courts. In present conditions, it is very doubtful whether it would be possible to secure agreement between the States and the central Governments in Australia and the United States to a reconstitution of all courts on a neutral—that is a non-State, non-federal basis, and it is certainly not difficult to envisage the fate of various federally created 'rights' in the United States if their enforcement and protection lay wholly in the control of State courts.

The merits of a federal court structure cannot be resolved on general, *a priori* grounds. The Australian record exposes very clearly the inconveniences of a two-tier jurisdiction and it should not be beyond the wit of man to refashion the Judicature Chapter of the Constitution and the legislation enacted thereunder so as to provide for the orderly administration of justice within the framework of a single integrated court system (which may include functionally specialized tribunals) free of the Gothic complexities of the law of federal jurisdiction.[108A]

---

[108A] A special committee has recommended to the Australian Constitutional Convention that further consideration be given to a unified system of Australian courts: *1977 Judicature Committee Report to Standing Committee D of the Australian Constitutional Convention*, p. 34.

# = 4 =

## *The Territorial Courts and Jurisdiction with Respect to the Territories*

'It would have been simple enough to follow the words of s.
122 and of ss. 71, 73 and 76 (ii) and to hold that the courts and
laws of a Territory were federal courts and laws made by the
Parliament. . . . But an entirely different interpretation has
been adopted, one which brings its own difficulties.'[1]

### I

Sec. 122 of the Commonwealth Constitution provides that 'the
Parliament may make laws for the government of any territory
surrendered by any State to and accepted by the Commonwealth,
or of any territory placed by the Queen under the authority of
and accepted by the Commonwealth, or otherwise acquired by the
Commonwealth, and may allow the representation of such
territory in either House of the Parliament to the extent and on
the terms which it thinks fit'. This is the general legislative power
with respect to Commonwealth Territories. In constituting courts
for the Territories it seems clear enough that sec. 71 of the Constitution could reasonably have been held to support the vesting
of the judicial power of the Commonwealth in federal courts
created by the Parliament for and within the Territories. Sec. 77
(i) authorizes the Parliament with respect to any of the matters
mentioned in secs. 75 and 76 to make laws defining the jurisdiction of any federal court other than the High Court. Secs. 75
and 76[2] mark out the actual and potential original jurisdiction
of the High Court. Sec. 76 (ii) authorizes the grant of jurisdiction
in any matter arising under any laws made by the Parliament,
and since sec. 122 authorizes the making of laws by the Parliament the jurisdiction of territorial courts could have been simply
enough defined under sec. 77 (i). Secs. 76 (ii) and 122 could have

---

[1] *The Queen v. Kirby, ex parte Boilermakers' Society of Australia* (1956) 94
C.L.R. 254, 290, *per* Dixon C.J., McTiernan, Fullagar and Kitto JJ.
[2] See pp. 4-5 *ante*.

been employed to invest the High Court with original jurisdiction in matters touching the Territories, and appeals from territorial courts to the High Court would have been authorized by sec. 73 (ii) which confers jurisdiction, subject to parliamentary control, to hear and determine appeals from all judgements, decrees, orders and sentences of *federal* courts other than the High Court. It is to be noted that if the territorial courts had been established as federal courts, they would have had to comply with the requirements of sec. 72 which, until its amendment in 1977, required life tenure for judges.[3] But, as the High Court observed in the *Boilermakers' Case*, an entirely different course was taken in relation to the territorial courts.

## II

There were three main categories of Commonwealth Territories—internal, external and trust Territories. The trust Territories were New Guinea (which from World War II was administered jointly with Papua as the Territory of Papua and New Guinea under the legislative authority of the Papua and New Guinea Act 1949) and Nauru which Australia administered on behalf of the three trusteeship powers, the United Kingdom, Australia and New Zealand. Nauru became independent in 1968[4] and Papua New Guinea obtained independence in 1975.[5] There are now no trust Territories administered by the Commonwealth.

In 1909 the Federal Capital Territory (now the Australian Capital Territory) was surrendered by New South Wales to the Commonwealth. This was confirmed by the Seat of Government Surrender Act 1909 (New South Wales) and by the Seat of Government Acceptance Act 1909 (Commonwealth). In 1915 Jervis Bay was similarly surrendered and sec. 4(2) of the Jervis Bay Territory Acceptance Act 1915 made the laws in force in the Australian Capital Territory applicable to the Jervis Bay Territory. The Seat of Government Acceptance Act 1909 declared, until provision was otherwise made, that within the Australian Capital Territory the High Court should have the jurisdiction formerly belonging to the Supreme Court of New South Wales. The Judiciary Act 1927 established a registry of the High Court within the Capital Territory and declared that in relation to the Territory the High Court should have the original jurisdiction exer-

---

[3] *Waterside Workers' Federation of Australia v. J. W. Alexander Ltd* (1918) 25 C.L.R. 434; *Boilermakers' Case* (1956) 94 C.L.R. 254, 290.

[4] Nauru Independence Act 1967.

[5] Papua New Guinea Independence Act 1975.

L

cised by the Supreme Court of New South Wales before 1911, together with such original jurisdiction, civil and criminal, as was from time to time conferred on the High Court by ordinance. The Seat of Government Supreme Court Act 1933 repealed the Judiciary Act 1927. (The title of the Act was altered to the Australian Capital Territory Supreme Court Act by the Statute Law Revision Act 1950.) It now provides (sec. 6) that the Supreme Court of the Territory consists of a Chief Justice and not more than two other judges, apart from those appointed as 'additional judges'. A judge ceases to hold office upon his attaining 70 years of age. Provision is made for appointment as additional judges of judges of other courts created by Parliament. An additional judge ceases to hold office if he no longer holds office as a judge of the other court. Prior to the enactment of the Federal Court of Australia Act there was provision for appeals and cases stated to the High Court. These matters are now regulated by the Federal Court of Australia Act 1976.

The Heard Island and McDonald Islands Act 1953[6] declares these islands to be a Commonwealth Territory. Sec. 5 provides that subject to the Act, the laws in force in the Australian Capital Territory, including the rules of common law and equity, shall be applicable to the Territory and by sec. 9 the Supreme Court of the Australian Capital Territory is invested with jurisdiction in the Territory, as if it were part of the Australian Capital Territory. Similar provision is made for the Australian Antarctic Territory by the Australian Antarctic Territory Act 1954.

The Northern Territory which, at the date of federation, was a Territory of South Australia and was so described in covering clause 6 of the Commonwealth Constitution Act, was acquired by the Commonwealth by the Northern Territory Acceptance Act 1910. The Supreme Court of the Northern Territory was established by ordinance in 1911, and was subsequently divided into two courts, the Supreme Court of North Australia and the Supreme Court of Central Australia.[7] In 1931, the Supreme Court of Central Australia was abolished and the Supreme Court of Northern Australia was continued as the Supreme Court of the Northern Territory.[8]

---

6 See (1953) 1 Sydney L.R. 374.

7 Northern Australia Act 1926, sec. 40.

8 Northern Territory (Administration) Act (No. 2) 1931. See Northern Territory (Administration) Act 1910 (as amended), sec. 18. Sec. 19 makes provision for magistrates and justices of the peace. See *Re Ballard, ex parte Wright* (1955) 1 F.L.R. 473 *per* Kriewaldt J. for an account of the history of the court.

The Supreme Court Ordinance 1911 of the Northern Territory and the amendments thereto were repealed by the Supreme Court Ordinance Repeal Ordinance 1965.[9] The Northern Territory Supreme Court Act 1961 abolished the Supreme Court existing immediately before the commencement of the Act (sec. 4) and established a superior court of record to be known as the Supreme Court of the Northern Territory of Australia. It consists of a Chief Judge and not more than three judges (apart from 'additional judges'). These judges hold office until they reach 70 years of age. Provision is made for the appointment of additional judges with the same qualifications and term of office as those for the Supreme Court of the Australian Capital Territory. Until 1976, appeals from the Supreme Court, which were to the High Court, were provided for in secs. 46 and 47 of the Act. Appeals are now regulated by the Federal Court of Australia Act 1976.

Linked with the Northern Territory are the Ashmore and Cartier Islands. By the Ashmore and Cartier Islands Acceptance Act 1933, these small islands off the north-west coast of Australia became a Commonwealth Territory, and sec. 6 of the Act provides that the Territory shall be deemed to form part of the Northern Territory and that the laws in force in the Northern Territory shall apply.[10]

Norfolk Island was accepted as a Commonwealth Territory by the Norfolk Island Act 1913 in anticipation of an Imperial Order-in-Council of 1914 by which it was placed by the King under authority of the Commonwealth. The Norfolk Island Act 1957, sec. 18 provides for the establishment of a Supreme Court to consist of a judge or judges appointed in accordance with the Act. Sec. 19 provides for the appointment as a judge of a person who is a judge of another court created by Parliament. The Coral Sea Islands Act 1969 declares those islands to be a Territory by name of Coral Sea Islands Territory. Under sec. 8 the courts of Norfolk Island have jurisdiction in and in relation to the Territory.

The Cocos (Keeling) Islands Act 1955 constituted these islands a Commonwealth Territory and sec. 16 authorized the making of ordinances regulating appeals from local courts to the High Court. However, since 1976 appeals are regulated by the Federal Court of Australia Act 1976.

The Christmas Island Act 1958 declares Christmas Island to be

9 1965, No. 42.
10 See Garran: The Law of the Territories of the Commonwealth (1935) 9 A.L.J. (Supplement) 28, 29.

a Territory under the authority of the Commonwealth (sec. 5). Sec. 11 creates the Supreme Court of Christmas Island and provides that it shall be constituted by ordinance. Sec. 16 authorized ordinances to provide for appeals to the High Court but these appeals are now regulated by the Federal Court of Australia Act 1976. The Supreme Court Ordinance 1958 as amended to 1976 provides in sec. 5 for the appointment of a person who is a judge of another court created by Parliament to be a judge of the Supreme Court. Provision is also made for the appointment of additional judges. A judge or an additional judge ceases to hold office if he ceases to hold office as a judge of any other court created by Parliament.

Under the Federal Court of Australia Act 1976 provision is made for appeals to the Federal Court of Australia from judgements of the Supreme Court of a Territory (sec. 24). Appeals to the High Court from Territory Supreme Courts now lie only with special leave given by the High Court (sec. 24(2)). Under sec. 26 of the Federal Court of Australia Act a Territory Supreme Court may state any case or reserve any question concerning a matter with respect to which an appeal would lie for the consideration of the Federal Court of Australia. Sec. 33 of the Act provides for appeals to the High Court from judgements of the Federal Court of Australia.

So far as the Australian Capital Territory is concerned, it was once considered that the appropriate constitutional provision was sec. 52 (i) which confers power on the Parliament to make laws for the peace, order and good government of the Commonwealth with respect to *inter alia* 'The seat of government of the Commonwealth . . .'.[11] In *Spratt v. Hermes*,[12] the High Court unanimously held that sec. 122 of the Constitution conferred a general power to legislate for the Australian Capital Territory and there was no limitation in sec. 52 (i) upon that power. While there has been no decision as to where in the Australian Capital Territory the seat of government is or on the ambit of that power,[13] the Court noted that there was a distinction between the seat of government and the Capital Territory and that sec. 125 referred to the seat of government as being 'within territory

11 *Federal Capital Commission v. Laristan Building and Investment Co. Pty Ltd* (1929) 42 C.L.R. 582. See also *Australian National Airways Pty Ltd v. Commonwealth* (1945) 71 C.L.R. 29, 83.

12 (1965) 114 C.L.R. 226.

13 This issue was discussed in *Coe v. Queensland Mines* (1974) 5 A.C.T.R. 53.

which shall have been granted to or acquired by the Commonwealth . . .'.[14]

The question has also arisen whether there is any legally significant distinction between external and internal Territories. In *Mitchell v. Barker*,[15] the High Court briefly discussed the question whether a magistrate's court in the Northern Territory was a federal court, so that an appeal lay under sec. 73 (ii) of the Constitution to the High Court. Griffith C.J. said: 'In *R. v. Bernasconi*[16] this Court held that the group of sections comprised in Chapter III of the Constitution do not apply to a Territory of the Commonwealth. If that is right in its largest sense, the Special Magistrates' Court is not a Federal Court and no appeal lies to this Court. *It may be that a distinction may some day be drawn between Territories which have and those which have not formed part of the Commonwealth.*'[17] In *Waters v. Commonwealth*,[18] Fullagar J. was called on to decide whether the High Court had original jurisdiction under sec. 75 (iii) of the Constitution in a matter, arising in the Northern Territory, in which the Commonwealth was a party.[19] He said: 'For the purpose of s. 122 of the Constitution no distinction can be drawn between Territories surrendered by a State and Territories otherwise acquired by the Commonwealth, but it may be that, for the purposes of s. 5 of the Constitution Act, a distinction is to be drawn between Territories which are "parts of the Commonwealth" and Territories which are not "parts of the Commonwealth".' Sec. 5 of the Constitution Act (one of the covering clauses) provides that the Constitution Act and all laws made by the Commonwealth Parliament under the Constitution shall be binding on the courts, judges and people of every State and of every part of the Commonwealth, notwithstanding anything in the laws of any State. These words suggest that the Commonwealth is not coterminous with the area of the States.

The supposed distinction would appear to be based on the fact that, at the time of federation, the Northern Territory was part of South Australia and the area of the Australian Capital Territory was part of New South Wales. In covering clause 6 of

---

14 (1965) 114 C.L.R. 226 at pp. 241, 257, 262, 269, 278 and see Ewens: Where is the Seat of Government? (1951) 25 A.L.J. 532.

15 (1918) 24 C.L.R. 365.

16 (1915) 19 C.L.R. 629. This case is discussed at pp. 149 ff. *post.*

17 Italics supplied.

18 (1951) 82 C.L.R. 188, 192.

19 He held following *R. v. Bernasconi* that it did not. This decision was overruled in *Spratt v. Hermes* (1965) 114 C.L.R. 226.

the Constitution Act 'the States' are defined to include 'South Australia, including the northern territory of South Australia'. The preamble to the Constitution Act states that 'the people of' the various colonies 'have agreed to unite in one indissoluble Federal Commonwealth'.

In *Spratt v. Hermes*,[20] the High Court seems to have rejected the view that, for constitutional purposes, there is any distinction between internal Territories and external Territories.[21]

The Commonwealth parliamentary draftsmen, until recent years, appear to have proceeded on the assumption that internal Territories were part of the Commonwealth while external Territories were not. In *Waters v. Commonwealth*,[22] Fullagar J. noted that sec. 8 of the Bankruptcy Act, in its then form, contemplated such a distinction. It provided that the Governor-General may by Proclamation declare that the Act shall, with such modifications as are prescribed, extend to any Territory which is not part of the Commonwealth. It was clearly assumed, however, that the Act applied without any such Proclamation to the Australian Capital Territory and the Northern Territory. Sec. 18, for example, purported to confer what was described as 'federal jurisdiction in bankruptcy' on *inter alia* the Supreme Courts of northern Australia and central Australia. The Australian Capital Territory was included in 'the District of New South Wales and the Australian Capital Territory' under sec. 12 of the Act.[23] A number of other Acts referred to Territories 'not being part of the Commonwealth' or 'not forming part of the Commonwealth' in sections that provided for the Acts' extension to such Territories.[24]

In *Spratt v. Hermes,* Barwick C.J., Menzies and Windeyer JJ. were of the view that, generally speaking, the Commonwealth included all the Territories of the Commonwealth, although some provisions of the Constitution that referred to the Commonwealth were not, because of their nature, applicable to the Territories. This latter question is discussed below. Kitto J. was of the contrary view. But none of the judges who discussed the question of

---

[20] (1965) 114 C.L.R. 226. See Zines: 'Laws for the Government of any Territory': Section 122 of the Constitution (1966) 2 F.L. Rev. 72.

[21] ibid. at p. 259. See also *Capital T.V. and Appliances Pty Ltd v. Falconer* (1971) 125 C.L.R. 591, 625.

[22] (1951) 82 C.L.R. 188, 192.

[23] Commonwealth Gazettes, 1928, p. 2199; 1938, p. 2533.

[24] E.g., Life Insurance Act 1945, sec. 6; The National Service Act 1951, sec. 5, Consular Privileges and Immunities Act 1972, sec. 4; Copyright Act 1968, sec. 4 and the Defence Act 1903 as amended, sec. 5A.

the meaning of 'the Commonwealth' for this purpose considered that any distinction should be made between internal and external Territories. Finally, in *Berwick Ltd v. Deputy Commissioner of Taxation*,[25] the Court held that the external Territories, except perhaps those held under United Nations Trusteeship, formed part of the Commonwealth of Australia.

The Statute Law Revision Act 1973[26] amended the various provisions referred to above by omitting phrases such as 'Territories not forming part of the Commonwealth' and inserting 'external Territories'. The Acts Interpretation Act was amended in 1973[27] to define 'Australia' and the 'Commonwealth', when used in a geographical sense, to exclude an external Territory (sec. 17(a)). 'External Territory' means 'a Territory, not being an internal Territory, for the government of which as a Territory provision is made by any Act' (sec. 17 (pd)). 'Internal Territory' means 'the Australian Capital Territory, the Jervis Bay Territory or the Northern Territory' (sec. 17 (pe)).

## III

In the United States, a distinction has been drawn between *constitutional* courts, established under Art. III of the Constitution, and *legislative* courts whose constitutional basis is found elsewhere in the Constitution.[28] The Supreme Court of the United States held in *American Insurance Co. v. Canter*[29] that the courts of the Territories were legislative courts organized outside the framework of Art. III, and therefore not capable of receiving an investment of jurisdiction under that Article. The constitution and jurisdiction of these courts depended upon 'the general right of sovereignty which exists in the government, or in virtue of that clause which enables Congress to make all needful rules and regulations respecting the territory belonging to the United States'. From this it was said to follow that the jurisdiction of the territorial courts could be extended beyond the cases and controversies enumerated in Article III and that the tenure of judges of these courts was not controlled by that Article.

25 (1976) 8 A.L.R. 580.

26 Act No. 216 of 1973.

27 Act No. 79 of 1973.

28 See Katz: Federal Legislative Courts (1930) 43 H.L.R. 894: Note: The Restrictive Effect of Article III on the Organization of the Federal Courts (1934) 34 Col.L.R. 344; The Judicial Power of Federal Tribunals Not Organised Under Article Three (1934) 34 Col.L.R. 746; Hart and Wechsler: The Federal Courts and the Federal System at pp. 340 *et seq.*

29 (1828) Pet. 511.

It is to be noted that the territorial courts are not the only tribunals within the category of legislative courts.[30]

Although the territorial courts are classified as legislative courts, it is long settled, notwithstanding a strong dissent by Taney C.J.,[31] that they are subject to the appellate jurisdiction of the Supreme Court of the United States. There is no elaborate exposition in the cases of the basis on which this appellate jurisdiction depends, and the fullest statement is to the effect that the United States exercises plenary authority over the Territories, that this includes ultimate legislative, executive and judicial power, from which it is said to follow that the Supreme Court has appellate jurisdiction over the courts established by Congress in the Territories.[32] This appellate jurisdiction does not depend upon the character of the court from which the appeal is taken, but on the nature of the proceeding in the lower court. It is only from *judicial* and not from *administrative* determinations of territorial courts that an appeal lies to the Supreme Court.[33] This is a rather odd chapter of the law. Though the legislative courts can exercise no part of the judicial power of the United States, and the Supreme Court can exercise only that power, the latter nonetheless can review judgements of the former.[34]

Special considerations arise with respect to the courts of the District of Columbia. The District of Columbia, under Art. I, sec. 8 of the United States Constitution, is the Seat of Government

[30] See *Ex parte Bakelite Corporation* (1929) 279 U.S. 438.

[31] *Gordon v. United States* (1865) 2 Wall. 561. This was posthumously printed twenty years after it was prepared. See the *Boilermakers' Case* (1956) 94 C.L.R. 291.

[32] *Freeborn v. Smith* (1864) 2 Wall. 160, 173; *United States v. Coe* (1894) 155 U.S. 76, 86. See Katz *op. cit.* at pp. 899, 903.

[33] Katz *op. cit.* at p. 903. Constitution of the United States of America, *op. cit.* at p. 594. See *National Mutual Insurance Co. v. Tidewater Transfer Co. Inc.* (1949) 337 U.S. 582. There was some difference of view in this case on the question whether the appellate jurisdiction of the Supreme Court depended on the matter being enumerated in the cases and controversies in Art. III, sec. 2. The majority (followed by Katz *op. cit.*, p. 902) said that the jurisdiction was not limited in this way, but Vinson C.J. and Douglas J. dissented. 'The appellate jurisdiction of this court is, in fact, dependent upon the fact that the case reviewed is of a kind within the Art. III enumeration. That Article, after setting out the cases of which inferior courts may take cognisance and the original jurisdiction of this Court, extends the appellate jurisdiction of the Supreme Court only as far as all other cases before mentioned. . . . We can no more review a legislative court's decision of a case which is not among those enumerated in Art. III than we can hear a case from a state court involving purely state law questions.'

[34] There is a short discussion of the American law on this subject in the majority judgement in the *Boilermakers' Case* (1956) 94 C.L.R. 254, 290-2.

of the United States. It is to be noted that in Australia, the Seat of Government is within, but is not coterminous with the Australian Capital Territory.[35] Through a long course of decisions, the courts of the District of Columbia were regarded as legislative courts[36] but in 1933 in *O'Donoghue v. United States*[37] the Supreme Court of the United States held that for purposes of tenure and the compensation of judges the courts of the District were constitutional courts within Article III. It was said that in establishing courts for the District of Columbia Congress was exercising dual powers: under Article III Congress had exercised the power to constitute courts inferior to the Supreme Court, and under Art. I, sec. 8 (the power to legislate for the District of Columbia) it had invested the District of Columbia courts with non-judicial as well as judicial functions.[38]

At no stage does there appear to have been any consideration of the possibility of conferring original jurisdiction on the Supreme Court of the United States in cases or controversies in or affecting the Territories.

## IV

The law relating to the Commonwealth territorial courts and to jurisdiction in the Territories has been profoundly affected by the 'extraordinary' decision[39] in *R. v. Bernasconi*.[40] That case was foreshadowed by *Buchanan v. Commonwealth*[41] where the High Court unanimously held that in legislating for the Northern Territory under sec. 122, it was not necessary to comply with sec. 55 of the Constitution which provides that laws imposing taxation shall deal only with the imposition of taxation and that laws imposing taxation, subject to defined exceptions, shall deal only with one subject of taxation. This prohibition of tacking was inserted to safeguard the position of the Senate. Barton A.C.J. dwelt on the inconvenience which would follow a restriction of the power to legislate for the Territories under sec. 122 by reference to sec. 55. The core of the argument was that the Senate

[35] See Ewens: Where is the Seat of Government? (1951) 25 A.L.J. 532, 533.

[36] They were expressly described as such by the Supreme Court of the United States in *Ex parte Bakelite Corporation* (1929) 279 U.S. 438.

[37] (1933) 289 U.S. 516.

[38] See the discussion in *National Mutual Insurance Co. v. Tidewater Transfer Co.* (1949) 337 U.S. 582.

[39] Sawer: Judicial Power under the Constitution, in: Essays on the Australian Constitution (Ed. Else-Mitchell, 2nd ed., 1961) at p. 77.

[40] (1915) 19 C.L.R. 629.

[41] (1913) 16 C.L.R. 315.

was protected as a *States'* House; that sec. 55 was linked to sec. 51 (ii) which confers power on the Parliament to legislate, subject to the Constitution, with respect to taxation, but so as not to discriminate between States or parts of States, and that sec. 55 was not therefore to affect the plenary powers of the Parliament in legislating for the Territories under sec. 122. In the words of Isaacs J., the Northern Territory 'is a territory of the Commonwealth . . . (but) . . . is not fused with it, and the provisions of secs. 53 and 55 of the Constitution intended to guard the Senate and the States have no application to the Northern Territory. The taxation involved in the Northern Territory Acts is quite outside the "taxation" referred to in sec. 55 of the Constitution.'[42]

The argument is not entirely convincing. It is true and notorious that the Senate was fashioned as a States' House, but it is a House of the *Parliament* which is invested with authority to legislate for the Territories under sec. 122. Sec. 122 provides that Parliament 'may allow the representation of such territory in either House of the Parliament to the extent and on the terms which it thinks fit'.[43] Secs. 55 and 53, it may reasonably be argued, were written into the Constitution to regulate the relations of the two Houses not only when the Parliament was legislating for the area comprised within the States, but whenever the Parliament was exercising its powers as such.

In *R. v. Bernasconi*, it was held that the exercise of Commonwealth legislative power under sec. 122, whether exercised directly by Parliament or through a subordinate agency, was not restricted by sec. 80 of the Constitution which provides that 'the trial on indictment of any offence against any law of the Commonwealth shall be by jury, and every such trial shall be held in the State where the offence was committed, and if the offence was not committed within any State the trial shall be held at such place or places as the Parliament prescribes'. As interpreted, sec. 80, which was designed to safeguard the right to trial by jury in serious criminal cases, is a very frail reed. It does not operate if the procedure of indictment is not adopted.[44] But the final words

---

[42] at p. 335.

[43] In *Western Australia v. Commonwealth* (1975) 7 A.L.R. 159, the High Court by a majority upheld the validity of the Senate (Representation of Territories) Act 1973 providing for the representation of the people of the Australian Capital Territory and the Northern Territory in the Senate. This decision was affirmed in *Queensland v. Commonwealth* (1977) 16 A.L.R. 487.

[44] See *per* Isaacs J. in *R. v. Bernasconi* (1915) 19 C.L.R. 629, 637; *R. v. Archdall and Roskruge* (1928) 41 C.L.R. 128; *R. v. Federal Court of Bankruptcy, ex parte Lowenstein* (1938) 59 C.L.R. 556; *Boilermakers' Case* (1956) 94 C.L.R.

of the section suggest the possibility of a trial at a place outside the area of a State.

Nevertheless in *R. v. Bernasconi* it was held that the trial in a Territory of a person on indictment for an offence against a law of the Commonwealth need not be by jury. The offence in that case was constituted by an ordinance of the Territory of Papua which excluded trial by jury and it was argued that a law passed by the legislature of a Territory under the authority of an Act of the Commonwealth Parliament could not properly be regarded as a law of the Commonwealth, but was more properly described as a 'law of the territory concerned',[45] and therefore not within the ambit of sec. 80. Griffith C.J., in whose judgement Rich and Gavan Duffy JJ. concurred, declined to decide the case on this narrow ground,[46] while Isaacs J. was of opinion that a territorial ordinance was a law of the Commonwealth 'because its present force subsists by virtue of the declared will of the Commonwealth Parliament'.[47]

In the view of Griffith C.J. sec. 80 was enacted to parallel in the case of indictable offences under Commonwealth laws those provisions in State laws which provided for trial by jury on indictment. From this he drew the broad conclusion that 'Chapter III is limited in its application to the exercise of the judicial power of the Commonwealth in respect of those functions of government as to which it stands in the place of the States, and has no application to territories'.[48] It is to be noted that Griffith C.J.'s judgement extended to the whole of Chapter III of the Constitution, that is to the Judicature Chapter. The Chief Justice's reasoning does not demonstrate very clearly why the operation of sec. 80 should be *geographically* limited to the area of the States, particularly in view of the fact that the words of sec. 80 contemplate the commission of an indictable offence outside that area. Isaacs J. advanced additional arguments of policy to support the conclusion that sec. 80 did not extend to the Territories. He observed that sec. 122 was an unqualified grant of power, complete in itself, which implied that a Territory was 'not yet in a con-

---

254, 290: 'As s. 80 has been interpreted there is no difficulty in avoiding trial by jury where it does apply.' More recently, however, Murphy J. has indicated his disagreement with this view and has suggested that sec. 80 guarantees trial by jury for serious criminal offences: *Beckwith v. The Queen* (1977) 51 A.L.J.R. 247.

45 See *Waters v. Commonwealth* (1951) 82 C.L.R. 188 at 191.

46 (1915) 19 C.L.R. 629, 634.

47 at p. 637.

48 at p. 635.

dition to enter into the full participation of Commonwealth constitutional rights and powers. It is in a state of dependency or tutelage, and the special regulations proper for its government until, if ever, it shall be admitted as a member of the family of States, are left to the discretion of the Commonwealth Parliament. . . . Parliament's sense of justice and fair dealing is sufficient to protect them, without fencing them round with what would be in the vast majority of instances an entirely inappropriate requirement of the British jury system.'[49]

It is fair comment that this is a sound policy reason for excluding the operation of jury trial in some of the Territories—though it makes no sense at all in the case of the Australian Capital Territory—but it is also fair comment to point out that such considerations should have been more appropriately addressed to those who were responsible for drafting the Constitution.[50] But there is no warrant in the actual terms of the Constitution for excluding the Territories from the operation of sec. 80, or for that matter from the operation of Chapter III as a whole.

The tendency, however, was to regard a Territory as being outside or subordinate to the Commonwealth proper and to give the Commonwealth unfettered power in the Territory; but, also, to support this view by an appeal to policy considerations relating to the particular provisions involved.

In *Porter v. The King; ex parte Yee*,[51] sec. 21 of the Supreme Court Ordinance 1911-1922 of the Northern Territory made under sec. 13 of the Northern Territory (Administration) Act 1910 provided for an appeal to the High Court from the Supreme Court of the Northern Territory. It was argued that the provision was void, first, because Chapter III of the Constitution did not apply to the Territories; a court of a Territory was, therefore, not a federal court within the meaning of sec. 73 which is included in Chapter III and which provides for an appeal to the High Court from judgements of, *inter alia*, a federal court. Secondly, Parliament could not confer appellate jurisdiction on the High Court under sec. 122 because it had been held in *In re Judiciary and Navigation Acts*[52] that the jurisdiction of the High Court was confined to such jurisdiction as was conferred or authorized by Chapter III.

The High Court (Isaacs, Higgins, Rich and Starke JJ.; Knox

---

[49] at pp. 637-8.
[50] Sawer *ante* note 39 at p. 77.
[51] (1926) 37 C.L.R. 432.
[52] (1921) 29 C.L.R. 257.

C.J. and Gavan Duffy J., dissenting) rejected these submissions and upheld its jurisdiction to hear the appeal on the ground that the exclusive and exhaustive nature of Chapter III, providing for the judicature and its functions, referred only to the federal system. Knox C.J. and Gavan Duffy J. dissented on the grounds that *In re Judiciary and Navigation Acts* established that the whole of the original and appellate jurisdiction of the High Court was to be found within Chapter III and that laws for the government of the Territory did not include a power to impose duties on persons or organizations (such as the High Court) not within the Territory.

The judgement of Higgins J., one of the majority in *Porter's Case*, was to cause difficulty later. Higgins J. had dissented in *In re Judiciary and Navigation Acts* on the grounds that the jurisdiction Parliament purported to confer in that case (the giving of advisory opinions) was within Chapter III and that even if it did not come within those provisions, Chapter III did not exhaustively describe the jurisdiction that could be vested in the Court. In *Porter's Case* Higgins J. did not distinguish *In re Judiciary and Navigation Acts* on the same basis as the other majority judges. Instead, he seemed to accept that decision as applicable to the High Court in relation to the Territories but declared that it was binding only in respect of the conferring of original—and not appellate—jurisdiction on the High Court.[53]

Putting aside the views of Higgins J., the opinions of the majority and minority judges in *Porter's Case* both involved the notion of the Territories power being in some sense separated from the rest of the Constitution. The Court considered that *R. v. Bernasconi* established that Chapter III did not extend to the Territories, which were governed under sec. 122 alone.

## V

A case which had great effect on the development of the law relating to jurisdiction in the Territories is *Lamshed v. Lake*,[54] where the High Court considered the operation of sec. 10 of the Northern Territory (Administration) Act 1910 which provided

---

[53] In *Federal Capital Commission v. Laristan Building and Investment Co. Pty Ltd* (1929) 42 C.L.R. 582, 585, Dixon J. said 'It thus appears that three of the six members of the Court who took part in the decision of *Porter v. The King; ex parte Yee* treated s. 122 as insufficient to empower the Legislature to invest the High Court with original jurisdiction in respect of a Territory'.

[54] (1958) 99 C.L.R. 132.

that trade, commerce and intercourse between the Northern Territory and the States, whether by means of internal carriage or ocean navigation, shall be absolutely free. The High Court held that that section validly operated in the States so as to override any inconsistent State law. As a result, it was held that a South Australian Act which prohibited carriers from using certain roads without a licence did not apply to a carrier in the course of a journey from Adelaide to Alice Springs because of the application of sec. 109 of the Constitution.

The State of South Australia had argued that under sec. 122 the Commonwealth Parliament was in the position of a local legislature in and for the Territory with its power limited to the area of the Territory. Dixon C.J. replied—

> To my mind s. 122 is a power given to the national Parliament of Australia as such to make laws 'for', that is to say 'with respect to', the government of the Territory. The words 'the government of any territory' of course describe the subject matter of the power. But once the law is shown to be relevant to that subject matter it operates as a binding law of the Commonwealth wherever territorially the authority of the Commonwealth runs.[55]

The Chief Justice pointed out that, on any view, it was necessary in applying sec. 122 to refer to some other parts of the Constitution. The reference to 'The Parliament' in sec. 122, for example, necessarily referred to Parts I, II, III and IV of Chapter I. Sec. 122 deals with Territories accepted by and placed under the authority of the 'Commonwealth', which word must refer to the executive government described in Chapter II.

His Honour saw no reason why, for example, sec. 116 (the religion clause) should not apply to laws made under sec. 122 and why sec. 120 (dealing with the custody of offenders against the laws of the Commonwealth) should not include offences created under sec. 122. Dixon C.J. even considered that there were a number of powers in sec. 51 that were applicable to the Northern Territory, e.g., the powers with respect to 'postal, telegraphic, telephonic, and other like services', 'the naval and military defence of the Commonwealth', 'fisheries in Australian waters beyond territorial limits', 'banking, other than State banking; also State banking extending beyond the limits of the State concerned', 'naturalization and aliens' and the incidental power.

Similarly, it was thought that a law operating in the Northern Territory which interfered with the freedom of inter-State trade, e.g., the carriage of goods between Queensland and Western

55 (1958) 99 C.L.R. 132, 141.

Australia, might be obnoxious to sec. 92. On this reasoning, sec. 10 of the Commonwealth Act was held to operate validly in South Australia and to be a 'law of the Commonwealth' within the meaning of sec. 109.

Where did this decision leave the earlier cases? Were they to be explained merely in the inappropriateness to the Territories of the particular constitutional provisions involved? Dixon C.J. did not expressly approve of *R. v. Bernasconi* or the view that Chapter III was inapplicable to the Territories. However, he said 'since Chapter III has been considered to be concerned with jurisdiction in relation to that division of powers [between a central and local State legislature] (*R. v. Bernasconi*) it may be treated as inapplicable so that laws made mediately or immediately under sec. 122 are primarily not within the operation of the Chapter'.[56]

A number of questions raised by *Lamshed v. Lake* were considered and some of them resolved in *Spratt v. Hermes*[57] and *Capital T.V. and Appliances Pty Ltd v. Falconer*.[58] It was held unanimously in the former case that sec. 72 of the Constitution did not apply to a magistrate sitting as a Court of Petty Sessions in the Australian Capital Territory to hear a charge alleging an offence under the Post and Telegraph Act 1901. All the judges followed *R. v. Bernasconi* to the extent that they considered that the magistrate was not exercising the judicial power of the Commonwealth within the meaning of sec. 71 of the Constitution. In *Capital T.V. and Appliances Pty Ltd v. Falconer* it was held that the Supreme Court of the Australian Capital Territory was not a federal court or a court exercising federal jurisdiction within the meaning of sec. 73 of the Constitution and that there was therefore no appeal as of right from that Court to the High Court under sec. 73.

All the judges in *Spratt v. Hermes* professed to follow the earlier cases in reaching their decision, but in other respects their judgements varied considerably. Barwick C.J. and Windeyer J. emphasized their view that the Territories were all part of the Commonwealth and that any general limitation on Commonwealth power applied in respect of sec. 122 unless it was shown that the limitation concerned was intended only to deal with 'federal' powers, i.e., those in secs. 51 and 52 of the Constitution

56 ibid. 142.
57 (1965) 114 C.L.R. 226. See Zines: 'Laws for the Government of any Territory': Section 122 of the Constitution (1966) 2 F.L. Rev. 72.
58 (1971) 125 C.L.R. 591.

which operated in the States. Sec. 71 was in the latter category and the reference there to 'federal courts' made this clear. Menzies J. went further. He regarded the Territories not only as parts of the Commonwealth but also as within 'the federal system'. No distinction, he thought, could be made between the Commonwealth in its federal and non-federal aspects. Generally there was no reason for regarding any provision as inapplicable to the Territories; however, His Honour felt constrained by prior decisions to hold that courts created under sec. 122 need not comply with the provisions of sec. 72.

None of these three judges was, however, prepared to accept in its entirety the broad statement in *R. v. Bernasconi* that the whole of Chapter III was inapplicable to the Territories. The Chief Justice pointed to the fact that an *inter se* question under sec. 74 could, for example, arise out of the exercise of power under sec. 122 because a law made under the latter section was a 'law of the Commonwealth' within sec. 109, as had been held in *Lamshed v. Lake*. On the other hand, Kitto and Taylor JJ. appeared to accept the broad statement in *R. v. Bernasconi* and Kitto J. in particular considered that 'the Commonwealth' had a *prima facie* meaning of 'federated States'. The emphasis in his judgement was on the unlimited power given by sec. 122 and the inapplicability of most of the provisions in the Constitution to the exercise of power under that section.

The conclusion of all judges of the Court that a territorial court was not a 'federal court' was affirmed in *Capital T.V. and Appliances Pty Ltd v. Falconer*, where the Court held that sec. 73 (ii) did not apply to judgements of the Supreme Court of the Australian Capital Territory.

## VI

In the *Capital T.V. Case* the order of the Supreme Court from which an appeal was sought was a conviction under the City Area Leases Ordinance which operated only in the Territory and could have no other basis of legislative power than sec. 122. In *Spratt v. Hermes*, however, the Court of Petty Session of the Australian Capital Territory was concerned with a charge under the Post and Telegraph Act which applied throughout the Commonwealth. In *Lamshed v. Lake*, Dixon J. had mentioned the post and telegraph power in sec. 51 (v) of the Constitution as among those powers in sec. 51 that were applicable to both the States and the Territories. It was argued, therefore, that a court must have federal jurisdiction to deal with such a matter. This argument was rejected but the reasons given were not stated very clearly. Barwick C.J. said that, in relation to this question, he agreed with the reasons of Kitto J. for deciding that a non-Chapter III court might enforce in a Territory a law made 'upon a subject matter falling within sec. 51 of the Constitution and intended to operate throughout the Commonwealth'.[59] Kitto J.'s statement was that the Act operated as a law in the Territory by force of sec. 122 'whereas it operates in the Commonwealth proper by force of sec. 51 (v) . . .'.[60] Windeyer J. made a similar comment.

In the *Capital T.V. Case*, Barwick C.J. based the distinction between federal and territorial jurisdiction partly on the constitutional powers under which the legislation which constituted the subject matter of the court's jurisdiction was enacted. Thus, he said, that a territorial court's jurisdiction 'could not be related to the Post and Telegraph Act so far as it derives its legislative force from sec. 51 of the Constitution'.[61] None of the other judges relied on this distinction. His Honour could have been stating, as Mr Comans suggests,[62] that sec. 51 is not a source of power to make laws for the Territories. Mr Comans was of the opinion that in *Tau v. Commonwealth*[63] the Court might be considered to have implicitly adopted that view. In that case a joint judgement of the Court held that the Commonwealth had power under sec. 122 to make laws for the compulsory acquisition of property in New Guinea without providing just terms within the meaning of sec. 51 (xxxi) of the Constitution.

The view that sec. 51 does not apply in the Territories is inconsistent with the judgement of Dixon C.J. in *Lamshed v. Lake* with which three other judges approved. As pointed out above, His Honour referred to several paragraphs in sec. 51 which, in his view, were applicable to the Territories. In *Berwick Ltd v. Deputy Commissioner of Taxation*,[64] Mason J., in reply to a submission that sec. 51 (ii) (the taxation power) did not apply to Norfolk Island, said 'The response to this submission is that sec. 122 is not disjointed from other provisions in the Constitution, that it has been acknowledged in some instances at least that the

59 (1965) 114 C.L.R. 226, 248.
60 at p. 259.
61 (1971) 125 C.L.R. 591, 600.
62 (1971) 4 F.L. Rev. 218 at p. 219.
63 (1969) 119 C.L.R. 564.
64 (1976) 8 A.L.R. 580.

M

legislative power conferred by sec. 51 must apply to the Territories and that there is every reason for regarding sec. 51 (ii) as one such power'.[65] Barwick C.J., McTiernan and Murphy JJ. agreed with Mason J.'s judgement and Jacobs J. expressed similar views, namely, that the provisions of the Income Tax Assessment Act in issue in that case were laws with respect to taxation within the meaning of sec. 51 (ii) and laws for the government of the Territory within sec. 122. Barwick C.J., after agreeing with Mason J., expressly stated that, in his opinion, 'sec. 51 (ii) was exercisable with respect to the income of residents of the Territory'. It would seem, therefore, that Barwick C.J.'s view in relation to territorial courts is that they can be given jurisdiction in respect of laws referable to sec. 122 even though they are also referable to sec. 51, but they cannot have jurisdiction in relation to laws that cannot be authorized by sec. 122.

## VII

Other issues that have arisen are

(1) whether laws that are made under sec. 122 are 'laws made by the Parliament' within the meaning of sec. 76 (ii) so that jurisdiction in relation to matters arising under such laws can be conferred on the High Court or (by virtue of sec. 77 (ii) and (iii)) on another federal court or a State Court exercising federal jurisdiction;

(2) if so, whether any of the jurisdiction of a territorial court is outside the scope of sec. 76 (ii);

(3) if the answer to the previous question is yes, whether original jurisdiction can be conferred under sec. 122 on the High Court or another federal court.

(1) In *Waters v. Commonwealth*,[66] Fullagar J., with some difficulty and hesitation, held that *R. v. Bernasconi* operated to shut out the operation of secs. 75 and 76, and that any recourse to the original jurisdiction of the High Court in a Territory must be authorized, if it were at all possible, by legislation under sec. 122. In that case, a resident of the Northern Territory claimed a declaration, injunction and other relief against the Commonwealth for an allegedly wrongful imprisonment in the Northern Territory. On the footing that the Commonwealth was properly made a party to the action,[67] Fullagar J. held, on the authority

[65] at p. 583.
[66] (1951) 82 C.L.R. 188.
[67] at p. 190.

of *R. v. Bernasconi,* that he did not have jurisdiction by virtue of sec. 75 (iii). He pointed to the difficulties in reconciling the cases relating to the Territories, and concluded that he must follow *R. v. Bernasconi* as authority for the broad proposition that Chapter III had no application where the facts giving rise to a cause of action occurred within a Territory. This reading of the ratio of *Bernasconi's Case* had the apparent approval of Kriewaldt J. in *Re Ballard,* though in two cases in the High Court,[68] jurisdiction was assumed in circumstances similar to those in *Waters v. Commonwealth.* One of these cases was decided before *R. v. Bernasconi,* while in the other the jurisdictional issue was not raised.

In *Spratt v. Hermes* all the judges expressed disapproval of *Waters v. Commonwealth.* They all agreed that the jurisdiction that was conferred on the High Court by sec. 75 or which might be conferred under sec. 76 was not restricted to jurisdiction in respect of acts, persons or things outside the Territories. *Spratt v. Hermes* came to the High Court as a result of a case stated pursuant to sec. 13 of the Australian Capital Territory Supreme Court Act. It therefore involved the exercise of original jurisdiction. As a constitutional question had been raised, all the judges (except Menzies J.) rested the validity of sec. 13 in its application to the particular case on sec. 76 (i).[69] Only Menzies J. had regarded it as valid under sec. 76 (ii). While, therefore, the case is authority for the proposition that the High Court has jurisdiction under sec. 75 in respect of matters occurring in a Territory and can have conferred upon it original jurisdiction under sec. 76 in relation to a Territory, it did not establish whether a law made under sec. 122 comes within the description of sec. 76 (ii). The only judge to deal expressly with this question in the *Capital T.V. Case* was Menzies J., who repeated the view he had previously expressed in *Spratt v. Hermes.*

It was affirmed in *Spratt v. Hermes* and the *Capital T.V. Case* by most of the judges that a law made under sec. 122 was a 'law of the Commonwealth', although in respect of sec. 80, *R. v. Bernasconi* should be followed as a matter of precedent. For example, Barwick C.J. in *Spratt v. Hermes* said 'the expression "law of the Commonwealth" embraces every law *made by the Parliament* whatever the constitutional power under or by reference to which

---

[68] *Strachan v. Commonwealth* (1906) 4 C.L.R. 455; *Carey v. Commonwealth* (1921) 30 C.L.R. 132.

[69] As Mr Comans states, *op. cit.,* 224, n. 21, the reference to sec. 76 (ii) in the judgement of Kitto J., pp. 249-50, must be an error.

that law is made or supported'.[70] In *Anderson v. Eric Anderson Radio & T.V. Pty Ltd*,[71] there was an action for damages, in respect of a negligent act committed in the Australian Capital Territory, brought in the District Court of New South Wales. It was argued that an Australian Capital Territory Ordinance abolishing the defence of contributory negligence was binding on the State court. It was said that the right of action was given by a law made by the Parliament and the Court was therefore exercising federal jurisdiction under sec. 39 of the Judiciary Act. The High Court held that the cause of action derived from State law, but they did not suggest that an action to enforce a law under an Ordinance of a Territory was not a matter within sec. 76 (ii). Taylor J., however, said that this issue 'may be open to question'.[72] In view of the general tendency to restrict the decision in *R. v. Bernasconi* and to reject the broad statement in that case that Chapter III does not apply to the Territories, it is suggested that Acts made under sec. 122 are 'laws made by the Parliament' within the meaning of sec. 76 (ii) of the Constitution[73] and jurisdiction relating to matters arising under such laws may be conferred on a federal court.

(2) It was assumed in the *Capital T.V. Case* that the jurisdiction of the Australian Capital Territory Supreme Court went beyond that which could be conferred on a federal court. Sec. 11 of the Act provides—

> 11. The Supreme Court—
> (a) has, subject to this as to any other Act or to any Ordinance, in relation to the Territory, the same original jurisdiction, both civil and criminal, as the Supreme Court of the State of New South Wales had in relation to that State immediately before the first day of January, One thousand nine hundred and eleven;
> (b) has such jurisdiction, both civil and criminal, and whether original or otherwise, as is from time to time vested in the Supreme Court by Act or by Ordinance; and
> (c) has jurisdiction, with such exceptions and subject to such conditions as are provided by Act or by Ordinance, to hear and determine appeals from all judgments, convictions, orders, and sentences of inferior Courts having jurisdiction in the Territory.

McTiernan J. said that 'it is clear that the jurisdiction thereby

---

[70] at p. 247. Emphasis supplied. See also Windeyer J. at pp. 275-6.
[71] (1965) 114 C.L.R. 20.
[72] at p. 37.
[73] Comans: Federal and Territory Courts (1971) 4 F.L. Rev. 218, 226.

defined is not jurisdiction which the Parliament of the Commonwealth has power under sec. 77 (i) of the Constitution to define.
The matters which are mentioned in sec. 11 are not limited to
matters enumerated in sec. 75 or sec. 76 of the Constitution'.[74]
Similarly, Menzies J. (although expressly accepting that laws made
under sec. 122 came within the description in sec. 76 (ii)) envisaged that jurisdiction could be conferred on the High Court
or another federal court under sec. 122 that went beyond the
matters set out in secs. 75 and 76 of the Constitution.[75] Walsh J.
seemed also to assume that the jurisdiction of the court went
beyond those matters.[76] Gibbs J., after setting out sec. 11 of the
Australian Capital Territory Supreme Court Act, said 'There can
be no doubt that the only power to create a court with jurisdiction of that kind is that conferred on the Parliament by sec.
122'.[77]

If the Commonwealth, on accepting a Territory, did not legislate in respect of the law that was immediately to apply to the new
Territory, it may be that the common law would operate to
apply so much of the law existing before acceptance as was applicable to the new situation, by analogy to the rules relating to the
cession of territory. Litigation relating to rights arising under that
law could not be said to be matters 'arising under any laws made
by the Parliament' for the purposes of sec. 76 (ii): they would
arise under the common law. But in fact the Commonwealth
Parliament has always legislated in the case of each Territory to
make statutory provision to apply the law of a State or other
Territory or the law previously operating at a particular date,
subject to future alteration by Act or Ordinance. In the case of
the Australian Capital Territory, for example, sec. 6 (1) of the
Seat of Government Acceptance Act 1909 provides—

> (1) Subject to this Act, all laws in force in the Territory im-
> mediately before the proclaimed day shall, so far as applicable, con-
> tinue in force until other provision is made.

In *Federal Capital Commission v. Laristan Building and Investment Co. Pty Ltd,*[78] Dixon J. said in respect of the Australian
Capital Territory—

> It may well be that all claims of right arising under the law in
> force in the Territory come within this description [i.e. within sec.

[74] (1971) 125 C.L.R. 591, 601.
[75] at p. 604.
[76] at p. 619.
[77] at p. 626.
[78] (1929) 42 C.L.R. 582.

76 (ii)] because they arise indirectly as the result of the Seat of Government Acceptance Act 1909 (see sec. 6), and the Seat of Government (Administration) Act 1910 (see secs. 4 to 7 and 12).[79]

Comans is of the view that if there are some matters arising in relation to the Territories that do not fall within sec. 75 or sec. 76 they are very rare.[80] Once, however, it is accepted that laws made under sec. 122 come within the description in sec. 76 (ii), it is difficult to conceive of any matter that may be tried in a territorial court, in pursuance of jurisdiction of the sort conferred by sec. 11 (a) of the Australian Capital Territory Supreme Court Act, which does not arise under an Act of Parliament. All the common law (including private international law) operating in a Territory has a statutory basis.

(3) Nevertheless there is a contrary assumption behind an argument of those judges who accept that sec. 76 (ii) does or might include matters arising under laws made in pursuance of sec. 122. This relates to the difference of opinion as to whether original jurisdiction may be conferred on the High Court or another federal court under sec. 122. Quite clearly, if the jurisdiction of all the territorial courts comes within the concept of 'matters arising under any laws made by the Parliament' within sec. 76 (ii), it is unnecessary to resort to sec. 122 for the purpose of investing a federal court with such jurisdiction.

As indicated above,[81] it was established in *Porter's Case* that Parliament may legislate under sec. 122 to provide for an appeal from a territorial court to the High Court of Australia.

The constitutional warrant for the appeal was stated by the High Court in the *Boilermakers' Case*.[82] 'By an exercise of legislative power derived from sec. 122 an appeal may be given to this Court from a court of a Territory. That was decided in *Porter v. The King, ex parte Yee*. . . . This seems at first sight to be inconsistent with the decision in *In re Judiciary and Navigation Acts* which was that the jurisdiction of the High Court, as of other federal courts when created, arises wholly under Chapter III of the Constitution. The reconciliation depends upon the

[79] at p. 585.

[80] *op. cit.*, p. 221.

[81] See pp. 152-3 *ante*.

[82] (1956) 94 C.L.R. 254, 290. The Privy Council in the *Boilermakers' Case* [1957] A.C. 288, 297, while acknowledging the divisions in the High Court in *Porter's Case* found the explanation of the right of appeal quite simple. 'There appears to be no reason why the Parliament having plenary power under section 122, should not invest the High Court or any other court with appellate jurisdiction from the courts of the territories. The legislative power in respect of the territories is a disparate non-federal matter.'

view which the majority adopted that the exclusive or exhaustive character of the provisions of that chapter describing the judicature and its functions has reference only to the federal system of which the Territories do not form a part.'

The view of the majority in *Porter's Case* is now beyond challenge.[83] However, in that case the Court was evenly divided on the question whether original jurisdiction could be conferred on the High Court under sec. 122. This was brought about by the fact that Higgins J. disagreed with the rest of the majority judges as to the effect of *In re Judiciary and Navigation Acts*.[84] Whereas the other majority judges based their judgements on the ground that Chapter III was not applicable to the Territories, Higgins J. distinguished *In re Judiciary and Navigation Acts* by declaring that it was binding only in respect of the original, and not the appellate, jurisdiction of the High Court. He observed that secs. 75 and 76 were so drafted as to carry the implication that the matters therein specified were the only matters in which original jurisdiction was or could be conferred on the High Court. Sec. 73 was differently drafted and simply declared that the Court should have jurisdiction to hear appeals from specified courts. 'The form of expression used is "the High Court shall have jurisdiction" etc., just as if it were "the High Court shall have a marshal"; this would not forbid other officers appointed under some other power.'[85] It was likewise competent to Parliament under sec. 122 to provide for the grant of additional appellate jurisdiction to the High Court from territorial courts.

In *Spratt v. Hermes* all the judges agreed that sec. 13 of the Australian Capital Territory Supreme Court Act (providing for a case stated to the High Court) could be read down to refer only to matters within secs. 75 and 76 of the Constitution. Nevertheless, the judges (assuming that sec. 13 conferred jurisdiction that went beyond those provisions) expressed their views whether original jurisdiction could be conferred on the High Court under sec. 122. Barwick C.J., Kitto and Menzies JJ. considered such jurisdiction could be conferred. Taylor, Windeyer and Owen JJ. took the opposite view. The Court was again evenly divided. In the *Capital T.V. Case* Menzies J. reiterated his earlier view and Walsh and Gibbs JJ. both stated that it might be possible under

[83] See *Chow Hung Ching v. The King* (1948) 77 C.L.R. 449, 475. Cf. *Musgrave v. Commonwealth* (1937) 57 C.L.R. 514, 532 *per* Latham C.J. and *Spratt v. Hermes* (1965) 114 C.L.R. 226.

[84] (1921) 29 C.L.R. 257.

[85] at p. 446.

sec. 122 to confer original jurisdiction on the High Court or another federal court.

It is difficult to understand why appellate and original jurisdiction should be treated differently. The reasoning of Higgins J. in *Porter v. The King* is, with respect, not very persuasive. It seems that the maxim *expressio unius exclusio alterius* should apply, if at all, to cases of original jurisdiction and appellate jurisdiction. It might be thought that the clear implication in sec. 73 is that it exhaustively marks out the appellate jurisdiction of the High Court. Windeyer J., in *Spratt v. Hermes*, expressed this view in the following terms: 'The distinction between appellate and original jurisdiction may seem slender if it is based on nothing more than the difference in the language between sec. 73 and secs. 75 and 76; for in each case the language of the grant of jurisdiction in the cases mentioned may seem to carry a negative implication'.[86] (However, he did go on to rely partly on the difference in language, 'slight though it is'.) The reasoning that was used to support appellate jurisdiction in the High Court was that Chapter III did not apply to the Territories and that the source of constitutional authority was to be discovered in sec. 122. As a matter of principle, it is difficult to see why that reasoning does not apply equally to original jurisdiction. This was in fact accepted by Barwick C.J., Kitto and Menzies JJ. in *Spratt v. Hermes*. The reasons given by Taylor, Windeyer and Owen JJ. for the opposite view varied. Taylor J. relied on 'the balance of authority'[87] and thought that view should be accepted. Owen J. considered that the justification for the distinction was to be found in Higgins J.'s judgement in *Porter's Case*.[88] Windeyer J. supported the appellate jurisdiction on the basis that 'The special position and function of this Court under the Constitution require that it should be able to declare the law for all courts that are within the governance of Australia'.[89] However, His Honour did not think that the same considerations applied in the case of original jurisdiction. He referred to the distinction as a 'workable anomaly'.

If, as suggested above, all or most matters that come before a territorial court are within sec. 76 (ii) of the Constitution, it may be that the issue of whether additional original jurisdiction may be conferred on the High Court or another federal court is,

[86] (1965) 114 C.L.R. 226, 277.
[87] at p. 265.
[88] at p. 279.
[89] at p. 277.

as Comans says, 'largely academic'[90] and that it will be necessary
to rely on sec. 122 only for the purposes of the appellate jurisdiction of the High Court. If, however, the contrary view is taken,
the reasoning of Barwick C.J., Kitto and Menzies JJ. is more
convincing and it should be open to Parliament to create a
federal court for the exercise of jurisdiction in a Territory if it
so desires.

## VIII

It was argued in the *Capital T.V. Case* that, although a territorial court is not a federal court, it may be invested with federal
jurisdiction. Sec. 71 of the Constitution vests the judicial power of
the Commonwealth in the High Court, such other federal courts
as the Parliament creates, and in such other courts as it invests
with federal jurisdiction. Sec. 73 (ii) authorizes appeals to the
High Court from courts exercising federal jurisdiction. Neither
section explicitly states that the sole repositories of vested federal
jurisdiction are *State* courts. Sec. 77 (iii) authorizes the investment
of *State* courts with federal jurisdiction in respect of the matters
enumerated in secs. 75 and 76.

In *Porter v. The King*,[91] Isaacs J. strongly supported the view
that a territorial court did not exercise federal jurisdiction. This
view was adopted by all the judges in the *Capital T.V. Case*. In
that case it was argued that, if the court derives its authority to
adjudicate from a law of the Commonwealth, its jurisdiction is
federal within the meaning of sec. 73. It was pointed out that
the Court had since *Lamshed v. Lake*[92] departed from the view
derived from *R. v. Bernasconi* that a law made under sec. 122 was
not for any purpose a 'law of the Commonwealth'. On this argument, a territorial court, though not a 'federal court' would be a
court exercising federal jurisdiction.

This argument was rejected. *R. v. Bernasconi* was followed to
the extent that it was held that federal jurisdiction did not mean
jurisdiction derived from any law made by the Parliament, but
only jurisdiction which was exercised by virtue of authority conferred under Chapter III.

*R. v. Bernasconi* has been much weakened as an authority since
*Lamshed v. Lake*. It is now clear that it cannot be said that for
all purposes Chapter III does not apply in respect of acts, persons

---

90 *op. cit.*, at p. 226.
91 (1926) 37 C.L.R. 432, 440.
92 (1958) 99 C.L.R. 132.

or things in the Territories. As a result of *Spratt v. Hermes*, it certainly does apply as far as secs. 75 and 76 are concerned and the same is probably true of secs. 74 and 78.[93] The force of precedent, however, was accepted in that case to the extent that a court of the Australian Capital Territory was not to be regarded as a 'federal court' within sec. 71 or one of 'the other courts created by the Parliament' within sec. 72. As a result, it is to be expected that there will be some anomalies in this area; however, it is suggested that it would be carrying a tolerance for inconsistency too far to argue that, on the one hand, a territorial court is not a 'federal court' *because* it is created outside Chapter III, but that its jurisdiction is 'federal' *despite* the fact that it is conferred by authority outside Chapter III. To put it around the other way, how could it be sensibly argued that the terms of office of the judges of the territorial court do not have to comply with sec. 72 even though they are judges of 'courts created by the Parliament', but that their jurisdiction is federal because it derives from a law made by Parliament? In any case, as a result of the *Capital T.V. Case*, it is clear that territorial courts are neither federal courts nor courts exercising federal jurisdiction.

The question then arises, what is the basis for determining whether a court is a territorial or federal court? It is suggested above[94] that sec. 51 can provide a source of power for making laws operating in a Territory. Nevertheless, it is clear that a territorial court is not prevented from hearing and determining a matter arising under a law merely because the law is referable to sec. 51 as well as to sec. 122. It has also been argued that jurisdiction in relation to a matter arising under a law made under sec. 122 comes within sec. 76 (ii) and therefore can be conferred on a federal court as federal jurisdiction. Further, assuming that there is jurisdiction that may be conferred under sec. 122 that does not come within sec. 76 (ii), it has been suggested above that it can be conferred on the High Court or other federal courts. How, therefore, does one determine whether a court created by Parliament with jurisdiction in relation to a Territory is a territorial court or a federal court?

Menzies J., who accepted all the above propositions, was of the view that the answer to this question depended upon legislative intention to be derived from the whole of the law establishing the court.[95] The main factors that indicated an intention to create

---

93 *Spratt v. Hermes* (1965) 114 C.L.R. 226 at pp. 245-6.
94 See pp. 156-8 *ante*.
95 (1971) 125 C.L.R. 591 at p. 603.

the Australian Capital Territory Supreme Court under sec. 122 as a territorial court were that it was constituted as a 'Supreme Court of the Territory', its jurisdiction was defined in sec. 11 (i) as being 'in relation to the Territory' and provision was made for the service of writs 'out of the jurisdiction of the Court'. The fact that the Act might have been construed as conferring life tenure on the judges of the court[96] did not outweigh the above factors. Walsh J., while regarding tenure as an important consideration, relied on the uncertainty of the operation of the provisions in the Act in this respect and the fact that before the Act was altered there were provisions for the appointment of acting judges for a term. Gibbs J., on the other hand, regarded it as 'unprofitable'[97] to consider whether the judges had life tenure as there was nothing to stop judges of territorial courts being appointed for life. While His Honour accepted that a federal court might have conferred upon it, under sec. 122, jurisdiction in respect of a Territory, he said, after reciting sec. 11 of the Australian Capital Territory Supreme Court Act, 'There can be no doubt that the only power to create a court with jurisdiction of that kind is that conferred on the Parliament by sec. 122'.[98] In view of His Honour's earlier assumption that jurisdiction under sec. 122 may be conferred on a federal court, this statement is difficult to understand. Comans suggests that he may have considered that a federal court must have *some* jurisdiction capable of falling within sec. 75 or sec. 76.[99] If so, the test is obviously fraught with uncertainty, raising questions of degree with no criterion of even the most general kind.

Nevertheless, these judges looked to the source of power to create the court. The nature of the court can only be determined by, *inter alia*, looking at its jurisdiction. If it is seen solely (or perhaps primarily) as a court in relation to a Territory, it will be regarded as being created under sec. 122 and as being therefore a territorial court.

Barwick C.J. referred to the 'other federal courts of which sec. 71 speaks' as 'those which are called into being by, and empowered to exercise jurisdiction under, laws made in pursuance of secs. 51 and 52'.[100] Mr Comans has stated that the view of Barwick C.J. differs from that of Menzies, Walsh and Gibbs JJ.

---

96 That question was not resolved.
97 at p. 625.
98 at p. 626.
99 *op. cit.*, at pp. 218-9.
100 at p. 599.

in that the former looks to the power supporting the legislation 'in relation to which the jurisdiction is exercised' while the latter looked to the power by virtue of which the jurisdiction was conferred.[101] It seems, however, from the passage from Barwick C.J.'s judgement referred to above that he is referring to the power to create ('call into being') the court and to the conferral of jurisdiction ('empowered to exercise jurisdiction') and to that extent his view is similar to that of the other judges.[102] The Chief Justice did give his opinion, however, that a territorial court could not exercise jurisdiction in matters arising under a law made under sec. 51 or sec. 52. It has been suggested above that this means laws which are not also authorized by sec. 122. This issue is considered below.

<h1 style="text-align:center">IX</h1>

It is clear that a territorial court is one which is created, and has jurisdiction conferred on it, under sec. 122 of the Constitution. If it has jurisdiction that cannot be supported by sec. 122, it will be either a federal court (the judges of which must be appointed in accordance with sec. 72) or a territorial court, part of the jurisdiction of which is not validly conferred. When is jurisdiction conferred 'in relation to a Territory' and therefore authorized by sec. 122?

Under general law, the jurisdiction of a court in relation to actions *in personam* does not depend on the subject matter but upon the amenability of the defendant to the writ of the court. Under common law, the writ does not run beyond the limits of the territorial jurisdiction of the court.[103] The jurisdiction of the Supreme Court of a State therefore extends to all cases (unless excepted by a valid Act) where a defendant is present in the State, whatever the subject matter of the suit. In the light of *Spratt v. Hermes* and the *Capital T.V. Case* there is, subject to one qualification mentioned below, little doubt that a similar jurisdiction conferred on a territorial court in relation to a Territory is

---

[101] *op. cit.*, at p. 222.

[102] Barwick C.J., however, is more explicit as to the origin of the power to create federal courts. It is difficult to see how this power could, in all cases, arise from sec. 51 or sec. 52 unless it be the incidental power in sec. 51 (xxxix). Quite a number of heads of federal jurisdiction do not relate to matters arising under laws made by the Parliament. It is established also that the power to confer federal jurisdiction can only come from sec. 77: *Collins v. Charles Marshall Pty Ltd* (1955) 92 C.L.R. 529; *In re Judiciary and Navigation Acts* (1921) 29 C.L.R. 257, 265.

[103] *Laurie v. Carroll* (1958) 98 C.L.R. 310.

within power conferred by sec. 122 of the Constitution. Sec. 11 (a) of the Australian Capital Territory Supreme Court Act confers on that Court in relation to the Australian Capital Territory 'the same original jurisdiction . . . as the Supreme Court of the State of New South Wales had in relation to that State immediately before the first of January 1911'. In the *Capital T.V. Case* all the judges considered that this conferral of jurisdiction was valid under sec. 122. In that case, however, Barwick C.J. stated that the Australian Capital Territory Supreme Court, being a territorial court, could not have jurisdiction 'related to the Post and Telegraph Act so far as it derives its legislative force from sec. 51 of the Constitution'. This would seem to suggest that in the case of a territorial court the mere presence or even residence of the defendant in the Territory is not sufficient if the subject matter of the suit concerned the operation of a federal law outside the Territory. Mr Comans gives an example of an action in a territorial court for the recovery of income tax owing by a resident of the Territory as income derived in a State while he was a resident of that State.[104] Many other examples could be given in relation to other Commonwealth laws.

In principle, there is no justification for treating the jurisdiction of territorial courts in this respect in a manner different from State courts. If laws providing for the jurisdiction of State courts are for 'the peace, order and good government' of the State, a law providing for a similar jurisdiction in relation to a Territory must be for 'the government of the Territory'.

Difficult issues, however, arise because, while the authority of a State only operates throughout the area of the State, it is the Commonwealth that is the 'sovereign' in relation to a Territory and a law for the government of a Territory 'operates as a binding law of the Commonwealth wherever territorially the authority of the Commonwealth runs'.[105]

In *Cotter v. Workman*[106] Fox J., in the Supreme Court of the Australian Capital Territory, considered the validity and effect of a rule of court which provided that writs issued out of the Court might be served anywhere in the Commonwealth without leave. It had been previously held by Gibbs J. in *Cope Allman (Australia) Ltd v. Celermajer*[107] that, as a result of these provisions, the Court had jurisdiction if the writ had been served on

---

104 *op. cit.*, at p. 228.
105 *Lamshed v. Lake* (1958) 99 C.L.R. 132, 141.
106 (1972) 20 F.L.R. 318.
107 (1968) 11 F.L.R. 488.

the defendant anywhere in the Commonwealth, even though the only connection with the Australian Capital Territory in that case was that a deed, out of which an action arose, was executed in Canberra. His Honour did not regard even that slight connection with the Territory as material. Fox J. held that the extension of the jurisdiction of the Court which followed from the provision for service was invalid as not authorized by sec. 122. Assuming that it was intended that any order of the court was to have effect throughout Australia, it is submitted, with respect, that the judge was clearly correct in holding that the commencement of an action by a plaintiff in a territorial court can hardly in itself provide a sufficient nexus with the Territory to constitute a provision purporting to confer such jurisdiction a law 'for the government' of the Territory. His Honour further held that 'when rules provide for service outside the Territory, the situations in which this can be done must be defined by the rules so that in each case there will exist a sufficient connection with the Territory'.

Mr Comans has suggested that the provisions for service outside the Territory without any other connection with the Territory might be valid if the court's order was not enforceable outside the Territory. It is in this way that State provisions for service outside the jurisdiction are upheld. The jurisdiction is referred to as 'assumed jurisdiction' and the orders given under that jurisdiction are not enforceable outside the State. It was similarly argued in *Cotter v. Workman* that the rules for service throughout the Commonwealth were valid, but the order was enforceable only in the Australian Capital Territory. Fox J. held that, in the light of the State and Territorial Laws and Records Recognition Act 1901 and Part IV of the Service and Execution of Process Act 1901, it was unlikely that any such result was intended. He went further, however, and said that in any case 'a legislative power which is limited by reference to territorial considerations cannot be the source of an assumed jurisdiction which does not satisfy those territorial limitations'. It is suggested that the considerations involved in the case of a State and a Territory are in this respect identical. In each case there must be a sufficient connection with the State or Territory concerned. If the 'assumed jurisdiction' is valid in the case of a State court—and it would appear that it is[108]—then it is valid in the case of a territorial court. As Barwick C.J. said in *Minister for Justice of Western Australia v. Australian National Airlines Commission*, 'the test of the validity of such a

108 *Ashbury v. Ellis* [1893] A.C. 339.

law [i.e. one made under sec. 122] must be whether the law is a law for the peace, order and good government of the Territory—treating the word "for" in sec. 122 as implying the concepts expressed in that traditional formula'.[109]

The question, however, as to what degree of connection is required to ensure the enforceability of an order of a territorial court outside the Territory is more uncertain. In recent times, in Commonwealth legislation operating throughout the Commonwealth, the Parliament has been careful to limit the jurisdiction of territorial courts so as to ensure an adequate nexus with the Territory. Thus, in the Bankruptcy Act 1966 an order of the Supreme Court of the Northern Territory has effect throughout the Commonwealth, but the Court has jurisdiction only if the facts of the case meet certain specified criteria relating to a connection with the Territory.[110] The Income Tax Assessment Amendment (Jurisdiction of Courts) Act 1976 limits the jurisdiction of the Supreme Court of the Australian Capital Territory and the Northern Territory to cases where the taxpayer[111] at the time of the suit or during part of the financial year in question was ordinarily resident in the Territory. Similar limitations on the jurisdiction of territorial courts were made in 1976 to the Trade Marks Act 1955 (sec. 112) and the Patents Act 1952 (sec. 146).[112]

There are, however, several Commonwealth Acts which purport to confer jurisdiction on territorial courts without requiring any specific connection with the Territory concerned. Sec. 11 (b) of the Australian Capital Territory Supreme Court Act, for example, provides that the Court 'has such jurisdiction, both civil and criminal, and whether original or otherwise, as is from time to time vested in the Supreme Court by Act or by Ordinance'. In deciding that the jurisdiction of the Australian Capital Territory Supreme Court was authorized by sec. 122 of the Constitution, the Court in the *Capital T.V. Case* did not give any relevant consideration to this provision. As the Australian Capital Territory Supreme Court has been held to be validly created under sec. 122, it is to be assumed that sec. 11 (b) will be 'read down' to include only jurisdiction that is authorized by sec. 122. Some of the jurisdiction that Commonwealth Acts have attempted

---

109 (1977) 12 A.L.R. 17, 21.
110 In respect of the earlier Act which had no such limitations on jurisdiction, see *Re Ballard, ex parte Wright* (1955) 1 F.L.R. 473 and Comans, *op. cit.*, at p. 231.
111 There are special provisions where the taxpayer is a trustee.
112 See also Foreign Takeovers Act 1975, secs. 34 (2) and 35 (9).

to confer may go beyond that constitutional provision, for example, the Crimes Act 1914, the Crimes (Aircraft) Act 1963, the Fisheries Act 1952, the Statutory Declarations Act 1959 and the Continental Shelf (Living Natural Resources) Act 1968, which purport to confer jurisdiction on territorial courts in respect of offences committed beyond the limits of the Commonwealth.[113] Unless these provisions can somehow 'be read down' under sec. 15A of the Acts Interpretation Act (and that is very doubtful), it would appear that they are invalid.

## X

The baroque complexities and many uncertainties associated with courts and jurisdiction in the Territories have come about partly as a result of conflicting theories and partly by a desire of the judges not to disturb earlier decisions. The general approach in *R. v. Bernasconi*, with its emphasis on the separation of the Territories from the Commonwealth and of sec. 122 from the rest of the Constitution, is fundamentally opposed to the approach of *Lamshed v. Lake*, which attacked this theory and underlined the fact that there is but one Commonwealth and that sec. 122 was meaningless unless read with other provisions of the Constitution. The *Bernasconi* view, however, survives at any rate to the extent that the term of office of Territorial judges need not comply with sec. 72 and there is no appeal under sec. 73 from judgements of territorial courts. Now that sec. 72 of the Constitution has been amended so that judges can be appointed until they attain 70 years of age or, in the case of federal courts other than the High Court, until a younger age if Parliament so provides, the policy arguments for treating territorial courts differently from other federal courts are not great and are far outweighed by the difficulties that face the Commonwealth where general Commonwealth laws operating throughout Australia and beyond are concerned. If the general approach of Menzies J. in the *Capital T.V. Case* is adopted, and it has been suggested above that it is the correct approach, it seems that the better course would be for the Commonwealth to declare an intention that the Supreme Courts of the Territories at any rate should be federal courts. It has been suggested that the Commonwealth would be unlikely to adopt that course as regards inferior courts,[114] but, as a result of the amendment of sec. 72, there is now no reason for that reluctance.

113 Comans, *op. cit.*, at p. 220.
114 ibid. at p. 235.

For such an approach to be followed, however, it is necessary that the High Court hold that original jurisdiction may under sec. 122 be conferred on a federal court other than the High Court (or, alternatively, that all the jurisdiction exercisable in relation to a Territory comes within the description in sec. 76 (ii) of matters arising under laws made by Parliament). Mr Comans has suggested that these propositions 'are not yet sufficiently supported by authority to make [the course suggested] safe'.[115] It is to be hoped that the Court will give Parliament the opportunity of adopting the proposed approach.

[115] ibid.

N

# = 5 =

## *The Autochthonous Expedient: The Investment of State Courts with Federal Jurisdiction*

### I

SEC. 71 of the Constitution vests the judicial power of the Commonwealth in the High Court, in such other federal courts as the Parliament creates, and in such other courts as it invests with federal jurisdiction. Although the section does not specifically name State courts as repositories of federal jurisdiction, it is settled that the only alternatives open to the Parliament are to create federal courts or to invest State courts with federal jurisdiction. As Griffiths C.J. said in the *Inter-State Commission Case*,[1] 'the provisions of sec. 71 are complete and exclusive and there cannot be a third class of courts which are neither Federal courts nor State courts invested with Federal jurisdiction.' This is confirmed by sec. 77 which, as we have seen, in sub-sec. (i) authorizes the legislative definition of the jurisdiction of any federal court other than the High Court. Sec. 77 (ii) provides for the definition of the extent to which the jurisdiction of any federal court shall be exclusive of that which belongs to or is invested in State courts, while sec. 77 (iii) authorizes the investment of any court of a State with federal jurisdiction.[2]

The use of State courts as repositories of federal jurisdiction was described by the High Court as an 'autochthonous expedient',[3] as indigenous or native to the soil. It has no counterpart in the American Constitution.

In the United States, Congress has on many occasions vested concurrently the enforcement of federal rights in State and federal courts. The Supreme Court of the United States has upheld the obligation of the State courts to enforce those rights where they are courts of general jurisdiction or their jurisdiction

---

[1] *New South Wales v. Commonwealth* (1915) 20 C.L.R. 54, 62.

[2] It has been held that a territorial court cannot exercise federal jurisdiction. *Capital T.V. and Appliances Pty Ltd v. Falconer* (1971) 125 C.L.R. 591.

[3] *Boilermakers' Case* (1956) 94 C.L.R. 254, 268.

is otherwise adequate under State law.[4] That does not mean,
however, that the State courts exercise federal jurisdiction in
the sense that that expression is used in sec. 77 (iii) of the Commonwealth Constitution nor does it enable Congress to legislate
in the manner that the Commonwealth Parliament has done in,
for example, sec. 39 of the Judiciary Act.[5]

We have seen[6] that in the American Constitutional Convention
arguments were advanced in favour of employing State courts as
courts of *general* original jurisdiction, so as to avoid any necessity
for the creation of inferior federal courts, but that these arguments failed to carry.

That a different view should have prevailed in Australia is
not surprising. There was no comparable apprehension of the
dangers which lurked in a federal court structure and the most
ardent Australian admirers of the American judicature accepted
a modification of that system whereby the High Court was
fashioned as a general court of appeal. The device of investing
State courts with federal jurisdiction was economical; as Bailey
has observed 'the burden which such a system (that is, the creation
of a hierarchy of federal tribunals) would have imposed on the
small population of Australia gave rise to the expedient adopted
in s. 77 (iii), of authorizing the Commonwealth Parliament to
make use for federal purposes of the existing judicial organization of the States, just as the Imperial Parliament made use of it
for Admiralty purposes'.[7] Economy alone does not explain the
departure from American precedent, for the United States was
small in population and resources in 1787; but the desire for
economy linked to a more willing acceptance of a unified judicial
system furnish an adequate explanation. This is underlined by
the comments of Quick and Garran in 1900.[8] The large original
and potentially original jurisdiction of the High Court, marked
out in secs. 75 and 76 of the Constitution, can most sensibly be

---

[4] Constitution of the United States of America: Analysis and Interpretation
(Eds. Small & Jayson, 1964) 725-7; Hart and Wechsler: The Federal Courts
and the Federal System (1953) 391-9.

[5] *Felton v. Mulligan* (1971) 124 C.L.R. 367, 393-4.

[6] See p. 105 *ante.*

[7] The Federal Jurisdiction of State Courts (1940) 2 *Res Judicatae,* 109.
See also *Commonwealth v. Limerick Steamship Co. Ltd, Commonwealth v.
Kidman* (1924) 35 C.L.R. 69, 90, *per* Isaacs and Rich JJ. where the power
conferred by sec. 77 (iii) is said to be 'obviously a very convenient means of
avoiding the multiplicity and expense of legal tribunals'.

[8] The Annotated Constitution of the Australian Commonwealth (1900) at
p. 804.

explained on the assumption that the Founding Fathers believed that the High Court would in all probability be the only general federal court. It is difficult otherwise to account for the translation of what in the American Constitution are matters of federal jurisdiction, though not for the most part matters within the original jurisdiction of the Supreme Court of the United States, into matters of original jurisdiction, actual or potential, of the High Court of Australia.[9]

There is a change of language from sec. 77 (i) to sec. 77 (iii) of the Constitution. The Parliament may *define* the jurisdiction of federal courts, while it may *invest* State courts with federal jurisdiction. There is a possible argument that 'definition' has a broader sweep than 'investment', in the sense that the exercise of the power to define carries with it power to regulate the structure of appeals, whereas investment suggests rather that the State courts must be taken as they are found, leaving the system of appeals to be regulated by State law. This is a matter of practical importance, because sec. 39 of the Judiciary Act, which is the most general exercise of the powers conferred by sec. 77 (iii), purports to regulate the system of appeals from State courts invested with federal jurisdiction. This, and other problems arising from sec. 39 of the Judiciary Act, will be considered more fully later, but it is clear on the authorities that there is no significance in the change of language from sec. 77 (i) to 77 (iii).[10] The federal jurisdiction which may be conferred on federal courts and on State courts also includes original and appellate jurisdiction, even though the subject-matters of such a grant must be within the nine matters of original or potential original jurisdiction of the High Court.[11]

## II

Apart from any investment of State courts with federal jurisdiction, it is clear that the State courts already possessed jurisdiction in respect of a number of matters within secs. 75 and 76. For example, the State courts had jurisdiction in matters between residents of different States; if the rules of service were satisfied, it was within the normal competence of a State court to try a case involving a Victorian plaintiff and a New South Wales de-

9 See p. 3 *ante.*

10 *Lorenzo v. Carey* (1921) 29 C.L.R. 243; *Commonwealth v. Limerick Steamship Co. Ltd* (1924) 35 C.L.R. 69, 89-93, 115-6; *Commonwealth v. Bardsley* (1926) 37 C.L.R. 393, 407-9. See Bailey, *op. cit. ante* note 7 at p. 184.

11 *Ah Yick v. Lehmert* (1905) 2 C.L.R. 593. See pp. 130-1 *ante.*

fendant. The operation of the Commonwealth Constitution intruded a new element, and sec. 5 of the Constitution Act provided that the Constitution and all laws made by the Parliament under the Constitution should be binding on the courts, judges and people of every State and every part of the Commonwealth notwithstanding anything in the laws of any State. This meant that, apart from any special enactment, a State court would have jurisdiction in a matter arising under the Constitution or involving its interpretation, in matters arising under laws made by the Parliament, and that the Commonwealth might come into the State courts as a plaintiff—all without any necessity for a grant of federal jurisdiction. The fact that a State court assumes jurisdiction on service under the Service and Execution of Process Act, a Commonwealth statute, does not mean that it is therefore exercising *federal* jurisdiction[12] and it is a misunderstanding of the notion of federal jurisdiction to describe the process by which a State court gives effect to rights arising under federal statutes in terms that 'when such rights are adjudicated upon, it is, in a sense, Federal jurisdiction which is being exercised'.[13] The confusion arises from an identification of federal jurisdiction with the application of federal law; it is clear that what determines whether there is an exercise of federal jurisdiction by a State court is the source of the *grant* of jurisdiction, not the source of the *law* being applied. 'To confer federal jurisdiction in a class of matters upon a State court is therefore not, if no more be added, to change the law which the court is to enforce in adjudicating upon such matters; it is merely to provide a different basis of authority to enforce the same law.'[14]

It appears, however, that there were matters, attendant upon the establishment of the Commonwealth, which State courts were not competent to entertain in the absence of an express grant of jurisdiction. In its State jurisdiction, a State court could not assume jurisdiction in a matter in which the Commonwealth was a defendant[15] and in *Ex parte Goldring*[16] it was held that the State

---

[12] See *A. Patkin and Co. Pty Ltd v. Censor and Hyman* [1949] A.L.R. 557; *Alba Petroleum Co. of Australia Pty Ltd v. Griffiths* [1951] V.L.R. 185.

[13] *Ex parte Australian Timber Workers' Union; Veneer Co. Ltd.* (1937) 37 S.R. (N.S.W.) 52, *per* Jordan C.J.

[14] *Anderson v. Eric Anderson Radio & T.V. Pty Ltd* (1965) 114 C.L.R. 20, 30.

[15] *Commonwealth v. Limerick Steamship Co. Ltd* (1924) 35 C.L.R. 69; *Commonwealth v. Bardsley* (1926) 37 C.L.R. 393, 405; Moore, Commonwealth of Australia (2nd ed., 1910) at pp. 212-3; Bailey, *op. cit. ante* note 7 at p. 111.

[16] (1903) 3 S.R. (N.S.W.) 260.

court had no power to issue *mandamus* or other order to command or prohibit a federal officer in the absence of any affirmative grant of jurisdiction by the Commonwealth Parliament. Within the framework of the Commonwealth Constitution, this means that any such grant must depend on an investment of federal jurisdiction pursuant to sec. 77 (iii). There is a qualified investment of federal jurisdiction in State courts in matters in which the Commonwealth is a defendant, by secs. 39 and 56 of the Judiciary Act, and these provisions are the federal source of the jurisdiction of State courts in such matters. Sec. 38 of the Judiciary Act defines the jurisdiction of the High Court to issue prohibition and *mandamus* against an officer of the Commonwealth as exclusive of that of the State courts. Sec. 9 (1) of the Administrative Decisions (Judicial Review) Act 1977 provides:

> 9 (1) Notwithstanding anything contained in any Act other than this Act, a court of a State does not have jurisdiction to review—
> (a)  a decision to which this Act applies;
> (b)  conduct that has been, is being, or is proposed to be, engaged in for the purpose of making a decision to which this Act applies; or
> (c)  a failure to make a decision to which this Act applies; or
> (d)  any other decision given, or any order made, by an officer of the Commonwealth or any other conduct that has been, is being, or is proposed to be, engaged in by an officer of the Commonwealth, including a decision, order or conduct given, made or engaged in, as the case may be, in the exercise of judicial power.

Sub-section (2) gives 'officer of the Commonwealth' the same meaning as in sec. 75 (v) of the Constitution and defines 'review' to mean review by way of (a) the grant of an injunction; (b) the grant of a prerogative or statutory writ (other than a writ of *habeas corpus*) or the making of orders of the same nature or effect; or (c) the making of a declaratory order.

With the exception of *habeas corpus*, therefore, it seems that State courts have no jurisdiction to issue any of the remedies mentioned in relation to administrative or judicial action by Commonwealth officers or judges or otherwise made under any Commonwealth law.

## III

A question arises as to the 'character' of State courts invested with federal jurisdiction. Secs. 71 and 77 draw a definite distinction between federal courts and courts invested with federal jurisdiction. It is clear therefore that federally invested State courts cannot properly be described as federal courts within the Australian constitutional framework. The answer to the further question whether State courts invested with federal jurisdiction are to be regarded as part of the 'Federal Judicature' is less certain. As Wynes points out[17] the answer is of more than academic interest, as it may affect the exercise of Commonwealth legislative power under sec. 51 (xxxix), which authorizes the making of laws with respect to matters incidental to the execution of any power vested by the Constitution in the Parliament, the executive government or *in the Federal Judicature* or in any department or officer of the Commonwealth. A conclusion that State courts invested with federal jurisdiction are not part of the federal judicature does not altogether deny the operation of sec. 51 (xxxix), for that power may and, as the cases establish, does operate upon the exercise of the legislative power which sec. 77 (iii) itself confers. The cases yield no clear indication of the character of State courts invested with federal jurisdiction.

In *R. v. Murray and Cormie*[18] Isaacs J. observed that the Constitution draws the clearest distinction between federal and State courts, and that while it enables the Parliament to utilize the judicial services of State courts, it recognizes in 'the most pronounced and unequivocal way that they remain state courts'. But in *Le Mesurier v. Connor*,[19] Isaacs J., dissenting, spoke of State courts invested with federal jurisdiction as '*pro hac vice*, a component part of the Federal Judicature'. In that case the majority, Knox C.J., Rich and Dixon JJ., appeared to prefer the earlier view expressed by Isaacs J. in *R. v. Murray and Cormie*. In *Lorenzo v. Carey*[20] the High Court described a court exercising federal jurisdiction as 'the judicial agent of the Commonwealth', while Starke J. in *Commonwealth v. Limerick Steamship Co. Ltd*[21] spoke of State courts invested with federal jurisdiction as 'substitute tribunals'. Of the writers, Wynes argues that the language of Chapter III and the general scheme of the Constitution support the view that such courts remain State courts and should not be regarded as part of the federal judicature.[22]

---

[17] Legislative, Executive and Judicial Powers in Australia (5th ed., 1976) at pp. 495-7.

[18] (1916) 22 C.L.R. 437, 452.

[19] (1929) 42 C.L.R. 481, 514.

[20] (1921) 29 C.L.R. 243, 252.

[21] (1924) 35 C.L.R. 69, 116.

[22] *op. cit. ante* note 17 at pp. 496-7. See also Lane: The Australian Federal System (1972) p. 361.

Bailey, to the contrary, is of opinion that the Constitution 'appears to treat a State court exercising federal jurisdiction as part of the federal judicature'[23] though he does not specifically relate the discussion to sec. 51 (xxxix).

Apart from sec. 51 (xxxix), the matter is of little importance, for the term 'federal judicature' appears only in that paragraph, and is not mentioned in Chapter III which is headed 'The Judicature'. It is believed that the better view is that State courts invested with federal jurisdiction are to be regarded as part of the federal judicature for the purposes of sec. 51 (xxxix). There is no clear warrant for regarding the federal courts and the federal judicature as coterminous; it would seem to be a better reading of the Constitution to regard all repositories of the judicial power of the Commonwealth as part of the system of federal judicature,[24] and there is no necessary inconsistency between the views expressed by Isaacs J. in *R. v. Murray and Cormie* and in *Le Mesurier v. Connor*. State courts invested with federal jurisdiction remain State courts, but, while acting in this capacity, are properly regarded as a component part of the federal judicature.

## IV

The limits of the power to invest State courts with federal jurisdiction are prescribed by sec. 77, so that a grant will be invalid unless it is with respect to a matter enumerated in secs. 75 and 76. In *Hooper v. Hooper*,[25] a question arose whether the investment of State Supreme Courts with jurisdiction in matrimonial causes by the Matrimonial Causes Act 1945 was within power, and it was argued that this was a bare grant of jurisdiction not referable to any of the heads of secs. 75 and 76. The High Court rejected the argument and pointed out that the grant of jurisdiction had to be read together with the choice of law rule in that statute directing the application of the *lex domicilii*; that the Act was to be construed as giving the force of federal law to the State laws, so that Parliament had effectively exercised its powers under secs. 51 (xxii) and 77 (iii), and that the grant of jurisdiction was therefore referable to sec. 76 (ii) of the Constitution.

There is a further broad constitutional restraint on the exercise of Commonwealth legislative power with respect to State

---

23 *op. cit. ante* note 7 at pp. 101-10.

24 *Commonwealth v. Limerick Steamship Co. Ltd* (1924) 35 C.L.R. 69, 105, *per* Isaacs and Rich JJ.

25 (1955) 91 C.L.R. 529.

courts. As Latham C.J. observed in *Federal Council of the British Medical Association in Australia v. Commonwealth*,[26] it is only by virtue of secs. 71 and 77 (iii) that the Commonwealth Parliament can invest a State court with jurisdiction so that the court becomes bound to exercise it. There is no constitutional provision under which the Parliament may require State courts to exercise any form of non-judicial power. So in *Queen Victoria Memorial Hospital v. Thornton*[27] it was held that the provisions of the Re-establishment and Employment Act 1945-1952, which purported to invest State courts with a very broad discretionary jurisdiction to determine questions of preference as between candidates for employment, were unconstitutional, since they purported to invest State courts with non-judicial power. It was observed: 'it would be strange indeed if the constitution contained a grant of legislative power which would enable the Parliament to require or to authorize State courts as such to exercise duties, functions or powers which were non judicial.'[28] The only source of legislative power to affect State courts outside Chapter III is sec. 51 (xxxix) which apparently confers legislative power in respect of matters incidental to the exercise of jurisdiction invested in State courts. It appears therefore that no power other than judicial power, and authority strictly incidental thereto, may be lawfully conferred by the Parliament on State courts.[29]

As sec. 77 (iii) is the exclusive source of power to invest State courts with federal jurisdiction it must be clear that any investment derives from that source. In *Peacock v. Newtown, Marrickville and General Co-operative Building Society No. 4 Ltd*[30] the purported investment of federal jurisdiction in State courts under the National Security (Contracts Adjustment) Regulations was held bad on the ground that the regulation-making power under the National Security Act, which in very broad terms authorized the making of regulations for defence purposes, did not expressly authorize the making of regulations for the purpose of investing State courts with federal jurisdiction. As it then stood, the National Security Act rested on sec. 51 and it may be on sec. 122 of the Constitution, and it could not therefore be regarded as authorizing the making of regulations for the investment of State

---

[26] (1949) 79 C.L.R. 201, 236.
[27] (1953) 87 C.L.R. 144.
[28] at p. 152.
[29] *Insurance Commissioner v. Associated Dominions Assurance Society Pty Ltd* (1953) 89 C.L.R. 78, 85, *per* Fullagar J.
[30] (1943) 67 C.L.R. 25.

courts with federal jurisdiction, which must depend on Chapter III.

The National Security Act was consequently amended in 1943 specifically to authorize the investment of judicial power by regulation. This raised the further question whether the power conferred by sec. 77 (iii) may be exercised in this way. The validity of the 1943 amendment was not judicially tested,[31] but there have been conflicting expressions of opinion in the High Court on the matter. In *Le Mesurier v. Connor*,[32] the High Court discussed the question whether sec. 18 (1) (b) of the Bankruptcy Act 1924-1928, which provided that the courts having jurisdiction in bankruptcy should be such State courts as were specially authorized by the Governor-General by proclamation to exercise that jurisdiction, was a law investing State courts with federal jurisdiction within sec. 77 (iii). The majority, Knox C.J., Rich and Dixon JJ., after observing that it was not necessary for the purposes of the case to decide the question, expressed the view that the power conferred by sec. 77 (iii) 'requires that the law made by the Parliament should not only define the jurisdiction to be invested but also identify the State Court in which the jurisdiction is thereby invested. The power is to make laws "investing", not, as in sec. 51, "with respect to" a subject-matter.'[33] For this reason it was not a case in which the Parliament, which was constituted to exercise plenary legislative power could, under the doctrine of such cases as *Hodge v. The Queen*,[34] *R. v. Burah*[35] and *Powell v. Apollo Candle Co.*,[36] delegate its powers in this way. Isaacs and Starke JJ. dissented on the broad ground that it was settled practice that the legislature could delegate its authority; as Starke J. said: 'The jurisdiction in the State Court is invested by the authority of the Act under which the proclamation was issued. Since the decision of the Judicial Committee in *Powell v. Apollo Candle Co.*, the position seems to me clear and beyond doubt.'[37]

---

[31] It was raised in argument in *R. v. Ray, ex parte Smith* [1948] S.A.S.R. 216, but the Court did not expressly deal with it. The regulation was, however, held valid. It was also referred to in *Ex parte Coorey* (1945) 45 S.R. (N.S.W.) 287, 302, where Jordan C.J. expressed his pleasure in not having to decide the point. See also Sawer: Australian Constitutional Cases (3rd ed., 1964) at p. 658.

[32] (1929) 42 C.L.R. 481.

[33] at p. 500.

[34] (1883) 9 App. Cas. 117.

[35] (1878) 3 App. Cas. 889.

[36] (1885) 10 App. Cas. 282.

[37] (1929) 42 C.L.R. 481, 521.

In *Peacock's Case*[38] three members of the High Court made a further offering of *dicta* on the subject. Latham C.J. said that the view of the majority in *Le Mesurier v. Connor*, if valid, applied only to an executive act, such as a proclamation, but would not apply to a regulation, legislative in character. Starke J. reaffirmed his position in *Le Mesurier v. Connor* and said that a denial of power to invest by regulation was 'plainly contrary'[39] to authority. Williams J. did not express a definite opinion, but said that he might feel obliged on grounds of principle and authority to follow the majority in *Le Mesurier v. Connor*. He doubted the validity of the distinction between 'executive' and 'legislative' regulations which, he said, was 'a fine one',[40] and suggested difficulties which might arise if the power of investment of State courts with federal jurisdiction and, by parity of reasoning, the power to define the jurisdiction of federal courts, were exercisable by delegated authority.

Certainly no clear statement of the law emerges from these *dicta*. In *Ex parte Coorey*,[41] Jordan C.J. referred to the division in the High Court, and declined to make any further contribution. 'Fortunately *non nostrum inter hos tantas componere lites*.' It is perhaps surprising that the validity of the National Security Act amendment of 1943 was not directly challenged in the High Courts though the argument was put to the Supreme Court of South Australia in *R. v. Ray, ex parte Smith*,[42] where it was virtually ignored by the Court, which upheld the validity of the investment of the local court under the National Security (Landlord and Tenant) Regulations.

In *Willocks v. Anderson*[43] the High Court was faced with regulations made under the Apple and Pear Organization Act 1948 which purported to confer jurisdiction on the High Court. Although the constitutional provision involved was sec. 76 (ii), the cases referred to above were discussed and a joint judgement of six members of the Court appeared to regard the questions whether Parliament could delegate under secs. 76 and 77 as involving the same issue. They expressly did not decide the question as they held that the Act did not authorize the making of the regulations conferring jurisdiction on the Court.

---

[38] (1943) 67 C.L.R. 25.
[39] at p. 44.
[40] at p. 51.
[41] (1945) 45 S.R. (N.S.W.) 287, 302.
[42] [1948] S.A.S.R. 216.
[43] (1971) 124 C.L.R. 293.

Wynes[44] supports the opinion of the majority in *Le Mesurier v. Connor*. The question turns on the significance of the change of language from laws 'with respect to' in sec. 51, to laws 'investing' in sec. 77 (iii). Distinctions drawn between regulations of 'executive' and of 'legislative' character are not persuasive, and raise some doubtful questions of law, and the practical arguments in favour of direct legislative investment by Williams J. in *Peacock's Case*,[45] while perhaps stronger, are not compelling. On a strictly grammatical reading, it is not easy to construe a law as *investing* jurisdiction unless a court can immediately be identified as the repository of the jurisdiction, but the broader arguments in favour of construing the grant of power so as to permit Parliament to provide for the investment of State courts by regulation are practical and strong. As Sir Owen Dixon has written in the context of the *general* power of Parliament to delegate: 'it seemed unbelievable that the executive should be forbidden to carry on the practice of legislation by regulation—the most conspicuous legal activity of a modern government,'[46] and it was on this broad basis that Isaacs and Starke JJ. strongly and dogmatically supported the view that Parliament might delegate its power under sec. 77 (iii). It is submitted that this is the preferable view.

## V

We have seen that the Constitution provides for the vesting of the judicial power of the Commonwealth exclusively in federal courts and in State courts invested with federal jurisdiction. There is no *tertium quid*; the Parliament may not avoid compliance with the constitutional requirements for the establishment of federal courts, prescribed by sec. 72, by remaking or reconstituting a State court whose judges, under State law, need not neces-

---

[44] *op. cit.* at p. 490-1. See also Howard: Australian Federal Constitutional Law (2nd ed., 1972) 244 and Lane, *op. cit.*, p. 567.

[45] (1943) 67 C.L.R. 25, 51. Williams J. said that if federal jurisdiction could be invested in State courts by regulation, the definition of federal jurisdiction under sec. 77 (i) could, by parity of reasoning, be effected by regulation. Such regulations are subject to disallowance by either House of Parliament under sec. 48 of the Acts Interpretation Act. This would mean that a federal court with judges appointed for life might be created by regulation, that could be subsequently disallowed with unfortunate practical consequences.

[46] The Law and The Constitution (1935) 51 L.Q.R. at 606. It may well be that this comment was directed only to powers to legislate 'with respect to' a particular matter, and was not intended to apply beyond that.

sarily have the tenure prescribed by sec. 72 of the Constitution.[47] Sec. 79 of the Constitution authorizes a specific measure of interference with State courts by providing that the federal jurisdiction of any court may be exercised by such numbers of judges as the Parliament prescribes.[48] Beyond this, the limits of permissible interference with State courts exercising federal jurisdiction are spelled out in the cases. It was stated early in the High Court that 'when the Federal Parliament confers a new jurisdiction upon an existing State Court it takes the Court as it finds it, with all its limitations as to jurisdiction unless otherwise expressly declared'.[49] There are also repeated statements in the cases that the Parliament in the exercise of its powers under secs. 77 (iii) and 51 (xxxix) may not affect or alter the constitution of a State court or the organization through which its jurisdiction and powers are organized. In *Le Mesurier v. Connor*[50] it was held, accordingly, that the provisions of the Bankruptcy Act 1924-1928 which purported to make registrars, acting as Commonwealth officers, part of the organization of State courts and which authorized them to exercise powers and functions as officers of the courts in the administration of their jurisdiction, were invalid. This was said to be an attempt to alter the constitution and structure of State courts, forbidden by the Constitution. The Constitution, it was held, envisaged the selection by Parliament of existing judicial organizations which depended alike for their structure and being on State law, and the investment of federal jurisdiction in such courts.

The principle stated in *Le Mesurier v. Connor* has been reaffirmed by the High Court and State courts on many occasions[51] and the limits of its operation have also been considered. In *Bond v. George A. Bond and Co. Ltd and Bond's Industries Ltd,*[52] the

---

[47] *Adams v. Chas S. Watson Pty Ltd* (1938) 60 C.L.R. 545, 554-5; *Peacock's Case* (1943) 67 C.L.R. 25, 37.

[48] Can Parliament prescribe a number *above* that prescribed by State law, *quaere.*

[49] *Federated Sawmill etc. Association (Adelaide Branch) v. Alexander* (1912) 15 C.L.R. 308, 313, *per* Griffith C.J.

[50] (1929) 42 C.L.R. 481.

[51] See e.g. *Bond v. George A. Bond and Co. Ltd and Bond's Industries Ltd* (1930) 44 C.L.R. 11; *Adams v. Chas S. Watson Pty Ltd* (1938) 60 C.L.R. 545; *Silk Bros Pty Ltd v. State Electricity Commission of Victoria* (1943) 67 C.L.R. 1; *Aston v. Irvine* (1955) 92 C.L.R. 353. See also *Ex parte Australian Timber Workers' Union; Veneer Co. Ltd* (1937) 37 S.R. (N.S.W.) 52; *Ex parte Coorey* (1945) 45 S.R. (N.S.W.) 287; *R. v. Ray, ex parte Smith* [1948] S.A.S.R. 216; *Russell v. Russell* (1976) 9 A.L.R. 103.

[52] (1930) 44 C.L.R. 11.

High Court upheld the validity of the Bankruptcy Act 1929, passed in consequence of the decision in *Le Mesurier v. Connor* which made registrars and deputy registrars independent of the State courts, required them to perform 'administrative' duties as directed by the State courts, and by sec. 24 gave registrars independent functions, including the power to hear debtors' petitions and to make sequestration orders. It was held that these amendments overcame the objections to the sections in the earlier Act; that sec. 77 (iii), considered with sec. 51 (xvii), authorized the grant by Parliament to State courts of all powers appropriate to the exercise of bankruptcy jurisdiction, and all authority incidental to the exercise of such powers, including the grant of authority to enable such courts to direct the performance of ministerial acts. The Court was prepared if necessary to read the authority to perform 'administrative' acts conferred by the amending Act as meaning 'ministerial' acts. Doubts were expressed as to the validity of sec. 24, on the ground that it conferred judicial power on the registrars, but it was held that the section was in any event severable.

Although the above cases establish that the Commonwealth in exercising power under sec. 77 (iii) cannot alter the structure or organization of a State court, it has also been held that it may not be able to make use of the existing organization of such a court in certain circumstances.

In *R. v. Davison*[53] Dixon C.J. and McTiernan J. pointed out that, although a court is composed of judges which form it, courts are provided with officers and, under a unitary system of government, it is not uncommon to find that certain duties falling to a court are executed, subject to judicial confirmation or review, by an officer of the court. They added that 'There is no distinct decision of this Court that under Chapter III no authority can be made by statute for the discharge in this way of the duties of a Federal court, although there are dicta to that effect'. The dicta referred to included that of Isaacs J. in *Le Mesurier v. Connor*[54] who distinguished judges comprising a court and the officers of the court. His Honour said that only the former constituted the court and therefore the judicial power of the Commonwealth, which, by sec. 71, is vested in courts, could not be exercised by the latter.

There has been no decision of the High Court in respect of officers of a federal court; however, the High Court has con-

[53] (1954) 90 C.L.R. 353, 365.
[54] (1929) 42 C.L.R. 481, 511, 512, 522-5.

sidered the purported exercise of judicial power by an officer of a State court exercising federal jurisdiction. In *Kotsis v. Kotsis*[55] it was held (Gibbs J. dissenting) that a deputy registrar of the Supreme Court of New South Wales did not have power to make an order in matrimonial causes under the Matrimonial Causes Act 1959 (Cth) directing the payment by the husband of the wife's interim costs in that cause. The main reason for the decision was that the deputy registrar, although an officer of the Supreme Court, was not part of that Court. This conclusion was arrived at by all the judges from an examination of the legislation relating to the constitution and organization of that Court. However, State legislation gave power to the judges by Rules to delegate certain authority and jurisdiction to the registrar (which included the deputy registrar), including jurisdiction to make an order of the sort made. When acting under this delegation, the registrar was 'deemed to be exercising the jurisdiction and powers of the Supreme Court'.[56]

The majority were of the view that, as sec. 77 (iii) authorized the investiture of jurisdiction only in a 'court of a State', a person who was a delegate of the court but not part of it could not exercise the jurisdiction. Gibbs J., however, was prepared to give the word 'court' under sec. 77 (iii) a wider and less technical meaning as including the organization of the court 'and particularly the officers of the court by which it exercises its functions under State law in analogous cases'.[57] The case of *Le Mesurier v. Connor* was relied on by both the majority and the minority, particularly the statement in that case that State law 'determines the constitution of the court itself and the organization through which its powers and jurisdiction are exercised'.[58]

The majority pointed to the clear distinction made between the 'constitution of the court' and 'the organization through which its powers and jurisdiction are exercised' for coming to the conclusion that the 'court' did not include the 'organization'. Gibbs J., on the other hand, reasoned that, as the Commonwealth could not alter either of these elements as laid down by State law, that must be because the 'court', upon which sec. 77 (iii) authorized the investiture of jurisdiction, included both.

The judgements of the majority are consistent with past decisions as to who, for general purposes, constitutes a court. On the

55 (1970) 122 C.L.R. 69.
56 Matrimonial Causes Act 1899 (as amended) (N.S.W.), sec. 4 (4).
57 at p. 104.
58 (1929) 42 C.L.R. 481, 495.

other hand, the decision in *Le Mesurier v. Connor* would seem to have involved a broader view for the purposes of sec. 77 (iii). Also, from an historical view point, officers of a court were, in 1900, exercising jurisdiction as delegates of English and Colonial courts and it might be argued that it was envisaged that, in exercising federal jurisdiction, a State court was intended to perform its functions through an organization and arrangement that was familiar when the Constitution was enacted.[59] Whatever might be said of the analytical or historical arguments, the decision of *Kotsis v. Kotsis* is unfortunate from a practical point of view. Additional burdens have been placed on the judges and an incongruous situation arises as a result of a State court being prevented from using, in the case of federal jurisdiction, the services of court officers who are available when State jurisdiction is involved. These practical consequences were adverted to by Gibbs J. He said:

> The exercise of federal jurisdiction is not necessarily any more difficult, complicated or important than the exercise of State jurisdiction, and in fact, of course, some matters which formerly fell within State jurisdiction are now within federal jurisdiction; matrimonial causes and bankruptcy are obvious examples. The nature of federal jurisdiction did not require any different kind of organization, and there was no less need for courts exercising federal jurisdiction to be organized so that their officers, acting subject to confirmation or review by the judges, might perform on behalf of the court judicial functions which were of a routine or comparatively minor character or which could for other reasons be safely entrusted to them. There is no reason of which I am aware why the exercise of federal jurisdiction should necessarily be less flexible and more costly than the exercise of State jurisdiction.[60]

Windeyer J. pointed to a method by which some of these consequences might be avoided to some degree and use made of the services of court officers. He said:

> I can see no reason why, assuming that the process of giving judgment is not taken from the court, matters arising before the hearing of the principal cause, or afterwards for working out the effect of a judgment, should not be inquired into and reported on by officers of the court. The court would not then confirm the decision of an officer. It would itself pronounce judgment on material he provided, which judgment might I suppose be in most cases in accordance with

[59] At any rate, in the absence of any federal rule to the contrary—see Gibbs J. at p. 109.
[60] at p. 110.

any recommendation emerging from the report, but would not necessarily be so.[61]

He gave instances of the sort of functions he had in mind, such as the taxation of costs, the taking of accounts, an inquiry as to damages for the purposes of reporting the result to the court to enable a judgement to be given and proceedings for a certificate of means pursuant to Matrimonial Causes Rules.

In *Knight v. Knight*[62] the Court applied the reasoning in *Kotsis v. Kotsis* in invalidating an order for maintenance pending a divorce suit made by the Master of the Supreme Court of South Australia. Barwick C.J. quoted with approval the passage of Windeyer J. referred to above.[63]

*Kotsis v. Kotsis* did not deal with the question whether a federal court might be empowered to delegate jurisdiction to an officer of the court and Gibbs J., in his dissenting judgement, said that the question was an open one. However, it is difficult to see how any distinction between these two cases can be made. The decision in *Kotsis v. Kotsis* did not rest on any ground related to 'federal principles' but on an interpretation of what is a 'court'. As sec. 71 vests the judicial power of the Commonwealth *inter alia* in 'federal courts' and sec. 77 (i) authorizes legislation defining the jurisdiction of 'any federal court other than the High Court', it would follow from *Kotsis v. Kotsis* that no judicial power can vest in, and no jurisdiction can be conferred on, an officer of a court as distinct from the court itself.

In both *Kotsis v. Kotsis* and *Knight v. Knight* the High Court found no intention in the State legislation to make the registrar or master a part of the Supreme Court. The question arises, however, of what would be the position if the State law had provided that the court was to consist of judges and, for some or all purposes, specified officers of the court. In those circumstances could federal jurisdiction be invested in the court and, if so, could it be exercised by such an officer? Barwick C.J. has stated that such a body would not constitute a 'court' for the purposes of either sec. 73 (ii) (appeals to the High Court) or sec. 77 (iii). He regarded the notion of a court composed only of judges as entrenched in 1900, together with the distinction between a court and its officers. So, 'If State law were to change this composition in a radical way what the State continued to call the Supreme

---

[61] at p. 92.

[62] (1971) 122 C.L.R. 114.

[63] See the observations of Carmichael J. in *Raymond v. Raymond* [1971] 1 N.S.W.L.R. 723.

O

Court would not satisfy, in my opinion, the references in the Constitution to the Supreme Courts of the States'.[64]

The other judges did not deal with this issue specifically, but the impression gained from the general reasoning of most of them is that they would not agree with the view of the Chief Justice. In addition to Gibbs J., Menzies J. said that 'Everything, there-fore, depends upon the laws of New South Wales constituting the Supreme Court'.[65] Owen J. considered that 'the short answer to the question asked is to be found by examining the New South Wales law under which the deputy registrar purported to act'.[66] Walsh J. was of the opinion that no question arose 'of considering whether a person might be a member of that Court although not called a judge',[67] but, nevertheless, he examined the State legislation at length to show that the registrar was not a member of the Court.

In *Knight v. Knight*[68] Gibbs J. mentioned these problems in a judgement in which he followed the majority view in *Kotsis v. Kotsis*. He said:

The question whether the master is a member of the Supreme Court of South Australia depends on the law of South Australia. If the question were answered in the affirmative further questions might arise. It might then be necessary to consider whether a Supreme Court whose membership was expanded to include persons other than judges would be a court within s. 77 (iii) of the Constitution, and whether, if so, the Commonwealth Act nevertheless discloses an in-tention that the federal jurisdiction in matrimonial causes with which the Supreme Courts are invested should only be exercised by judges and, if it does, whether the Constitution permits the Parlia-ment to impose conditions of that kind when effecting an investiture of federal judicial power. These questions were debated but not de-cided in *Kotsis v. Kotsis*.[69]

It would be unfortunate if the view were accepted that the addition of registrars or masters as constitutive members of a court meant that it was no longer a court within the meaning of the various provisions of the Constitution. This is, it is suggested, the very sort of development that should be left to a legislature to pursue if it so desires. Consideration of such a proposal should not be bedevilled by having to consider the consequences of hav-

64 (1971) 122 C.L.R. 69 at p. 77.
65 at pp. 84-5.
66 at p. 94.
67 at p. 97.
68 (1971) 122 C.L.R. 114.
69 at pp. 131-2.

ing a court upon which no federal jurisdiction could be invested or judgements from which there could be no appeal to the High Court. The composition that courts had in 1900 might be considered as either part of the connotation (which cannot change) or denotation (which can) of the term 'court' in the Constitution. Certainly formal logical or analytical reasoning does not supply the answer. This is an area in which it is suggested that some room be left to the States to experiment with new forms. It is possible, of course, to imagine radical changes that would convert what was a court into what might appropriately be regarded as a political inquisition or worse; but that is no reason for making more burdensome any alteration of the conditions pertaining in 1900 if a government should feel modern conditions require it.

Sec. 79 of the Constitution authorizes parliamentary control of the number of judges who may exercise the federal jurisdiction of a State court. But before any question of the operation of sec. 79 arises, there is a question whether there has been an investment of a State court under sec. 77 (iii) and the choice of designated *persons* who may be qualified to constitute State courts is not a valid investment under this power. So in *Silk Bros Pty Ltd v. State Electricity Commission of Victoria*[70] regulations constituting Fair Rents Boards provided that they might be constituted by police magistrates and, if the Governor-in-Council deemed fit, by two other persons. It was not specifically required that such other persons should be justices of the peace, so that it was possible to appoint a Fair Rents Board which could not constitute a court of Petty Sessions. The Governor-in-Council appointed police magistrates for the time being assigned to adjudicate at courts of Petty Sessions to constitute Fair Rents Boards, and in the metropolitan area specified police magistrates were appointed as Fair Rents Boards. It was held that the investment was bad on the ground that there was no investment of State courts of Petty Sessions as such, but an appointment of particular persons, described as police magistrates, to be Fair Rents Boards at places at which courts of Petty Sessions were held.

In *Ex parte Coorey*,[71] Jordan C.J. said that sec. 79 did not authorize the Parliament to select one among several judges, each of whom was capable of constituting a State court, and to provide that he alone should constitute the court when exercising federal jurisdiction. If this means that Parliament may not direct that the federal jurisdiction of a State court of summary jurisdiction

70 (1943) 67 C.L.R. 1.
71 (1945) 45 S.R. (N.S.W.) 287, 304-5.

shall be exercised by members of that court possessing specified qualifications, as, for example, a stipendiary magistrate, it is contrary to the clearly expressed view of the High Court. If it means that Parliament may not declare that the federal jurisdiction of a State court shall be exercised by a *named* judge of that court, it is not easy to see how this case can be distinguished from the one immediately preceding. It has been held that if federal jurisdiction is conferred in terms on a justice of a Supreme Court, and not upon a Supreme Court, *eo nomine*, it will be a valid exercise of power if the true construction of the grant is that the jurisdiction is conferred on the judge *as a member of the Supreme Court*, and if he, as a single judge, is capable of constituting the court. In such a case, the designation of the single judge is an exercise of power under sec. 79.[72]

Various Commonwealth statutes purport to invest State courts with federal jurisdiction and to prescribe that that jurisdiction shall be exercised by judges described by a particular qualification. The most obvious example is sec. 39 of the Judiciary Act which provides in sub-paragraph (2) (d) that:

> The Federal jurisdiction of a court of summary jurisdiction of a State shall not be judicially exercised except by a Stipendiary or Police or Special Magistrate, or some Magistrate of the State who is specially authorized by the Governor-General to exercise such jurisdiction.

Similar provision is made by sec. 68 (3) of the Judiciary Act, and in other Acts, such as the Fisheries Act 1952 and the Continental Shelf (Living Natural Resources) Act 1968.

On their face such provisions do not appear to be exercises of power under sec. 79, which authorizes prescription of the *number*, not of the *qualification*, of judges who may exercise the federal jurisdiction of State courts. In *Ex parte Coorey*,[73] Jordan C.J. said that 'so far as s. 39 (2) (d) and s. 68 (3) [of the Judiciary Act] purport to enable the Governor-General to select a particular magistrate of the State and specifically authorize him to exercise Federal jurisdiction as a State court, I am of opinion that they are *ultra vires* the Constitution as interpreted by the High Court'. The difficulty in this view, as a matter of authority, is that in such cases as *Baxter v. Commissioner of Taxation, New South Wales*,[74] *Lorenzo v. Carey*,[75] and *Commonwealth v. Lime-*

---

[72] *Aston v. Irvine* (1955) 92 C.L.R. 353.
[73] (1945) 45 S.R. (N.S.W.) 287, 305.
[74] (1907) 4 C.L.R. 1087.
[75] (1921) 29 C.L.R. 243.

*rick Steamship Co. Ltd,*[76] the High Court discussed sec. 39 of the
Judiciary Act in terms which, though not specifically directed to
sec. 39 (2) (d), assumed its validity. In *Queen Victoria Memorial
Hospital v. Thornton,*[77] where jurisdiction was conferred on
police, stipendiary or special magistrates under the Reestablish-
ment and Employment Act 1945-1952 the High Court, while holding the investment bad on other grounds,[78] stated in the clearest
terms, and by reference to the authorities cited above, that sec.
39 (2) (d) was valid. 'Whether the power to enact s. 39 (2) (d) of
the Judiciary Act arises under s. 51 (xxxix) of the constitution or
under s. 79 need not be considered, for the validity of the provision has been upheld.'[79]

The matter has also been considered by the Full Supreme
Court of South Australia in *R. v. Ray, ex parte Smith.*[80] In an
action brought under the National Security (Landlord and
Tenant) Regulations in a local court, the court rejected the
argument that there was any right to a trial of the issue by a court
constituted by a special magistrate and two justices of the peace
in accordance with the terms of the State Local Courts Act, because the National Security (Landlord and Tenant) Regulations
specifically provided that such jurisdiction should be exercised
by a special magistrate sitting alone. Napier C.J. said:

> It was contended that the Commonwealth, when it invests the court
> of a State with Federal jurisdiction must take the court as it finds it,
> but that does not compel the Commonwealth to adopt rules of proce-
> dure which it regards as inapplicable or inappropriate. If the State
> Court is so organized as to function in different ways for different
> purposes, I think that the Commonwealth must have the power to
> commit Federal jurisdiction to the State court functioning in the
> manner that is, or is considered to be, best suited to its purpose *(Troy
> v. Wigglesworth; Lorenzo v. Carey).* Once the jurisdiction becomes
> Federal, the Commonwealth can at will regulate the procedure and
> control the method of the relief.[81]

The Court did not specify the constitutional authority to prescribe the composition of State courts invested with federal jurisdiction, but the language of Napier C.J.'s judgement suggests that
it is to be discovered in sec. 51 (xxxix), rather than in sec. 79. It
appears to have been the Court's view that the regulation of the

---

76 (1924) 35 C.L.R. 69.
77 (1953) 87 C.L.R. 144.
78 See pp. 180-1 *ante.*
79 (1953) 87 C.L.R. 144, 152.
80 [1948] S.A.S.R. 216.
81 at p. 223.

composition of State courts is a matter of procedure, and that it is open to the Federal Parliament to control the procedure to be adopted by a State court invested with federal jurisdicton. The breadth of the proposition stated by Napier C.J. suggests that it also is open to Parliament, *pace* Jordan C.J. in *Ex parte Coorey*, to designate a particular judge (or judges) to exercise the federal jurisdiction of a State court, and it is not easy to distinguish that case from such legislation as sec. 39 (2) (d) which the High Court has expressly declared to be valid. In *Kotsis v. Kotsis*[82] Gibbs J., referring to sec. 39 (2) (d), said: 'Although the grounds on which that provision was treated as valid were not made altogether clear I see no reason to doubt the correctness of the opinion expressed by seven members of the Court' (in *Queen Victoria Memorial Hospital v. Thornton*).

There is much to be said for the practical outcome which upholds the Commonwealth legislative policy that matters arising in the exercise of federal jurisdiction by a State court of summary jurisdiction should be entrusted to specially qualified magistrates rather than to lay justices of the peace. There is some difficulty however in locating the constitutional authority to control State courts in this way, and the High Court in *Queen Victoria Memorial Hospital v. Thornton* pointed to the alternative sources of secs. 51 (xxxix) and 79, but was content to rest on authority which itself does not carry the matter forward. It strains the language of sec. 79 to make 'number' include 'qualification' of judges. This suggests recourse to sec. 51 (xxxix), but the constitutional scheme generally, and notably the express terms of sec. 79, suggest a very limited power of recourse to the incidental power to authorize interference with the composition of State courts exercising federal jurisdiction. The law on this matter is apparently settled, though the source of constitutional power remains obscure.

Other difficulties arise from the holding that the Parliament may validly prescribe the qualification of judges of State courts invested with federal jurisdiction. It may be that a State court of summary jurisdiction will exercise federal jurisdiction without knowing it, and, indeed without any reasonable opportunity of finding out.[83] A further question arises as to the consequences of a failure by a State court of summary jurisdiction to constitute itself in accordance with sec. 39 (2) (d) of the Judiciary Act when it exercises federal jurisdiction. Does such an omission constitute a failure to exercise federal jurisdiction altogether; or is there an

---

[82] (1970) 122 C.L.R. 69, 111.
[83] See p. 88 *ante*.

exercise of federal jurisdiction, albeit an unlawful one, so that an appeal lies as prescribed by sec. 73 of the Constitution and the Judiciary Act as from a State court exercising federal jurisdiction? In *Troy v. Wigglesworth*,[84] a majority in the High Court held that this was not the usurpation of a non-existent federal jurisdiction, but was a wrongful exercise of an existing jurisdiction. Whatever the analytical difficulties, this may now be regarded as settled law.[85]

While Parliament may not reshape State courts which it invests with federal jurisdiction and must, subject to the qualifications already noted, respect their constitutions and organizations as prescribed by State law, it may fix and control the *jurisdiction* of those courts in investing them with federal jurisdiction. Unless there is an express declaration to the contrary, the limitations of jurisdiction prescribed by State law will be respected,[86] but by such express declaration 'the Federal Parliament may in conferring jurisdiction in respect of Federal subject matter, extend or limit the jurisdiction of a State Court in respect of persons, locality, amount or otherwise, as it may think proper'.[87] Thus in *Peacock's Case*[88] regulations under the National Security Act which increased the amount recoverable in a New South Wales district court invested with federal jurisdiction beyond the limits prescribed by State law were held not to be invalid on this ground. In *Adams v. Chas S. Watson Pty Ltd*[89] it was held that federal law could prescribe limitation periods which a State court invested with federal jurisdiction must recognize in disregard of limitation periods imposed by State law. The Fisheries Act 1952 (sec. 15) and the Continental Shelf (Living Natural Resources) Act 1968 (sec. 19) confer jurisdiction on State courts of summary jurisdiction to try offences against the Act committed outside Australia. Those provisions would appear to have extended the locality of the jurisdiction of such courts although in all other respects the Acts expressly confine the jurisdiction within the limits prescribed by State law. Similarly, sec. 85E of the Crimes Act 1914 (as amended), in investing State courts with federal jurisdiction 'within the limits of their several jurisdictions', expressly excludes 'limits having effect by reference to the

---

84 (1919) 26 C.L.R. 305.

85 See *Keetley v. Bowie* (1951) 83 C.L.R. 516, 520.

86 *Federated Sawmill etc. Association (Adelaide Branch) v. Alexander* (1912) 15 C.L.R. 308, 313.

87 *Peacock's Case* (1943) 67 C.L.R. 25, 39, *per* Latham C.J.

88 (1943) 67 C.L.R. 25.

89 (1938) 60 C.L.R. 545.

place at which offences are committed'.[90] Sub-sec. (4) further provides that 'The trial on indictment of an offence against this Act, not being an offence committed within a State, may be held in any State or Territory'.[91] Under sec. 68 (5) of the Judiciary Act 1903 (inserted in 1976) the jurisdiction vested in State or territorial courts with respect to offences against the laws of the Commonwealth is expressly declared to be conferred 'notwithstanding any limits as to locality of the jurisdiction of the court under the law of the State or Territory'.

## VI

The Court has drawn a distinction between an attempted alteration of the constitution of a State court or the organization through which its jurisdiction and powers are exercised (which, as we have seen, is outside the limits of Commonwealth power) and legislating to make the investiture of federal jurisdiction effective (which is within Commonwealth power).

In *Lorenzo v. Carey*[92] a judgement of five members of the Court approved a statement by Isaacs J. in *Baxter v. The Commissioner of Taxation*[93] that 'Once the jurisdiction became federal the Commonwealth Parliament could at will regulate the procedure and control the method and extent of relief'. As in the case of sec. 39 (2) (d) of the Judiciary Act there has been no general agreement among the judges as to the source of this power. Isaacs and Rich JJ. in *Commonwealth v. Limerick Steamship Co. Ltd*[94] considered the power was derived from sec. 51 (xxxix) because of their view that the State courts exercising federal jurisdiction were part of the 'Federal Judicature' within the meaning of that provision. On the other hand, in *Bond v. George A. Bond and Co. Ltd*,[95] Rich and Dixon JJ. considered that sec. 77 (iii) together

---

[90] See also Crimes (Aircraft) Act 1963 (sec. 22) and Statutory Declarations Act 1959 (sec. 12).

[91] In *R. v. Bull* (1974) 131 C.L.R. 203, the High Court considered the jurisdiction of the Supreme Court of South Australia in 1911 in respect of offences committed at sea for the purposes of determining the jurisdiction of the Supreme Court of the Northern Territory. While the particular exercise of jurisdiction was upheld in that case—a customs matter—the reasons of the judges varied greatly: McTiernan, Menzies and Gibbs JJ. considered that the Supreme Court of South Australia had in 1911 jurisdiction in respect of all offences against local laws committed at sea. Stephen and Mason JJ. confined their reasoning to customs laws and Barwick C.J. dissented.

[92] (1921) 29 C.L.R. 243.

[93] (1907) 4 C.L.R. 1087 at p. 1145.

[94] (1924) 35 C.L.R. 69.

[95] (1930) 44 C.L.R. 11 at p. 22.

with the particular substantive head of power in sec. 51 provided the constitutional authority. They said that 'Sec. 77 (iii) considered with sec. 51 (xvii) confers ample power upon the Parliament to bestow upon State Courts all powers appropriate to bankruptcy jurisdiction and all authority incidental to the exercise of such powers'. Menzies J. in *Kotsis v. Kotsis*[96] seemed to agree with this view when he said that a provision of the Matrimonial Causes Act which authorized the Governor-General to make rules relating to the practice and procedure of courts with jurisdiction under the Act was an exercise of power under sec. 51 (xxii). In *Russell v. Russell*[97] Gibbs J. left the source of authority to deal with procedure undecided;[98] Stephen J. appeared to regard it as within the incidental area of power granted by sec. 77 (iii); on the other hand, Mason J. and Jacobs J.[99] preferred to rely on the particular subject in sec. 51 under which the substantive rules were made. Mason J. said:

> For my part, I should be inclined to think that the general powers to legislate in s. 51 confer authority to enact procedural as well as substantive rules of law upon the topics there enumerated and that a vesting under s. 77 (iii) in a State court of federal jurisdiction in matters arising under a Commonwealth statute gives that court authority and imposes upon it a duty to hear and determine those matters according to the substantive and procedural rules thereby enacted without the need for co-operative assistance from s. 51 (xxxix). However, this is a matter which need not be explored, for the existence of the legislative power to regulate the procedure to be followed in the exercise of federal jurisdiction by State courts has been frequently and authoritatively asserted in the past.[100]

It is suggested that (contrary to the view expressed by Stephen J.) rules of procedure for a court invested with federal jurisdiction cannot easily be described as incidental to the act of investing the court with jurisdiction and are more appropriately seen as incidental to the actual exercise of judicial power granted by sec. 71 of the Constitution and therefore 'incidental to the execution of any power vested by this Constitution in . . . the Federal Judicature . . .' within the meaning of sec. 51 (xxxix) if, as has been suggested, State courts exercising federal jurisdiction are within the concept of the 'Federal Judicature'.[101] Alternatively, or

96 (1970) 122 C.L.R. 69 at p. 89.
97 (1976) 9 A.L.R. 103.
98 at pp. 130-1.
99 at pp. 135 and 151 respectively.
100 at p. 135.
101 Lane, *op. cit.*, pp. 234-361.

perhaps additionally, the subject matters mentioned in the various paragraphs in sec. 51 would, for the reasons stated by Mason J., provide a source of power.

The distinction between laying down rules of procedure and attempting to interfere with the structure of the court or the organization through which it operates is not always a clear one. In the Family Law Act 1975 sec. 97 (1) provided that, with certain exceptions, all proceedings in the Family Court or in another court, when exercising jurisdiction under the Act, should be heard in a closed court. Sec. 97 (4) provided that neither the judge nor counsel in respect of proceedings under the Act should robe. In *Russell v. Russell*[102] the Court held that, in relation to State courts exercising jurisdiction under the Act, sec. 97 (1) was invalid (Barwick C.J., Gibbs and Stephen JJ.; Mason and Jacobs JJ. dissenting) and sec. 97 (4) was valid (Stephen, Mason and Jacobs JJ.; Barwick C.J., and Gibbs J. dissenting).

Barwick C.J. and Gibbs J. considered that both provisions went beyond mere practice and procedure and interfered with the nature and organization of the Court. Mason and Jacobs JJ. were equally clear that both those provisions were procedural rules which had nothing to do with the constitution or organizational structure of State courts. Stephen J. was of the view that the provision regarding the non-wearing of robes was procedural but that relating to the closure of courts intruded into the constitution and organization of the court.

The issues of robes for judges and counsel and whether courts should be closed in family law cases clearly have relevance to matrimonial causes and the settlement of disputes involving husband, wife and children. The conflicting interests involved—the dignity of the court as against the advantage of informality—the privacy and delicacy of family matters as against the ideal of open justice—should be primarily for resolution by the legislature that has power with respect to the matters being litigated. To deny that Parliament can carry out the policy it determines if it wishes to use State courts for the hearing of suits is to make less effective and useful the arrangements for which the Constitution provides. Courts open to the public have been traditional in our legal system and the social reason for open courts has always been regarded as important, as Stephen J. showed in his judgement in *Russell v. Russell*. It is suggested with respect, however, that the importance of a rule relating to how a court operates does not in itself mean that the 'character', 'structure' or 'organization' of

102 (1976) 9 A.L.R. 103.

the court has been changed if that rule is altered. There can be countervailing reasons and policies, as is shown by the fact that judges have always had power to sit in a closed court in exceptional circumstances. The determination of the appropriate policy in the case of particular suits such as matrimonial causes should, it is submitted, be a matter for the Commonwealth Parliament when it legislates in respect of that subject even if it wishes to invest State courts with jurisdiction to determine the suit under the Act.

## VII

Some of the more difficult problems affecting the investment of State courts with federal jurisdiction arise from sec. 39 of the Judiciary Act which may conveniently be set out in full:

39. (1) The jurisdiction of the High Court so far as it is not exclusive of the jurisdiction of any Court of a State by virtue of section 38, shall be exclusive of the jurisdiction of the several Courts of the States except as provided in this section.

(2) The several Courts of the States shall within the limits of their several jurisdictions, whether such limits are as to locality, subject matter or otherwise, be invested with federal jurisdiction, in all matters in which the High Court has original jurisdiction or in which original jurisdiction can be conferred upon it, except as provided in section 38, and subject to the following conditions and restrictions:

(a) A decision of a Court of a State, whether in original or in appellate jurisdiction, shall not be subject to appeal to Her Majesty in Council, whether by special leave or otherwise.[103]

(b) . . .[104]

(c) The High Court may grant special leave to appeal to the High Court from any decision of any Court or Judge of a State notwithstanding that the law of the State may prohibit any appeal from such Court or Judge.

(d) The federal jurisdiction of a Court of summary jurisdiction of a State shall not be judicially exercised except by a Stipendiary or Police or Special Magistrate, or some Magistrate of the State

---

[103] Before its amendment by Act No. 134 of 1968, paragraph (a) provided:
'Every decision of the Supreme Court of a State, or any other Court of a State from which at the establishment of the Commonwealth an appeal lay to the Queen in Council shall be final and conclusive except so far as an appeal may be brought to the High Court.'

[104] Before its omission by Act No. 164 of 1976, paragraph (b) provided:
'Wherever an appeal lies from a decision of any Court or Judge of a State to the Supreme Court of the State, an appeal from the decision may be brought to the High Court.'

who is specially authorized by the Governor-General to exercise such jurisdiction.

Sec. 39 (1) purports to be an exercise of power under sec. 77 (ii) of the Constitution, while sec. 39 (2) rests on sec. 77 (iii). In *Lorenzo v. Carey*[105] Higgins J. observed that only sub-paragraph (d) of sec. 39 (2) was aptly described as a condition of the exercise of the jurisdiction invested by that sub-section; while sec. 39 (2) (a) and (c) and former paragraph (b) were more appropriately described as substantive enactments relating to appeals from State courts *after* they had exercised federal jurisdiction. A contrary view was expressed by Isaacs and Rich JJ. in *Commonwealth v. Limerick Steamship Co. Ltd.*[106] They held that these paragraphs were a valid exercise of power under sec. 77 (iii), in so far as regulation of the right to appeal from any State court invested with federal jurisdiction was appropriately construed as a limitation on that court's jurisdiction, and that sec. 77 (iii) therefore authorized the investment of such courts with federal jurisdiction, subject to defined and limited rights of appeal. It is to be noted, however, that sec. 39 (2) (c) does not, of itself, *confer* rights of appeal to the High Court. Sec. 73 (ii) of the Constitution allows a right of appeal to the High Court from State courts invested with federal jurisdiction and sec. 39 (2) (c) is properly construed as a 'regulation' of that appeal within sec. 73 requiring special leave to appeal.[107]

The legislative policy which sec. 39 of the Judiciary Act was designed to accomplish has been discussed many times, and in *Minister of State for the Army v. Parbury Henty and Co. Pty Ltd*[108] it was described by Dixon J. in the following terms:

> The provision was meant to cover the whole field of Federal jurisdiction so that the conditions embodied in the four paragraphs of sub-sec. 2 should govern its exercise whether the cause of action, the procedure and the liability to suit arose under existing or future legislation. To that end it invested State courts with the full content of the original jurisdiction falling within the judicial power of the Commonwealth and, as it has been held, some of the appellate jurisdiction. The limits of jurisdiction of any courts so invested found their source in State law, and, I presume, any change made by the State in those limits would, under the terms of s. 39 (2) *ipso facto* make an identical change in its Federal jurisdiction. An acknowledged purpose was to exclude appeals as of right to the Privy Council, and it was in-

---

[105] (1921) 29 C.L.R. 243, 255.
[106] (1924) 35 C.L.R. 69.
[107] *Wishart v. Fraser* (1941) 64 C.L.R. 470, 480, *per* Dixon J.
[108] (1945) 70 C.L.R. 459, 505.

tended to exclude them over the whole field of Federal jurisdiction. That jurisdiction was, therefore, conferred in its entirety, leaving it to future legislation to bring into being new subject matters and deal with procedure and liability to suit.

So far as this passage suggests that every investment of a State court with federal jurisdiction falls within the ambit of sec. 39, and is subject to the control of that section, its correctness is open to question. In the *Parbury Henty Case*, three members of the Court were of opinion that the State courts were invested with federal jurisdiction in that case by the National Security (General) Regulation in question and not by sec. 39. But discussion of this question may be postponed for the present. Subject to this quali-fication, sec. 39 has a very broad operation. Isaacs J. in *Le Mesurier v. Connor*[109] spoke of it as 'a standing provision con-stantly speaking in the present', and in a later case the High Court characterized the section as a law operating upon the courts of the States as those courts exist from time to time, and said that its operation was to invest those courts with federal jurisdic-tion.[110] The section has an ambulatory operation and in the *Par-bury Henty Case*, Dixon J. expressed this in terms that any change made by State law in the limits of the jurisdiction of the State courts would *ipso facto* make an identical change in the federal jurisdiction of those courts.[111] In *Commonwealth v. Dis-trict Court of the Metropolitan District*[112] it was unsuccessfully argued that the federal jurisdiction of the New South Wales dis-trict courts conferred by sec. 39 was fixed as at the date of the Judiciary Act 1903, so that the Commonwealth could not sue to recover an amount which was not recoverable in that State juris-diction in 1903, although the jurisdictional amount had been substantially raised by subsequent law.

The section is also ambulatory in the sense that it applies to a State court which has come into existence since the date of the Judiciary Act,[113] but this does not mean that sec. 39 (2) operates as a delegation of power to the States to invest a court with federal jurisdiction, so that it does not raise afresh the issues de-bated in the High Court in *Le Mesurier v. Connor*[114] and in

---

109 (1929) 42 C.L.R. 481, 503.
110 *Commonwealth v. District Court of the Metropolitan District* (1954) 90 C.L.R. 13, 22.
111 (1945) 70 C.L.R. 459, 505.
112 (1954) 90 C.L.R. 13.
113 *Collins v. Charles Marshall Pty Ltd* (1955) 92 C.L.R. 529, 536.
114 (1929) 42 C.L.R. 481.

*Peacock's Case*[115] touching the power of Parliament to delegate its power to invest under sec. 77 (iii). As was pointed out in *Commonwealth v. District Court of the Metropolitan District*,[116] sec. 39 (2) does not delegate any power to the States to invest courts with federal jurisdiction; for the transformation into federal jurisdiction is effected directly by the section. Notwithstanding Isaacs J.'s arguments by analogy to sec. 39 (2) in dissent in *Le Mesurier v. Connor*,[117] the cases are different; the law in question in *Le Mesurier v. Connor* purported to empower the Governor-General to select any court of a State, and by naming it to effect an investment of federal jurisdiction. Whatever the validity of such an exercise of power, it is plainly distinguishable from a law which, according to its terms, operates to confer federal jurisdiction on State courts of a given description as they are brought into existence, and as the limits of their respective jurisdictions are defined and redefined.

The operation of sec. 39 on the jurisdiction of State courts calls for closer examination. Sec. 38 of the Judiciary Act, an exercise of power under sec. 77 (ii), declares certain matters to be within the *exclusive* jurisdiction of the High Court. Sec. 39 (1), also an exercise of power under sec. 77 (ii), then declares the jurisdiction of the High Court to be exclusive of that of State courts, so far as it has not already been rendered exclusive by sec. 38. Sec. 39 (2), pursuant to sec. 77 (iii), invests State courts with federal jurisdiction in *all* matters enumerated in secs. 75 and 76, except as provided in sec. 38. It appears, therefore, that there is not a perfect correspondence between the *divesting* operation of sec. 39 (1) and the *vesting* operation of sec. 39 (2). Sec. 77 (ii) can only operate to declare the jurisdiction of the High Court exclusive of that of State courts in respect of those matters in sec. 76 in which the Parliament has conferred original jurisdiction on the High Court. Under sec. 77 (iii), at least on the face of the section, Parliament could invest State courts with federal jurisdiction in respect of *all* matters within secs. 75 and 76, whether or not original jurisdiction had been conferred on the High Court by legislation under sec. 76. Sec. 39 (2) purports to invest State courts with jurisdiction in respect of all such matters, so that it appears for example, that in respect of sec. 76 (ii), matters arising under laws made by the Parliament, where original jurisdiction has not been generally conferred on the High Court,

115 (1943) 67 C.L.R. 25.
116 (1954) 90 C.L.R. 13, 22.
117 (1929) 42 C.L.R. 481, 504-5.

State courts are invested with federal jurisdiction, without any divestment of their jurisdiction to try such matters, which arise apart from any grant of federal jurisdiction, by reason of the obligation imposed upon them by sec. 5 of the Commonwealth of Australia Constitution Act.[118]

The question arose early whether sec. 39 (2) could have this operation; that is to say, could confer federal jurisdiction on State courts in respect of all matters in secs. 75 and 76. In *In re the Income Tax Acts, Outtrim's Case*,[119] the question was whether the salary of a Commonwealth officer was liable to State income tax, a matter which raised issues arising under the Constitution or involving its interpretation, in respect of which original jurisdiction had been conferred on the High Court by sec. 30 of the Judiciary Act under authority of sec. 76 (i) of the Constitution. Hodges J., in the Supreme Court of Victoria, upheld the defendant's claim to immunity, but granted leave to appeal to the Privy Council. This was a case in which, in the absence of sec. 39 of the Judiciary Act, the Supreme Court would have had jurisdiction without any investment of federal jurisdiction. Sec. 39 would have operated in this case to withdraw State jurisdiction and to invest the Supreme Court with federal jurisdiction only, subject to the condition imposed by sec. 39 (2) (a), shutting out any appeal as of right to the Privy Council. Hodges J. in granting leave to appeal offered what he described as 'a few crude observations'[120] on the constitutional issues. So far as those observations bear on the power of the Commonwealth Parliament to qualify, alter or in part repeal any Imperial Order-in-Council authorizing appeals from the Supreme Court to the Privy Council, discussion may be postponed for the present. Hodges J. directed attention to the divesting and the investing provisions of sec. 39, and observed that it was not open to the Commonwealth Parliament under sec. 77 to take away jurisdiction which 'belonged to' a State court, and then to return it in the form of federal jurisdiction with conditions attached. The investing clauses 'repeal the provision which takes the jurisdiction away, and it is back, belonging,

---

118 '5. This Act, and all laws made by the Parliament of the Commonwealth under the Constitution, shall be binding on the courts, judges, and people of every State and of every part of the Commonwealth, notwithstanding anything in the laws of any State; and the laws of the Commonwealth shall be in force on all British ships, the Queen's ships of war excepted, whose first port of clearance and whose port of destination are in the Commonwealth.'

119 [1905] V.L.R. 463.

120 at p. 465.

as it originally belonged, to the State Courts'.[121] On this view of sec. 77 (iii) Parliament could only invest State courts with federal jurisdiction in respect of those matters which, apart from such a grant, were not within their jurisdiction.

In *Webb v. Outrim*,[122] the Privy Council allowed the appeal on the merits, but expressly adopted the reasoning of Hodges J. in granting leave to appeal, and amplified those reasons very little. In *Baxter v. Commissioner of Taxation (N.S.W.)*,[123] the High Court treated *Webb v. Outrim* as a decision not on the vesting provisions of sec. 39 (2), but on the condition imposed by sec. 39 (2) (a). Conceding, without deciding, the invalidity of sec. 39 (2) (a), the Court offered an alternative construction of the vesting provisions of sec. 39, which was subsequently adopted and amplified by the High Court in *Lorenzo v. Carey*.[124] That case and *Baxter's Case* raised questions touching the right of appeal from State courts to the High Court under sec. 39 (2). In *Lorenzo v. Carey*, Mr Dixon, for the State of Victoria intervening, unsuccessfully argued[125] that sec. 39 was invalid in whole for the reason stated by Hodges J. in *Outtrim's Case*. The High Court upheld the general validity of the section, expressing no opinion as to sec. 39 (2) (a) which was said to be severable in any event. The Court's favourable view of sec. 39 called for a definition of federal jurisdiction:

> The phrase 'Federal jurisdiction' as used in secs. 71, 73 and 77 of the Constitution means jurisdiction derived from the Federal Commonwealth. It does not denote a power to adjudicate in certain matters, though it may connote such a power; it denotes the power to act as the judicial agent of the Commonwealth, which must act through agents if it acts at all. An agent may have a valid authority from a number of independent principals to do the same act. A State Court must recognize the laws of the Commonwealth and be guided by them in exercising its State jurisdiction, and precisely the same duty or a diverse duty may fall upon it by virtue of a grant of Federal jurisdiction under sec. 77 (iii). But even if the duty to be performed under the two jurisdictions be identical, the two jurisdictions are not identical: they are not one but several. When Federal jurisdiction is given to a State Court and the jurisdiction which belongs to it is not taken away, we see no difficulty in that Court exercising either

[121] at p. 468.
[122] [1907] A.C. 81, 91-2.
[123] (1907) 4 C.L.R. 1087, esp. at 1141 *et seq.*
[124] (1921) 29 C.L.R. 243.
[125] at pp. 245-6. He argued further that the decision in *Webb v. Outrim* that sec. 39 (2) (a) was invalid, involved the whole section in invalidity, on the ground that sec. 39 (2) (a) was not severable.

jurisdiction at the instance of a litigant. The position of such Courts is no more anomalous than that of the Courts of Australia and other parts of the British Empire which have administered law and equity in distinct proceedings before the same tribunal.[126]

On this view, there is no analytical difficulty in the concurrent possession of State and federal jurisdiction by a State court in respect of a particular matter, nor in the withdrawal of State jurisdiction and the investment of federal jurisdiction in respect of the same matter. Federal jurisdiction is properly viewed from the standpoint of the *source* of authority to adjudicate, not from the standpoint of the *subject-matter* of adjudication. Moreover the language of sec. 77 (iii) supports this view of federal jurisdiction; it authorizes the investment of State courts with federal jurisdiction with respect to *any* of the matters mentioned in secs. 75 and 76.[127] It is clear that State courts possessed State jurisdiction in respect of some of these matters; but the grant of power authorizes the investment of State courts without distinguishing between such matters and those which specifically required a grant of jurisdiction to State courts.

There may be good practical sense in the conclusion reached by Hodges J. and unsuccessfully argued by Mr Dixon in *Lorenzo v. Carey.* It is absurd that a State court should possess two separate jurisdictions with differing incidents, in respect of the same matter. It is a safe guess that the Founding Fathers did not foresee these complications when they drew sec. 77 (iii); while it makes sense to authorize the definition of jurisdiction in sec. 77 (i) and (ii) by reference to *any* of the matters mentioned in secs. 75 and 76, there was no call for a grant of power to invest State courts with federal jurisdiction—assuming any need to introduce a concept of *federal* jurisdiction here at all—except in respect of those matters which lay outside the ordinary jurisdiction of State courts, such as matters in which the Commonwealth was a defendant, or where some order was sought against a Commonwealth officer, in which latter case anyway, the jurisdiction of the High Court was defined as exclusive by sec. 38 of the Judiciary Act. The power to invest State courts with federal jurisdiction should have been separated from the other two sub-sections of sec. 77, and should have been more narrowly drawn to ensure that State courts should have been competent to exercise jurisdiction

---

126 at pp. 251-2. See also *Commonwealth v. Limerick Steamship Co. Ltd* and *Commonwealth v. Kidman* (1924) 35 C.L.R. 69; *Commonwealth v. Kreglinger and Fernau Ltd* and *Commonwealth v. Bardsley* (1926) 37 C.L.R. 393.

127 Hodges J. in *Outtrim's Case* did not consider this problem. See Bailey: The Federal Jurisdiction of State Courts (1940-1) 2 *Res Judicatae* at p. 116.

P

in matters enumerated in secs. 75 and 76, otherwise outside their competence, which might be the subject of a *supplementary* grant of jurisdiction by Parliament. It is beyond belief that there was an intention to give State courts the same subject-matter jurisdiction twice over. This, however, beats the air; power was conferred in terms of sec. 77 (iii), and as a construction of constitutional language, it is not easy to fault the reasoning in *Lorenzo v. Carey.*

In *Baxter v. Commissioner of Taxation (N.S.W.)*[128] the High Court did not consider sec. 39 (2) (a), and in *Lorenzo v. Carey* the Court referred to *Webb v. Outrim* as deciding that sec. 39 (2) (a) was invalid so far as it purported to take away the right to appeal to the Privy Council. Until 1968 sec. 39 (2) (a) provided:

> Every decision of the Supreme Court of a State, or any other Court of a State from which at the establishment of the Commonwealth an appeal lay to the Queen in Council shall be final and conclusive except so far as an appeal may be brought to the High Court.

In *Baxter's Case* and in *Lorenzo v. Carey*, the discussion of sec. 39 proceeded on the basis that sec. 39 (2) (a) was, in any event, severable. It is now accepted that sec. 39 (2) (a) is valid. As Dixon J. said in *McIlwraith McEacharn Ltd v. Shell Co. of Australia Ltd*,[129] 'in this Court, which considered that by reason of s. 74 of the Constitution it was not a matter for the Privy Council to decide, the provision has been treated as valid'. This conclusion was accepted in *Commonwealth v. Queensland.*[130]

The reasoning by which this result has been achieved has been remarkable in its sweep.[131] *Webb v. Outrim* was a matter involving the interpretation of the Constitution, and on the reasoning developed in *Lorenzo v. Carey*, sec. 39 of the Judiciary Act operated in such a case to invest the Supreme Court of Victoria with federal jurisdiction only. The matter had appeared differently to Hodges J., and his reasoning led to the conclusion that sec. 39 would not operate, because sec. 77 (iii) did not authorize the investment of federal jurisdiction where, as in this case, the State courts already possessed jurisdiction without any grant under sec. 77. On the view that Hodges J. was exercising State jurisdiction, it was clear that there was no power to cut off

[128] (1907) 4 C.L.R. 1087.
[129] (1945) 70 C.L.R. 175, 209.
[130] (1975) 7 A.L.R. 351.
[131] Sawer: Essays on the Australian Constitution (Ed. Else-Mitchell, 2nd ed., 1961) at p. 85 says that 'the attempts at distinguishing the disapproval of the scheme voiced by the Privy Council in *Webb v. Outrim* have verged on the disingenuous'.

the appeal from a State Supreme Court to the Privy Council. Hodges J. gave as a further reason for holding sec. 39 (2) (a) bad that, even assuming that the Supreme Court was invested with federal jurisdiction, sec. 77 (iii) should not be construed as authorizing the Parliament to take away a right of appeal conferred by Order-in-Council under the Imperial Judicial Committee Act 1844, in the absence of direct authority so to do. 'If there was no direct authority for such legislation, I should say that the British Parliament never intended or authorized so important an end to be attained by indirect or circuitous methods. In such an important matter, direct authority would be given or none at all. And none is directly given.'[132] The question of the relationship of sec. 39 (2) (a) as an exercise of power under sec. 77 (iii) to the Order-in-Council under the Judicial Committee Act may have been thought to raise a question of repugnancy under the Colonial Laws Validity Act; yet as Irvine C.J. noted in *Kreglinger and Fernau Ltd v. Commonwealth*[133] that Act was not cited or expressly referred to in *Outtrim's Case*. Hodges J.'s judgement suggests that the question, though perhaps not very carefully analysed, was regarded as raising a question of *ultra vires*, concerned with the affirmative limits of the power conferred by sec. 77 (iii).[134]

The reasoning of Hodges J. was expressly approved, and quoted in part by the Privy Council in *Webb v. Outrim*. The holding that sec. 39 (2) (a) could not foreclose an appeal as of right from the State Supreme Court to the Privy Council rested therefore on two grounds; one that the State court was not exercising federal jurisdiction, and that sec. 39 could not convert State into federal jurisdiction, and that it was not possible to bar an appeal from the exercise of State jurisdiction to the Privy Council: the other based on a view of the affirmative limits of sec. 77 (iii), assuming an exercise of federal jurisdiction by the State Supreme Court. These questions arose again in two groups of cases: *Commonwealth v. Limerick Steamship Co. Ltd* and *Commonwealth v. Kidman*,[135] and *Commonwealth v. Kreglinger and Fernau Ltd* and *Commonwealth v. Bardsley*.[136] All these cases except *Commonwealth v. Kidman*, in which the Commonwealth was the plaintiff, were actions by private parties against the Common-

---

132 [1905] V.L.R. 463, 467.
133 [1926] V.L.R. 310, 320.
134 See Bailey, *ante* note 127 at p. 191.
135 (1924) 35 C.L.R. 69.
136 (1926) 37 C.L.R. 393.

wealth. *Commonwealth v. Kidman* was therefore the only case in the group precisely covered by *Webb v. Outrim*, at least on the point of the exercise of *State* jurisdiction by the State Supreme Court. In the other three cases, the Commonwealth being a defendant, the reasoning of Hodges J. would have led to the conclusion that sec. 39 operated to confer federal jurisdiction, so that the validity of sec. 39 (2) (a) fell inevitably to be considered by reference to the limits of sec. 77 (iii), and the relation of sec. 39 (2) (a) to the Imperial Order-in-Council.

In *Commonwealth v. Limerick Steamship Co. Ltd* and *Commonwealth v. Kidman,* the Supreme Court of New South Wales gave leave to appeal to the Privy Council from its judgements, and the parties appealed against these orders. In *Commonwealth v. Kreglinger and Fernau Ltd* and *Commonwealth v. Bardsley* (the *Skin Wool Cases*), the actions were tried by Cussen J. in the Supreme Court of Victoria. On appeal from his judgement for the defendants to the Full Supreme Court,[137] the majority held that they were bound by *Parkin v. James*[138] to hold that sec. 39 (2) (a) of the Judiciary Act, if valid, precluded an appeal to the Full Supreme Court, and required it to go direct to the High Court. On this view, the majority had to consider the argument that sec. 39 (2) (a) was invalid in so far as it prevented appeals to the Privy Council from State courts exercising federal jurisdiction. They upheld this argument, refusing to follow the *Limerick Case* and purporting to follow *Webb v. Outrim,* and further held that sec. 39 (2) (a) was inseverable, with the consequence that the section was wholly invalid. They then dismissed the appeal from Cussen J. on the merits. The plaintiffs then appealed to a differently constituted Full Court for leave to appeal to the Privy Council, which was granted in view of the court's previous holding that sec. 39 (2) (a) was invalid. The defendants appealed to the High Court against the order granting leave.

In the *Limerick Case*, a closely divided High Court (Isaacs, Rich and Starke JJ.; Knox C.J. and Gavan Duffy J. dissenting) discharged the orders of the Supreme Court of New South Wales. Knox C.J. and Gavan Duffy J. regarded themselves as bound by *Webb v. Outrim* to hold sec. 39 (2) (a) invalid. The majority held that sec. 77 (iii) authorized the definition and restriction of the right of appeal from a State court invested with federal jurisdiction and this then squarely raised a question of repugnancy between sec. 39 (2) (a) and the Imperial Order-in-Council. On the

137 [1926] V.L.R. 310.
138 (1905) 2 C.L.R. 315.

view that sec. 77 (iii) authorized the regulation of appeals from
a State court invested with federal jurisdiction, it was said that
the question of repugnancy arose as between an Imperial Act
of 1844 authorizing orders-in-council regulating appeals to the
Privy Council and an Imperial Act of 1900, the Constitution Act,
authorizing the regulation of appeals from State courts invested
with federal jurisdiction. On this construction, the conflict was
between the authority of two Imperial Acts, and on established
rules of interpretation the later in time prevailed.

The majority held further that *Webb v. Outrim* was not controlling; that it could be distinguished as a decision on the vesting
provisions of sec. 39; that is to say, that the section could not
operate to replace existing State jurisdiction with federal jurisdiction. The difficulties in this argument are that *Webb v. Outrim*
did not rest exclusively on this ground, and that in any event any
such distinction could not apply to *Kidman's Case* to which the
arguments touching the vesting provisions of sec. 39 applied as
they applied to *Webb v. Outrim*. The majority argued by reference to sec. 38 of the Judiciary Act that *Kidman's Case* must be
taken to be decided in federal jurisdiction, but there does not
appear to be any satisfactory basis on which that case can be
convincingly distinguished from *Webb v. Outrim*.[139]

A question immediately arises as to the limits of the repugnancy argument as formulated in the *Limerick Case* and *Kidman's Case*. As stated there, it might appear that any Commonwealth legislation enacted pursuant to the authority of the Constitution would prevail over inconsistent Imperial legislation
enacted prior to 1900. That this broad proposition did not cor-
rectly state the law was established by the High Court's decision
six months after the *Limerick Case* in *Union Steamship Co. of
New Zealand v. Commonwealth*[140] where it was held that Commonwealth legislation enacted pursuant to secs. 51 (i) and 98 of
the Constitution was void under the Colonial Laws Validity Act
for repugnancy to the Merchant Shipping Act 1894. When the
matter arose in the High Court in the *Skin Wool Cases*, it was
argued that the *Union Steamship Co. Case* had destroyed the
majority argument denying repugnancy in the *Limerick Case*
and *Kidman's Case*. In the *Skin Wool Cases*, the High Court by a
majority of six to one discharged the Full Court's order giving
leave to appeal. Knox C.J., Gavan Duffy and Powers JJ. held that
the validity of sec. 39 (2) (a) raised an *inter se* question, in

139 Bailey *ante* note 127 at p. 196.
140 (1925) 36 C.L.R. 130.

which by secs. 38A and 40A of the Judiciary Act, the High Court had exclusive jurisdiction, so that when the issue was raised in the Full Court, that Court should have proceeded no further, and that its order granting leave to appeal to the Privy Council was therefore a nullity. Isaacs, Rich and Starke JJ. agreed, and Higgins J. alone dissented. Isaacs J., in a judgement with which Rich J. expressly agreed, developed an elaborate and remarkable argument on the issue of repugnancy. He expressly accepted the authority of the *Union Steamship Co. Case*, which he explained on the ground that the Imperial Merchant Shipping Act 1894 dealt with a subject of Empire-wide concern, and that there could not be spelled out of the Constitution any implied authority to authorize legislation inconsistent with it, even though the Constitution was an Imperial Act later in date than the Merchant Shipping Act. The control of appeals from Australian courts was a different case; it was a matter of distinctively Australian concern and, applying the principles of responsible government—which in this context meant the development of Dominion status—a construction of the Constitution which enabled the Commonwealth Parliament to control all litigation on federal matters and to make provision for appeals inconsistent with British legislation earlier in date than the Constitution was justified. Isaacs J. developed this argument with a characteristic sweep and concluded that sec. 77 (iii) 'must be read as modifying the earlier instrument, at least to the extent of leaving the will of the Australian national Parliament on the subject of civil rights in Australia, in relation to federal matters specifically enumerated in the constitution, free from the control of Imperial ministerial discretion'.[141]

Isaacs and Rich JJ. also argued that on their proper construction the Imperial Orders-in-Council applied only to the exercise of State jurisdiction by a State Supreme Court. This is open to the objection that on their face the Orders apply clearly to both State and federal exercises of jurisdiction.[142] The broad argument of Isaacs J. is more persuasive; it has been said to bear 'all the marks of judicial legislation . . . [but] . . . the grasp of principle is sure and the application, though unexpected, does not seem . . . either strained or unconvincing'.[143] Bailey argues further that it is supported by the decisions of the Privy Council in *Nadan v.*

---

[141] (1926) 37 C.L.R. 393, 414-5.
[142] Bailey *ante* note 127 at pp. 186-7.
[143] *op. cit.* at p. 190.

*The King*[144] and *British Coal Corporation v. The King.*[145] In the
earlier case, the holding was that it was beyond the competence
of the Canadian Parliament, at that time, to abolish the *prerogative* appeal in criminal cases to the Privy Council, but it was
common ground in argument before the Privy Council that there
was power to abolish the appeal as of right. It was the appeal as
of right which was in issue in *Webb v. Outrim* and in the High
Court cases. In *British Coal Corporation v. The King*, the Privy
Council upheld similar Canadian legislation passed after the
enactment of the Statute of Westminster 1931. It had been argued,
notwithstanding the Statute of Westminster, that there was no
power in the Dominion legislature to abrogate the prerogative
appeal in the absence of express authority or necessary intendment. This argument was rejected by the Privy Council and Lord
Sankey, in language strikingly reminiscent of Isaacs J.'s judgement in the *Skin Wool Cases*, pointed to the development of
Dominion status in aid of the conclusion that a broad and liberal
interpretation should be given to Dominion powers in such
respects as these.

In light of these decisions, it has been argued that *Webb v.
Outrim* would be differently decided by the Privy Council at the
present day, in favour of sec. 39 (2) (a), and it may very well be
that this is so.[146] *Webb v. Outrim* dealt only with the appeal as of
right, and it was not argued that sec. 39 (2) (a) affected the prerogative appeal. By the Judiciary Act 1968, however, sec. 39 (2) (a)
was amended so as expressly to abolish the prerogative appeal
from State courts exercising federal jurisdiction. It now provides:

> A decision of a Court of a State, whether in original or in appel-
> late jurisdiction, shall not be subject to appeal to Her Majesty in
> Council, whether by special leave or otherwise.

Since the State of Westminster Adoption Act 1942, it is clear that
the Commonwealth has power to abolish the prerogative appeal
from State courts exercising federal jurisdiction.[147]

It is another question whether the attempts at distinguishing
*Webb v. Outrim* which were made in the High Court cases can
be supported. It seems clear enough that the distinction between
the Privy Council decision and *Kidman's Case* cannot be main-

144 [1926] A.C. 482.
145 [1935] A.C. 500.
146 Bailey *ante* note 127 at p. 194.
147 *Cooperative Committee on Japanese Canadians v. Attorney-General for
Canada* [1947] A.C. 87. This is implicit in the judgement of Gibbs J. in *Commonwealth v. Queensland* (1975) 7 A.L.R. 351.

tained; but Bailey argues that there is a 'technically valid'[148] distinction between the other three cases and *Webb v. Outrim*, which rests on the argument that the jurisdiction exercised in the High Court cases, whether tested by the reasoning of Hodges J. in *Outtrim's Case* or by the principles stated by the High Court in *Lorenzo v. Carey*, must have been exclusively federal. Sawer, to the contrary, has little doubt that in *Webb v. Outrim* the Privy Council intended to hold sec. 39 (2) (a) invalid in relation to federal jurisdiction, though his argument that *Webb v. Outrim* was a case involving the interpretation of the Constitution and therefore within secs. 30 and 39 of the Judiciary Act ignores the basis on which Hodges J. held it not to be a case in which federal jurisdiction could lawfully be invested in the State court. But it seems that the *ratio decidendi* of *Webb v. Outrim* was two-pronged; on one line of argument, assuming the exercise of State jurisdiction, the Privy Council appeal could not be abolished; on the other, assuming the exercise of federal jurisdiction, it was still beyond power to abolish the appeal. This makes it very difficult to support any convincing distinction between *Webb v. Outrim* and the High Court cases, and in *McIlwraith McEacharn Ltd v. Shell Co. of Australia Ltd*[149] Dixon J. preferred to accept the authority of the High Court cases—despite the close division on the validity of sec. 39 (2) (a)—without any attempt to distinguish *Webb v. Outrim*.

In *McIlwraith McEacharn Ltd v. Shell Co. of Australia Ltd*, Dixon J. said that *Webb v. Outrim* was not binding on the High Court because of the operation of sec. 74 of the Constitution. In the four High Court cases, it was argued that the issue of inconsistency between sec. 39 (2) (a) and the Orders-in-Council raised a question of the limits *inter se* of the powers of the Commonwealth and a State within sec. 74. On this view, which had the support of the majority in the High Court in *Baxter's Case*, *Webb v. Outrim* did not bind the High Court on any view of its *ratio decidendi*. These arguments were developed in the judgements in the *Skin Wool Cases*. Isaacs J. argued that the State constitution included all the rules derived from all sources which affected the powers of the Supreme Court; that behind all governmental powers in Australia lay the ultimate authority of the United Kingdom Parliament, and that there was therefore a conflict between the legislative power of the Commonwealth to forbid an appeal to the Privy Council and the judicial power of the State

---

[148] *ante* note 127 at p. 195.
[149] (1945) 70 C.L.R. 175, 209.

to grant it. Higgins J. disagreed; his view was that the exercise of power by a State court in granting leave to appeal depended on the Imperial Order-in-Council; that this was not an exercise of the constitutional power of a State, so that the only conflict was between the powers of the Commonwealth Parliament and the King-in-Council. This view apparently commanded the support of Knox C.J. and Gavan Duffy J. who in the *Limerick Case* and *Kidman's Case* held *Webb v. Outrim* to be controlling; while Rich J. supported Isaacs J., the two remaining judges in the cases, Starke and Powers JJ., did not express their views on the matter. Dixon J.'s brief statement in the *McIlwraith Case* appears to support the argument of Isaacs J.

The decision in *Felton v. Mulligan*[150] was based on the view that sec. 39 (2) (a) was valid. In *Commonwealth v. Queensland* (the *Queen of Queensland Case*)[151] Gibbs J. (with whose judgement Barwick C.J., Stephen and Mason JJ. agreed), adopted the statement of Dixon J. in the *McIlwraith Case*. He said that 'The power given by sec. 77 has been held to enable the Parliament to enact legislation having the effect that no appeal may be brought to the Judicial Committee from the decision of a State Court given in the exercise of federal jurisdiction. . . .'[152] It seems clear that the question of the validity of sec. 39 (2) (a) is now settled.[153]

In the first edition of this book[154] the question was discussed whether sec. 39 (2) (a), as it then existed, allowed in accordance with State law an appeal from a single judge of a State Supreme

---

[150] (1971) 124 C.L.R. 367.

[151] (1975) 7 A.L.R. 351.

[152] pp. 362-3.

[153] Mr Justice Murphy has held that since the enactment of the Privy Council (Appeals from the High Court) Act 1975 the implication should be drawn that the Privy Council may not receive appeals on any questions from any court in Australia including a State court, whether exercising State or federal jurisdiction (*Commonwealth v. Queensland* (1975) 7 A.L.R. 351, 381). Murphy J.'s argument rests on the basis that, if there is no appeal from the High Court, there can be no appeal to the Privy Council from any court from which an appeal to the High Court may be taken. The reasoning behind this approach is that 'The existence of two ultimate Courts of Appeal on any question would not be only incongruous but mischievous. Any difference of opinion between the Privy Council and the High Court on non-*inter se* questions would naturally be exploited by litigants' (p. 381).

No other judge of the High Court has, as yet, adopted this approach. As appeals to the Privy Council from State courts exercising federal jurisdiction are now no longer possible, Murphy J.'s approach is as a practical matter of importance only where those courts are exercising State jurisdiction.

[154] pp. 179-81.

Court invested with federal jurisdiction to the Full Supreme Court. This issue arose because that provision stated that every decision of a Supreme Court 'shall be final and conclusive except so far as an appeal may be brought to the High Court'. It was held in *Minister of State for the Army v. Parbury Henty and Co. Pty Ltd*[155] that sec. 39 did not affect the internal system of appeals in a State Supreme Court.

This question does not arise under the amendment made to sec. 39 (2) (a) in 1968 which merely provides that a decision of a court of a State exercising federal jurisdiction shall not be subject to appeal to Her Majesty in Council, whether by special leave or otherwise.

## VIII

Further problems arise in connection with the investment of State courts with federal *criminal* jurisdiction. Sec. 39 of the Judiciary Act is expressed in general terms, and, on its face, applies equally to civil and criminal jurisdiction. There are, however, specific statutory provisions with respect to criminal jurisdiction, notably sec. 68 of the Judiciary Act. The historical background is of some interest. The Punishment of Offenders Act 1901 was a temporary measure which was to cease to have effect when the High Court was established. It provided that the laws in each State respecting the arrest and custody of offenders, and the procedure for their summary conviction or for their examination and commitment for trial on indictment or information, or for the grant of bail, should apply so far as applicable to persons charged with offences against the laws of the Commonwealth committed within the State. The courts and magistrates of each State exercising jurisdiction in these matters were given the like jurisdiction with respect to persons charged with offences against the laws of the Commonwealth, subject to the proviso that jurisdiction should only be exercised with respect to summary conviction, or examination and commitment for trial, by stipendiary, police or special magistrates or by a State magistrate specially authorized by the Governor-General. The Act then gave appellate jurisdiction 'to the Court and in the manner provided by the law of that State for appeal from the like convictions, judgements, sentences or orders in respect of persons charged with offences against the laws of the State'.

It was necessary to make some temporary provision until the establishment of the High Court. Sec. 73 (ii) of the Constitution

[155] (1945) 70 C.L.R. 459.

allowed an appeal to the High Court from State courts invested with federal jurisdiction, but that depended upon the establishment of the High Court. The appeals section of the Punishment of Offenders Act bridged the gap[156] but on the inauguration of the High Court, the force of the Act was spent. The Judiciary Act 1903, however, included not only sec. 39, but also sec. 68 which substantially reproduced the provisions of the Punishment of Offenders Act, except that the appeal section was not re-enacted. Following the decision of *Seaegg v. The King*,[157] sec. 68 was amended in 1932. It was further amended in 1976 and now reads as follows:

68. (1) The laws of each State or Territory respecting the arrest and custody of offenders or persons charged with offences, and the procedure for—

(a) their summary conviction; and

(b) their examination and commitment for trial on indictment; and

(c) their trial and conviction on indictment; and

(d) the hearing and determination of appeals arising out of any such trial or conviction or out of any proceedings connected therewith

and for holding accused persons to bail, shall, subject to this section, apply and be applied so far as they are applicable to persons who are charged with offences against the laws of the Commonwealth committed within that State or Territory, or whose trial for offences committed elsewhere may lawfully be held therein.

(2) The several courts of a State or Territory exercising jurisdiction with respect to—

(a) the summary conviction; or

(b) the examination and commitment for trial on indictment; or

(c) the trial and conviction on indictment;

of offenders or persons charged with offences against the laws of the State or Territory, and with respect to the hearing and determination of appeals arising out of any such trial or conviction or out of any proceedings connected therewith, shall have the like jurisdiction with respect to persons who are charged with offences against the laws of the Commonwealth committed within the State or Territory or who may lawfully be tried within the State or Territory for offences committed elsewhere:

(3) Provided that such jurisdiction shall not be judicially exercised with respect to the summary conviction or examination and commitment for trial of any person except by a Stipendiary or Police or

156 *Ah Yick v. Lehmert* (1905) 2 C.L.R. 593, 606-7.
157 (1932) 48 C.L.R. 251.

Special Magistrate, or some Magistrate of the State or Territory who is specially authorized by the Governor-General to exercise such jurisdiction.

(4) The several Courts of a State or Territory exercising the jurisdiction conferred upon them by this section shall, upon application being made in that behalf, have power to order, upon such terms as they think fit, that any information laid before them in respect of an offence against the laws of the Commonwealth shall be amended so as to remove any defect either in form or substance contained in that information.

(5) In relation to offences committed elsewhere than in a State or Territory (including offences in, over or under any area of the seas that is not part of a State or Territory), the jurisdiction conferred by sub-section (2) is conferred notwithstanding any limits as to locality of the jurisdiction of the court concerned under the law of the State or Territory.

(6) Where a person who has committed, or is suspected of having committed, an offence against a law of the Commonwealth, whether in a State or Territory or elsewhere, is found within an area of waters in respect of which sovereignty is vested in the Crown in right of the Commonwealth, he may be arrested in respect of the offence in accordance with the provisions of the law of any State or Territory that would be applicable to the arrest of the offender in that State or Territory in respect of such an offence committed in that State or Territory, and may be brought in custody into any State or Territory and there dealt with in like manner as if he had been arrested in that State or Territory.

(7) The procedure referred to in sub-section (1) and the jurisdiction referred to in sub-section (2) shall be deemed to include procedure and jurisdiction in accordance with provisions of a law of a State or Territory under which a person who, in proceedings before a court of summary jurisdiction, pleads guilty to a charge for which he could be prosecuted on indictment may be committed to a court having jurisdiction to try offences on indictment to be sentenced or otherwise dealt with without being tried in that court, and the reference in sub-sections (1) and (2) to 'any such trial or conviction' shall be read as including any conviction or sentencing in accordance with any such provisions.

(8) Except as otherwise specifically provided by an Act passed after the commencement of this sub-section, a person may be dealt with in accordance with provisions of the kind referred to in sub-section (7) notwithstanding that, apart from this section, the offence would be required to be prosecuted on indictment, or would be required to be prosecuted either summarily or on indictment.

(9) Where a law of a State or Territory of the kind referred to in sub-section (7) refers to indictable offences, that reference shall, for the purposes of the application of the provisions of the law in accordance with that sub-section, be read as including a reference to

an offence against a law of the Commonwealth that may be prosecuted on indictment.

(10) Where, in accordance with a procedure of the kind referred to in sub-section (7), a person is to be sentenced by a court having jurisdiction to try offences on indictment, that person shall, for the purpose of ascertaining the sentence that may be imposed, be deemed to have been prosecuted and convicted on indictment in that court.

(11) Nothing in this section excludes or limits any power of arrest conferred by, or any jurisdiction vested or conferred by, any other law, including an Act passed before the commencement of this sub-section.

The 1932 amendments affected sub-secs. (1) and (2), and conferred *appellate* jurisdiction on State courts in respect of offences against the laws of the Commonwealth. This raises questions as to the relationship between secs. 39 and 68 of the Judiciary Act, and the general question of the extent to which sec. 39 applies to criminal matters. In *Ah Yick v. Lehmert*[158] the issue was whether a Victorian court of General Sessions was competent to entertain an appeal from a conviction by a police magistrate under the Commonwealth Immigration Restriction Act 1901. The High Court held that the appeal lay, that it was authorized by sec. 39 of the Judiciary Act, that under sec. 77 (iii) federal appellate jurisdiction could validly be conferred on the court,[159] and that sec. 68, which at that time made no investment of appellate criminal jurisdiction, should not be construed as a limitation on the scope and operation of sec. 39. Griffith C.J. said:

Now, if secs. 68 and 39 of the Judiciary Act 1903 covered precisely the same ground, there might be some force in that argument,[160] though it would still be contrary to the accepted canons of construction to hold that, where there are two affirmative enactments in the same Act each dealing with the same matter, one is to be taken as negativing the other. But on examination it will be seen that secs. 68 and 39 probably do not cover the same ground. Sec. 39 applies only to the nine classes of cases enumerated in secs. 75 and 76 of the Constitution. Sec. 68 applies to all persons charged with offences against the laws of the Commonwealth. Now, unless it can be asserted that there can be no offence against the laws of the Commonwealth which does not fall within one of the nine classes of cases enumerated in secs. 75 and 76 of the Constitution, sec. 68 of the Judiciary Act 1903 was necessary. I should be very sorry to affirm that secs. 75 and 76 of the Constitution do cover every possible case of offences against the laws of the Commonwealth. They cover every offence against the

158 (1905) 2 C.L.R. 593.
159 See p. 131 *ante*.
160 That is, that no appeal lay under sec. 39.

Statutes of the Commonwealth as they at present exist, so far as I know, but I apprehend that many cases may arise in which it will be at least doubtful whether those sections cover them.[161]

Barton J. expressed agreement with this view. The meaning of the passage is not altogether clear, and Griffith C.J. did not find it necessary to develop the argument. The limits of the power to invest State courts with federal jurisdiction are expressly defined by reference to the nine matters enumerated in secs. 75 and 76, and it follows therefore that any such investment whether by sec. 39 or 68 of the Judiciary Act may not transcend these limits. It does not follow, of course, that jurisdiction with respect to offences against the laws of the Commonwealth will necessarily be referable to sec. 76 (ii)—matters arising under laws made by the Parliament; jurisdiction in respect of offences against the common law of the Commonwealth may properly be referable to sec. 75 (iii)—matters in which the Commonwealth is a party.[162]

While an investment of State courts with federal jurisdiction may not extend beyond the limits fixed by secs. 75 and 76, it is clear that secs. 39 and 68 of the Judiciary Act do not cover precisely similar ground. In *Seaegg v. The King*,[163] it was held that the vesting provisions of sec. 39 of the Judiciary Act did not convert a right of appeal conferred by State law to a State court in respect of offences under *State* law into a right of appeal to that court in respect of an offence under *federal* law. The question was whether a person convicted of an offence against a law of the Commonwealth by a New South Wales court of Quarter Sessions could appeal to the Supreme Court of New South Wales as a Court of Criminal Appeal under the provisions of the Criminal Appeal Act 1912. The High Court held that on its proper construction, the statutory right of appeal was confined to convictions on indictment preferred according to State law. The Court held further that sec. 68 of the Judiciary Act, as then enacted, did not confer a right of appeal in such a case.

This decision led to the amendment of sec. 68 in 1932. The amendments, as Dixon J. pointed out in *Williams v. The King (No. 2)*,[164] were 'intended to confer upon the Courts of Criminal Appeal of the States a jurisdiction to hear and determine appeals in the case of Federal offences such as existed in the case of State offences'. It is clear that in its amended form sec. 68 confers a more extensive jurisdiction on State courts than do the vesting

---

[161] (1905) 2 C.L.R. 593, 607-8.
[162] See *R. v. Kidman* (1915) 20 C.L.R. 425. See pp. 7-8 *ante*.
[163] (1932) 48 C.L.R. 251.
[164] (1934) 50 C.L.R. 551, 559.

provisions of sec. 39. The scope of the amended sec. 68 was considered by the High Court. In *Williams v. The King (No. 1)*,[165] the Court unanimously held, reversing the New South Wales Court of Criminal Appeal, that sec. 68 did not entitle the Attorney-General of the *State*, who, under the terms of the Criminal Appeal Act, was authorized to appeal to the Court of Criminal Appeal against any sentence pronounced by the Supreme Court or any court of Quarter Sessions, to appeal against a sentence imposed for an offence against *federal* law. Thereupon the Attorney-General for the *Commonwealth* appealed to the Court of Criminal Appeal against the sentence imposed on the prisoner, and the court increased the sentence. On an application to the High Court for special leave to appeal, the Court in *Williams v. The King (No. 2)*[166] was equally divided so that leave to appeal was refused. Rich, Starke and Dixon JJ. held that the amendments to sec. 68 of the Judiciary Act operated on the New South Wales statute which conferred power on the State Attorney-General to appeal against sentence imposed on convictions under State law, to permit the Attorney-General for the Commonwealth to bring the like appeal to the State court against sentence imposed on a conviction for a federal offence. As Dixon J. said: 'When sec. 68 (2) speaks of the "like jurisdiction with respect to persons who are charged with offences against the laws of the Commonwealth", it recognizes that the adoption of State law must proceed by analogy. The proper officer of the Crown in right of the Commonwealth for representing it in the Courts is the Federal Attorney-General. I do not feel any difficulty in deciding that, under the word "like" in the expression "like jurisdiction", the functions under sec. 5D of the State Attorney-General in the case of State offenders fall to the Federal Attorney-General in the case of offenders against the laws of the Commonwealth.'[167] Gavan Duffy C.J., Evatt and McTiernan JJ. rested the contrary argument partly on the construction of the words of sec. 68, but mainly on the view that the grant of any right of appeal to the Crown against sentence should be discovered only on a clear and unequivocal expression of intention in sec. 68. The matter was raised again in *Peel v. The Queen*[168] and this time there was a majority of four to three in favour of the view of Rich, Starke and Dixon JJ. Menzies, Windeyer, Owen and Gibbs JJ. (Barwick C.J., Mc-

---

165 (1934) 50 C.L.R. 536.
166 (1934) 50 C.L.R. 551.
167 at pp. 561-2.
168 (1971) 125 C.L.R. 447.

Tiernan and Walsh JJ. dissenting) held that sec. 68 (2) of the Judiciary Act operated upon sec. 5D of the Criminal Appeal Act (N.S.W.) so as to enable the Commonwealth Attorney-General to appeal to the Court of Criminal Appeal against a sentence pronounced by the Supreme Court or a Court of Quarter Sessions upon conviction of a party charged with an offence against Commonwealth law.

The matter is, of course, one of statutory interpretation rather than constitutional power. While the language of sec. 68 is obscure, it is suggested that the majority view is preferable. That interpretation, as Dixon J. pointed out, ensures that federal criminal law is administered in each State upon the same footing as State law and avoids the establishment of two independent systems of criminal justice.[169]

This view was expounded by Mason J. in *The Queen v. Loewenthal; ex parte Blacklock*[170] as follows:

> Although the distinction between federal and State jurisdiction has created problems, they were largely foreseen by the authors of the Judiciary Act. Part X of the Act provided a solution to the difficulties arising from a duality of jurisdiction by applying to criminal cases heard by State courts in federal jurisdiction the laws and procedure applicable in the State (s. 68). The purpose of the section was, so far as possible, to enable State courts in the exercise of federal jurisdiction to apply federal laws according to a common procedure in one judicial system.

Sec. 68 (2) (b) of the Judiciary Act purports to confer on the courts of a State exercising jurisdiction with respect to the examination and commitment for trial on indictment of persons charged with offences against the laws of the State 'the like jurisdiction with respect to persons who are charged with offences against the laws of the Commonwealth'. It is clearly established that the act of an examining magistrate in determining whether an accused should be discharged or committed to prison or admitted to bail to await trial is purely an executive act.[171] It might be argued therefore that the provision is invalid in attempting to invest a State court with non-judicial power. In *Pearce v. Cocchiaro*[172] the Court was concerned with sec. 273 (2) of the Bankruptcy Act 1966, which provides that where proceedings for certain offences under the Act are brought in a

[169] *Williams v. The King (No. 2)* (1934) 50 C.L.R. 551, 560.
[170] (1974) 48 A.L.J.R. 368, 370.
[171] *Amman v. Wegener* (1972) 129 C.L.R. 415 and cases cited therein by Gibbs J. at p. 435.
[172] (1977) 14 A.L.R. 440.

court of summary jurisdiction, the court may either determine
the proceedings or commit the defendant for trial. Gibbs J. (with
whom Stephen, Jacobs and Aickin JJ. agreed) stated that in so
far as the power which a special magistrate was invested is judicial
power, it is validly enacted under sec. 77 (iii) of the Constitution.
In so far as it confers power of a non-judicial kind (being the
same sort of power that he already exercises in relation to
offences against State law), it is a valid law with respect to those
matters in relation to which the Parliament created the criminal
offences. In that case the relevant power was sec. 51 (xvii). It
was made clear in that case that a magistrate exercising either
power was properly described as a court. This reasoning would
also apply to sec. 68 (2) of the Judiciary Act and, on that basis,
para. (b) of that sub-section is valid. Sec. 68 (3), however, provides that the jurisdiction referred to in sub-sec. (2) shall not be
'judicially exercised' with respect to the summary conviction or
examination and commitment for trial of any person except by a
magistrate of the type set out in that provision. In *Pearce v.
Cocchiaro* Gibbs J. said as to that provision:

> There can be no doubt that a special magistrate conducting an
> examination for the purpose of deciding whether an alleged offender
> should be committed for trial would come within the description
> of a court within s 68 (2) and it appears that the Parliament, in
> enacting s 68 (3), proceeded on the assumption that a magistrate
> exercising such a function would be exercising the jurisdiction ju-
> dicially. It is immaterial whether this assumption was right or wrong,
> for the only substantive requirement of s 68 (3) is that a person
> charged with an offence against a law of the Commonwealth shall
> not be summarily convicted, or examined and committed for trial,
> except by a magistrate of one of the kinds described. The intention
> was to preclude the exercise of this jurisdiction by justices of the
> peace who are not such magistrates.[173]

It would seem to follow that para. (b) of sec. 68 (2) is valid. It
should be noted, however, that on this reasoning the Commonwealth has imposed non-judicial power on a State officer. It
seems doubtful whether the Constitution permits such action, at
any rate where there is no State legislative provision authorizing
it. But the Court did not examine that question in detail.

Sec. 39 (2) (b) of the Judiciary Act operated to authorize an
appeal to the High Court from a conviction by a State court
invested with federal jurisdiction for an offence against federal
law. Paragraph (b) of sec. 39 (2) was repealed by the Judiciary

[173] at pp. 446-7.

Q

(a) shall be taken to be invested subject to the provisions of paragraph (a) of sub-section (2) of the last preceding section; and

(b) shall be taken to be invested subject to the provisions of paragraphs (b), (c) and (d) of that sub-section (whether or not it is expressed to be invested subject to all or any of those provisions), so far as they are capable of application and are not inconsistent with a provision made by or under the Act by or under which the jurisdiction is invested,

in addition to any other conditions or restrictions subject to which the jurisdiction is expressed to be invested.

(2) Nothing in this section or the last preceding section, or in any Act passed before the commencement of this section, shall be taken to prejudice the application of any of sections seventy-two to seventy-seven (inclusive) of this Act in relation to jurisdiction in respect of indictable offences.

A special statutory provision may, of course, exclude the operation of sec. 39A but, in the light of the wording of that section, the court would probably insist on a clear expression by Parliament of an intention to do so.

## X

An 'unnecessary piece of mystification'[182] remains to be clarified. In *Lorenzo v. Carey*[183] the High Court said that it could see no difficulty in a State court exercising either State or federal jurisdiction at the instance of a litigant. This involved the rejection of earlier views that it was only possible under sec. 77 (iii) to invest State courts with federal jurisdiction in respect of matters which, apart from any such investment, lay outside their competence, and the acceptance of a definition of jurisdiction in this context as a *source* of authority, so that a State court might at any one time be seised concurrently of State and federal jurisdiction in respect of such a matter.

Such was the problem which confronted the Supreme Court of Victoria in *Booth v. Shelmerdine*.[184] This case involved the validity of a judgement of a Victorian court of Petty Sessions which was exercising jurisdiction in respect of a matter arising under a law made by the Commonwealth Parliament. The court was constituted by a magistrate and honorary justices, and if it was exercising federal jurisdiction it was not constituted in ac-

---

182 Sawer: Essays on the Australian Constitution (Ed. Else-Mitchell, 2nd ed., 1961) at p. 86.
183 (1921) 29 C.L.R. 243, 253.
184 [1924] V.L.R. 276.

cordance with sec. 39 (2) (d) of the Judiciary Act. On the
authority of *Lorenzo v. Carey*, this was a matter in which sec.
39 (2) conferred federal jurisdiction on the State court, but in
which sec. 39 (1) did not deprive it of the jurisdiction which
belonged to it, because the matter was not one in which original
jurisdiction had been conferred on the High Court under sec. 76
(ii). McArthur J. experienced rather more difficulty in reaching a
conclusion than the High Court had apparently thought possible
in *Lorenzo v. Carey*, but concluded that the State court was not
exercising federal jurisdiction. The result was reached by an
examination of the intention of the parties and the court. The
search after intent does not carry conviction; and a better resolution of the difficulty might have been achieved by resort to a presumption in favour of validity: sec. 39 (2) (d) not being satisfied,
it should be presumed that the court was exercising its State
jurisdiction.[185]

The surprising thing is that this problem has not arisen more
frequently in the reported cases.[186] It is obvious that the possession of concurrent jurisdiction can raise other difficulties posed
by the provisions of sec. 39 (2) (a) and (c) in relation to appeals to
the Privy Council and the High Court, where it may not be
enough to rely on presumptions of validity.

Dixon J. in *Ffrost v. Stevenson*[187] suggested that a solution to
these problems, or at least some of them, might be found in sec.
109 of the Constitution. He said:

> It has always appeared to me that, once the conclusion was
> reached that Federal jurisdiction was validly conferred, then under
> sec. 109 it was impossible to hold valid a State law conferring juris-
> diction to do the same thing, whether subject to no appeal or sub-
> ject to appeal in a different manner or to a different tribunal or tri-
> bunals or otherwise producing different consequences.

In the *Parbury Henty Case*[188] Latham C.J. referred to these
observations, and added that in such cases when one law permits
an appeal and another prohibits an appeal in the same proceedings there is a stronger case for holding that the laws are inconsistent than when each of two laws permits different appeals in
a proceeding.

In *Felton v. Mulligan*[189] a widow sought a declaration in the

185 Sawer, *ante* note 182 at p. 85.
186 ibid.
187 (1937) 58 C.L.R. 528, 573.
188 (1945) 70 C.L.R. 459, 483.
189 (1971) 124 C.L.R. 367.

by Parliament'.[195] But on the line of reasoning in *Lorenzo v. Carey* it could only be performed by giving the High Court or some other federal court all the jurisdiction in sec. 76 of the Constitution—a rather drastic step for curing a problem that has, as a practical matter, not proved to be too great.

The majority judges in *Felton v. Mulligan* did not consider this question of power, as distinct from the operation of sec. 109. However, while the reasoning is unsatisfactory, the result is certainly desirable. The basic difficulty, as mentioned above, is the distinction made between federal and State jurisdictions to deal with the same matter. Once that distinction is accepted, and sec. 39 (2) of the Judiciary Act is regarded as valid, the attempted solution provided by *Lorenzo v. Carey* is, for the reasons stated by Walsh J., obviously impractical or, if one litigant could determine the jurisdiction to be exercised, unjust. No other solution can be readily envisaged short of the legislative solution of giving concurrent jurisdiction to the High Court or the Federal Court of Australia. The solution put forward by at least three judges in *Felton v. Mulligan*, although intellectually unsatisfying, has the merit of removing an absurd situation.

## XI

One area of jurisdiction of State courts that is still obscure is that of Admiralty. This matter was touched on in Chapter 1,[196] where it was explained that since 1939 the High Court does not have any jurisdiction conferred on it under sec. 76 (iii)—matters 'Of Admiralty and maritime jurisdiction'—but exercises Admiralty jurisdiction under the Colonial Courts of Admiralty Act 1890 (Imp.). It has been held that since that date the State Supreme Courts are also Colonial Courts of Admiralty under that Act.[197]

In so far as matters within the jurisdiction conferred by the Imperial 1890 Act are included within those covered by sec. 76 (iii) of the Constitution, they fall *prima facie* within the operation of sec. 39 (2) of the Judiciary Act, and therefore are within federal jurisdiction. In so far as the State court's jurisdiction is federal, sec. 39 (2) (a) prevents appeals to the Privy Council; on the other hand, if it is jurisdiction under the Colonial Courts of Admiralty Act, sec. 6 of that Act confers, subject to some

195 *ante* note 182 at p. 86.

196 See pp. 67-72 *ante*.

197 *McIlwraith McEacharn Ltd v. The Shell Co. of Australia Ltd* (1945) 70 C.L.R. 175; *Lewmarine Pty Ltd v. The Ship 'Kaptayanni'* [1974] V.R. 465.

exceptions, a right of appeal to the Privy Council where there is as of right no right of local appeal. The question then is whether in any particular case a State court is exercising jurisdiction under the Colonial Courts of Admiralty Act 1890 or sec. 39 of the Judiciary Act. These matters were referred to by Dixon J. in *McIlwraith McEacharn Ltd v. The Shell Co. of Australia Ltd*:

> When s. 39 was passed, the *Statute of Westminster* 1931 (Imp.) had not been enacted, and, having regard, not only to the many inconveniences that would result, but also to the conflicts with the provisions of the *Colonial Courts of Admiralty Act* which would ensue from an attempt to make the jurisdiction thereunder of this Court exclusive of that of the Supreme Courts and then to invest them with Federal jurisdiction of the same character as would otherwise belong to them as Colonial Courts of Admiralty, I do not think that the general words of s. 39 should be interpreted as applying to the special case of the jurisdiction of Colonial Courts of Admiralty. In any case, from the decision already cited, viz. *Richelieu and Ontario Navigation Co. v. Owners of S.S. Cape Breton* [[1907] A.C. 112], it follows that par. (a) of sub-s. (2) of s. 39 could not operate against s. 6 of the *Colonial Courts of Admiralty Act*. If, therefore, the cause falls within the jurisdiction conferred by the *Colonial Courts of Admiralty Act*, which in effect means if it is one which would have been brought within the jurisdiction of the High Court of Admiralty by s. 13 of the *Admiralty Court Act* 1861, then, in my opinion, it is not affected by s. 39 and the appeal to the Full Court was competent.[198]

This passage is in many ways difficult to interpret. If sec. 39(1) were construed as making exclusive of State courts the jurisdiction of the High Court under the Colonial Courts of Admiralty Act and sec. 39 (2) operated to invest State courts with federal jurisdiction in those matters, it would follow that all the jurisdiction conferred on State courts under the Colonial Courts of Admiralty Act would be exercisable only as federal jurisdiction. Apart from other 'inconveniences' that might result from this situation—which he does not explain—Dixon J. raised doubts as to the validity of such an attempt, having regard to the fact that sec. 39 was enacted before the Statute of Westminster and there would be inconsistency between that section and the Colonial Courts of Admiralty Act. It does not seem, however, that sec. 77 (ii) and (iii) would enable this result to be achieved because sec. 77 refers only to matters mentioned in secs. 75 and 76. So far as Admiralty jurisdiction is concerned, sec. 77 (ii) enables the Parliament to make exclusive only the jurisdiction of the High Court referred to in sec. 76 (iii) which authorizes Par-

existence of sec. 76 (iii) of the Constitution, which specifies matters of Admiralty and maritime jurisdiction as matters of federal jurisdiction.

In *McIlwraith McEacharn Ltd v. The Shell Co. of Australia Ltd* Dixon J. said that, because of the decision of the Privy Council in *Richelieu and Ontario Navigation Co. v. Owners of S.S. Cape Breton*,[209] sec. 39 (2) (a) 'could not operate against section 6 of the Colonial Courts of Admiralty Act' granting a right of appeal to the Privy Council.[210] It was held in that case that a Canadian Act declaring judgements of the Supreme Court to be final could not affect the right of appeal conferred by sec. 6 of the Colonial Courts of Admiralty Act. The Canadian case could be distinguished, as his Honour pointed out earlier in his judgement (in relation to sec. 73 of the Constitution), on the basis that the Commonwealth Constitution is later in point of time than the 1890 Act. On the interpretation suggested above, however, sec. 39 does not operate to impose its conditions directly on jurisdiction conferred by the Colonial Courts of Admiralty Act. The relevant jurisdiction invested by sec. 39 (2) is that which 'can be conferred' on the High Court under sec. 76 (iii), not jurisdiction that has been conferred under the 1890 Act. In any case, sec. 39 (2) (a) was amended in 1968, that is, after the Statute of Westminster Adoption Act, to substitute a new provision for the old one, and making it clear that federal jurisdiction under sec. 39 was invested subject to the condition that there was no appeal to Her Majesty in Council, whether by special leave or otherwise.

On the basis that the Constitution as a later Imperial statute prevails over the earlier 1890 Imperial Act, it would seem that on an application of the reasoning in *Felton v. Mulligan*[211] the federal jurisdiction of State courts, having been vested in pursuance of sec. 77 of the Constitution, operates to the exclusion of jurisdiction under the 1890 enactment. Sec. 109 of the Constitution cannot be used, as it was in that case, to resolve the issue as it is not a case of conflict between Commonwealth and State laws. In principle, however, there does not seem any reason for applying a narrower test to the question of inconsistency of laws passed by the same legislature than that which is applicable to laws enacted by the Commonwealth and State Parliaments. Indeed, in *Clyde Engineering Co. Ltd v. Cowburn*[212] Isaacs J. in in-

209 [1907] A.C. 112.
210 (1945) 70 C.L.R. 175, 210.
211 (1971) 124 C.L.R. 367.
212 (1926) 37 C.L.R. 466.

terpreting sec. 109 relied on ordinary rules of construction and English decisions on the issue of whether two Acts are inconsistent.

If the Colonial Courts of Admiralty Act is regarded as overriding because of the Colonial Laws Validity Act and notwithstanding the Constitution, it is of course clear that the Commonwealth can, since the Statute of Westminster Adoption Act, invest State courts with federal jurisdiction on conditions of appeal that are inconsistent with the earlier Act and to the exclusion of the other jurisdiction. It is doubtful whether the amendments made to sec. 39 of the Judiciary Act since 1942 could be regarded as a re-enactment of the vesting provisions.[213]

It is true that many cases have affirmed the existence in State courts of jurisdiction under the Colonial Courts of Admiralty Act. It is also probably the case that one of the reasons for amending the Judiciary Act in 1939 was to ensure that State courts acquired jurisdiction under that Act.[214] Nevertheless, the effect of the decision in *Felton v. Mulligan* could be that the States have no such jurisdiction. The doubts and difficulties that exist in relation to this issue should be resolved by the enactment of Commonwealth legislation.

---

[213] To take the view that sec. 73 (iii) of the Constitution does not prevail over the 1890 Act as a later enactment could lead to some surprising results outside the area of the investing of State courts with federal jurisdiction. It has been assumed that the Privy Council (Appeals from the High Court) Act 1975, if valid, has a result of abolishing all appeals to the Privy Council from decisions of the High Court. The Act provides that special leave of appeal to Her Majesty in Council from a decision of the High Court shall not be asked. The provisions of the Act have regard to secs. 73 and 74 of the Constitution. Sec. 73 makes all judgements of the High Court in its appellate jurisdiction final and conclusive. Sec. 74 empowers the Parliament to make laws limiting the matters in which special leave of appeal from the High Court to the Privy Council may be asked. Sec. 6 of the Colonial Courts of Admiralty Act, however, grants a *right* of appeal to the Privy Council in certain circumstances if a local appeal has been had. An appeal from a State Supreme Court to the High Court is a local appeal for the purpose of the Act: *McIlwraith McEacharn Ltd v. The Shell Co. of Australia Ltd* (1945) 70 C.L.R. 175. If the provisions of sec. 73 making judgements of the High Court in its appellate jurisdiction final and conclusive do not prevail over sec. 6 of the Colonial Courts of Admiralty Act, the Privy Council (Appeals from the High Court) Act 1975 has not abolished that appeal. It is also clear that sec. 74 of the Constitution does not give any power to abolish it as that provision refers only to cases where special leave to appeal is sought. In those circumstances it may be that the external affairs power or sec. 2 of the Statute of Westminster could be called in aid to achieve the object of abolishing the appeal.

[214] See p. 67 *ante*.

Q

# INDEX